STRATEGIC
BENCHMARKING

STRATEGIC BENCHMARKING

How to Rate Your Company's Performance against the World's Best

Gregory H. Watson

John Wiley and Sons, Inc.
New York • Chichester • Brisbane • Toronto • Singapore

Library of Congress Cataloging-in-Publication Data:

Watson, Gregory H.
    Strategic benchmarking : how to rate your company's performance against the world's best / by Gregory H. Watson.
        p. cm.
    "Published simultaneously in Canada"—T.p. verso.
    Includes index.
    ISBN 0-471-58600-5 (alk. paper)
    1. Organizational effectiveness.   2. Performance.   3. Strategic planning. I. Title.
HD58.9.W378   1993
658.4'012—dc20   92-41907

To my dear cousin Ethel Baker
who will always be "extra special" to me.

Preface

Benchmarking is the most recent quality practice that has captured the interest of business.

The underlying reason for benchmarking is to learn how to improve business processes and increase competitiveness. More than any other quality practice, it can deliver returns quickly to the bottom line. The premise is simple: companies choose to benchmark outstanding companies whose business processes are analogous to their own. Benchmarking identifies those practices that have enabled the successful companies' superior performance and that can be adapted to the benchmarking companies' business applications. Thus, benchmarking is an operational process of continuous learning and adaptation that results in the development of an improved organization.

As a formal topic for public business discussion, benchmarking is relatively new. The first book on this subject appeared in 1989: *Benchmarking: The Search for Industry Best Practices That Lead to Superior Performance* by Robert C. Camp of Xerox Corporation.[1] In 1992, four benchmarking books were released in the following order: Michael J. Spendolini, *The Benchmarking Book;*[2] Gregory H. Watson, *The Benchmarking Workbook: Adapting Best Practices for Performance Improvement;*[3] Gerald J. Balm, *Benchmarking: A Practitioner's Guide for Becoming and Staying Best of the Best;*[4] and Kathleen H. J. Leibfried and C. J. McNair, *Benchmarking: A Tool for Continuous Improvement.*[5] Each of these books addressed the implementation of benchmarking at the "how to" or process level, rather than as a strategic approach for business process improvement.

This book takes a different approach. It is intended to elevate the discussion of benchmarking to the level of executives. It addresses the implementation of benchmarking as a business process improvement strategy within the context of strategic planning. Through four "classic" benchmarking case studies, it examines approaches for studying business processes. Finally, it provides guidance on alternatives for the implementation of benchmarking.

My agreement to undertake a trade book on benchmarking was prompted by my observation of several companies that were attempting to implement this process. For instance, senior managers were treating benchmarking like many of the other quality techniques. They were requiring that benchmarking studies be conducted for every process or were requesting only the "benchmark" measure of a process, not the enabling behaviors that allowed the performance to be achieved. Neither of these senior management behaviors is particularly advantageous: the first is not cost-effective and the second results in a measure without a context. These problems need to be both addressed and eliminated.

Regarding the cost-effectiveness of the proliferation of benchmarking studies, a study of benchmarking practices by the American Productivity & Quality Center (APQC), in Houston, Texas, indicated that benchmarking studies can be expensive.[6] Internal costs could range up to $60,000, not including the cost of external consulting services. Some companies have reported extensive benchmarking studies that cost over $100,000. At that rate, few companies can afford the cost of benchmarking all their business processes. Even when companies prudently identify key business processes, ten to fifteen processes may still need to be benchmarked, and the cost could be prohibitive, particularly for small businesses.

An appropriate activity for senior management is the guidance of the benchmarking efforts so that they remain focused on strategic issues related to the improvement of key business processes and thereby obtain the maximum return on the investment in the studies. This emphasis on *strategic benchmarking* or management-directed change can be stimulated by learning from companies that have formed long-term strategic alliances for business process improvement.

What happens when a manager wants only the data and not an understanding of how the process was enabled to achieve its level of performance? Typically, the result is an exhortation to achieve "stretch goals," but the enabling process capability to achieve those goals is not provided. Failure to achieve the goal, as well as demoralization of the work force, can then be expected.

One of the key advantages of a well-structured benchmarking study is its illumination of process features that can be implemented to achieve improved performance. Observation of the success at another company provides confidence within the benchmarking company that similar, or increased, performance can be achieved by implementing related process improvements. Without an understanding of the factors that enabled the improved performance at the benchmark company, it will be difficult to stimulate similar process performance improvement. If management makes the appropriate request of benchmarking teams—the discovery of both the benchmark and the process enablers—the study team will be more likely to successfully complete the benchmarking study project.

This book is for management. It is intended to identify better ways to use interbusiness cooperation to improve strategic planning and thereby increase competitiveness. The first four chapters describe the theory of benchmarking; the remaining chapters apply benchmarking in a variety of situations. Major case studies of benchmarking applications from Hewlett-Packard, Ford, General Motors, and Xerox are included. The cases are supplemented by examples from service industries and trade associations, to illustrate how benchmarking applies to any type of organization. The appendix materials may be helpful in implementing benchmarking: the Benchmarking Code of Conduct, from the International Benchmarking Clearinghouse (IBC) of the APQC; a listing of secondary research tools; the APQC Benchmarking Recognition Award Criteria; a sample benchmarking procedure, which describes the administrative aspects for implementation of benchmarking; a bibliography of books, reports, and articles on benchmarking; and a glossary of benchmarking terms.

The various elements of this book have been brought together to support management in making a long-term commitment to learning the applications of strategic benchmarking. Strategic benchmarking is a tool that will yield continuous business improvement. Continuous improvement is not limited to steady, incremental improvement; it also implies a need for rapid, breakthrough improvement. Today's pace of business is fast and is accelerating rapidly. Strategic benchmarking can help businesses keep up with this pace by improving the "time-to-market" for implementation of business change. As C. Jackson Grayson, Chairman of the APQC, has said: "In today's globally competitive world, you benchmark and improve . . . or you don't survive."[7] It is my earnest hope that this book will help all of the potential survivors of today's turbulent business environment to become even more competitive in their business practices.

GREGORY H. WATSON

Victor, New York
January 1993

Acknowledgments

Just as benchmarking is a team exercise, so is the production of a book of this scale. Many expressions of gratitude for support, assistance, and guidance are in order. I would like to begin by thanking Mike Hamilton of John Wiley & Sons, Inc., for his encouragement to produce a book for the trade press and for his constructive prodding to complete its production. Dick Luecke proved to be a most capable researcher and compatriot in developing the case studies. My father-in-law, Joe Brandon, also deserves a word of appreciation for critiquing the "process as preached" and helping to make it more understandable to those outside the quality profession. The talents of APQC research librarian Joy Holland contributed the benchmarking bibliography. Carla O'Dell, Director of the APQC International Benchmarking Clearinghouse (IBC) has been an enthusiastic cheerleader, as have friends Jeramy Bede, Jan Case, Chuck Elliott, Lucy Freedman, Jim Heidbreder, Lisa Marshall, Debra Maymi, William Miller, Gary Taylor, and Joe Wexler.

Special recognition goes to the many individuals who assisted us in developing the case study materials: Ron Benton and Frank Yockey (Hewlett-Packard); Penny C. Paquette (Amos Tuck School, Dartmouth College); Charles Gumushian (Ford Motor Company); Steven Wells and Bruce Pince (Sandy Company); Carlisle Davis (General Motors); Robert C. Camp and Warren Jeffries (Xerox Corporation); Larry Anderson (International Facilities Management Association); Obie LeFlore and Joseph Spadaford (First National Bank of Chicago); Keith L. McCandless (The Healthcare Forum); and Ron Malone (APQC). Thank you all.

G.H.W.

Contents

Vision without action is just a dream.
Action without vision is just activity.
Vision and action together can change the world.

—Joel Barker
President
Infinity, Ltd.

1

Introducing Benchmarking

In recent years, the business world has been accosted by a flurry of acronymic assaults; among them are:

MBO	Management by Objectives;
SQC	Statistical Quality Control;
TQM	Total Quality Management;
DOE	Design of Experiments;
QFD	Quality Function Deployment.

Some of these methods have been launched by the professional quality community, after studying Japanese business practices, in an attempt to help businesses improve their competitive performance in delivering products and services to customers. However, too many of these methods were oversold and were not put into an appropriate business context that would define their true contribution. The net effect of these assaults has been the development, among senior managers, of a somewhat jaundiced or skeptical view toward any newly promoted hot topic.

Benchmarking is the latest hot topic to come onto the quality playing field—and benchmarking has no acronym. Unlike many of its quality acronym predecessors, benchmarking has its roots in fundamental business activities that have been practiced widely for years. Upon discovering the meaning and application of benchmarking, many senior managers sense déjà vu—they recognize that this method represents something similar to their competitive analysis techniques and feel comfortable implementing it. This, in part, helps to account for the rapidly expanding management interest; benchmarking has caught on more quickly than other quality tools and has infiltrated the work processes of senior managers. To account for this success of benchmarking, we must first understand how benchmarking is defined.

BENCHMARKING DEFINED

Roger Milliken has called benchmarking "stealing shamelessly."[1] Motorola even used the code name "Bandit" to identify its pocket pager product line, which was built by combining the best practices of many companies into a single product design and production capability.[2] However, benchmarking is not just copying from other companies. As W. Edwards Deming has stated: "It is a hazard to copy. It is necessary to understand the theory of what one wishes to do."[3] Benchmarking is more than just copying.

Westinghouse envisions benchmarking as an integrated tool within its Total Quality Improvement Process for "identifying best practices, wherever they exist, implementing and communicating those practices throughout Westinghouse to improve competitive performance and preserve our core competencies."[4] The Westinghouse Productivity & Quality Center's course on benchmarking uses the following definition:

> Benchmarking is a continuous search for and application of *significantly better practices* that leads to superior competitive performance. [italics added][5]

Westinghouse does not require teams to discover the very best practice; finding significantly better practices is sufficient to drive the improvement efforts.

Another twist on the benchmarking definition was provided by Fred Bowers, corporate benchmarking program manager for Digital Equipment Corporation, who suggested a futuristic definition of benchmarking. In a presentation at an American Productivity & Quality Center (APQC) benchmarking conference, Bowers defined benchmarking in terms of the direction it appears to be growing: "The process by which organizations learn, modeled on human learning process."[6] We will build on his definition, which links benchmarking to the learning organization, as we consider a manager's perspective of the value of benchmarking.

Many definitions have been proposed for benchmarking, but one developed at APQC by the International Benchmarking Clearinghouse (IBC) Design Steering Committee represents a consensus among some 100 companies:

> Benchmarking is a systematic and continuous measurement process; a process of continuously measuring and comparing an organization's business processes against business process leaders anywhere in the world to gain information which will help the organization take action to improve its performance.[7]

Although benchmarking is a measurement process and results in comparative performance measures, it also describes how exceptional performance is attained. The practices that lead to exceptional performance are called enablers.[8] Thus, the process of benchmarking results in two types of outputs: benchmarks, or measures of comparative performance, and enablers. Applying Deming's logic, the enablers represent the theory behind the process performance.

Another piece of advice from Deming also applies: "Adapt, don't adopt."[9] Process enablers are developed to meet a specific business need within the context of a particular business environment and company culture. No two businesses are exactly alike in these areas, and practices from one business are not directly transferable to another without rigorous examination of areas that need to be translated to fit a different environment and culture. Thus, stealing shamelessly can cause trouble if the business practices of one organization don't translate to those of another.

AN OVERVIEW OF THE BENCHMARKING PROCESS

Benchmarking follows a basic four-step approach. The four steps follow the fundamental quality method as described by the Shewhart or Deming cycle: plan, do, check, act (Figure 1–1).[10] In the first step, planning the benchmarking study, it is necessary to select and define the process that is to be studied; identify the measures of process

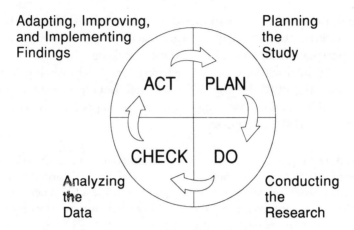

Figure 1–1.   The Benchmarking Process Compared with the Deming Cycle

performance; evaluate one's own capability at this process; and determine which companies should be studied.

The first step can be reduced to answering two fundamental questions:

1. What should we benchmark?
2. Whom should we benchmark?

The second step in benchmarking is to conduct secondary and primary research. This includes an investigation of public disclosures about the particular process at target companies. It is important to learn as much as possible before making any direct contact, because many companies are completely unaware of what has been written about them in the press and trade publications. Direct communication with companies may consist of telephone surveys, written questionnaires, or site visits to make detailed observations.

The third step in benchmarking is analysis of the gathered data to determine study findings and recommendations. The analysis consists of two aspects: determining the magnitude of the performance gaps between companies, using the benchmarking metrics identified during the planning step; and identifying the process enablers that facilitated the performance improvements at the leading companies.

The final step in benchmarking involves the adaptation, improvement, and implementation of appropriate benchmark process enablers. The objective of benchmarking is to change an organization in a way that increases its performance. Thus, benchmarking is a process with a built-in bias for action; it goes beyond just conducting a business process study or obtaining a relative measure of business performance.

A BRIEF HISTORY OF BENCHMARKING

As early as the late 1800s, Frederick Taylor's work on the application of the scientific method of business had encouraged comparison of work processes. During World War II, it became a common business practice for companies to "check" with other companies to determine standards for pay, work loads, safety, and other business hygiene factors. In his book describing the development of the Toyota production system, Taiichi Ohno, former vice president of manufacturing for Toyota, described the post-World War II efforts at benchmarking:

> Following World War II, American products flowed into Japan—chewing gum and Coca-Cola, even the Jeep. The first U.S.-style supermarket appeared in the mid-1950's. And as more and more Japanese people visited the United States, they saw the intimate relationship between the supermarket and the style of daily life in America. Consequently, this type of store became the rage in Japan due to Japanese curiosity and fondness for imitation.[11]

Ohno further applied his observations of the supermarket by using shelf restocking as an analogy for his development of the just-in-time (JIT) inventory management method. "From the supermarket we got the idea of viewing the earlier process in a production line as a kind of store."[12] The supermarket analogy provided Ohno with an example of an enabling process from which he developed the *kanban* system for inventory flow management.

Many observers have described Japanese businesspeople as "copycats" who have excelled only in the art of imitation. This is not true—the Japanese have been applying the practice of benchmarking to their product and process developments as a means to shortcut the time it takes to implement improvements and reduce the time it takes to get products to market. Paul Howell has observed:

> The Japanese excel at benchmarking, at exhaustively analyzing the best companies in each industry, then continually improving on their performance until the Japanese products and services then become the best.[13]

I believe that benchmarking has evolved to a fourth generation in its development as a business process. Its evolutionary process has resembled the classic "art-transitioning-to-science" model for development of a new management discipline (Figure 1–2). This transition, occurring through four generations of development from the time of Taiichi Ohno's supermarket study application, is interpreted in light of the publication of Xerox Corporation's practice of benchmarking in the late 1980s, in response to Xerox's being the winner of the 1989 Malcolm Baldrige National Quality Award.

As shown in Figure 1–2, the first generation of benchmarking may be construed as product-oriented reverse engineering or competitive

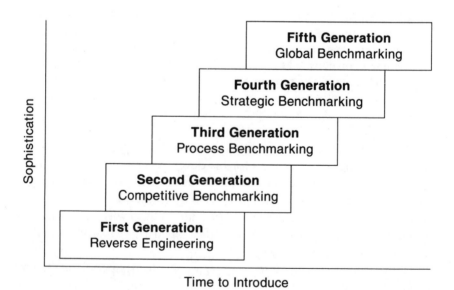

Figure 1–2.   Benchmarking as a Developing Science

product analysis. As an illustration of the emphasis in this area, by 1990 about 800 articles had been published in which benchmarking was listed as a key word. These articles were almost entirely in the fields of civil engineering or product comparisons for performance of software or hardware. Fewer than 20 of the articles dealt with process benchmarking, and almost all were describing the Xerox experience.[14] In this first generation, comparisons of product characteristics, functionality, and performance were made with similar products or services from competitors. Reverse engineering, which tends to be a technical, engineering-based approach to product comparisons, includes tear-down and evaluation of technical product characteristics. In contrast, competitive product analysis compares market-oriented features to evaluate the relative capabilities of the competitive product offerings. These methods are in use at most companies.

The second generation, competitive benchmarking, was refined into a science at Xerox during the 1976–1986 decade. Competitive benchmarking moved beyond product-oriented comparisons to include comparisons of processes with those of competitors. Xerox developed this capability after finding that the manufacturing cost of its products equaled the sales price of competitors' products. Xerox needed to understand what processes its competitors were using to deliver their products more efficiently.

The third generation of benchmarking developed during 1982–1988, as more quality leaders recognized that they could learn more easily from companies outside their industry than from competitive studies. Companies that compete have natural boundaries beyond which they will not (and cannot, because of trade restrictions) share process information. These boundaries and restrictions do not apply for companies that are not direct competitors. The depth of knowledge available among noncompetitors is as detailed as their ability to share process information. The absence of any information-sharing restriction has led to a shift that has broadened benchmarking applications: Instead of targeting only competitors, they target companies with recognized strong practices independent of the industry. However, this shift also required more in-depth knowledge of the similarities among businesses that may appear greatly different on the surface, in order to understand how to apply lessons learned across these industry boundaries. Such process benchmarking is based on the development of analogies between the business processes at two or more companies. For instance, to be able to have a useful result from its study of the order fulfillment process, Xerox formed an analogy for the shipment of copier products by using the L. L. Bean process for shipment of fishing boots and equipment (see Chapter 8 for more details). One of the features of process benchmarking is the identification of particular business processes that are targets for analysis. These processes can be carefully defined as "the order booking process" or "the month-end book closing process" or more broadly defined as "the order fulfillment process" or "the cash flow management process." The larger the scope of the study, the greater the extent of resources required to conduct this type of investigation.

The fourth generation of benchmarking is referred to in Figure 1–2 as strategic benchmarking. I define strategic benchmarking as a systematic process for evaluating alternatives, implementing strategies, and improving performance by understanding and adapting successful strategies from external partners who participate in an ongoing business alliance. Strategic benchmarking differs from process benchmarking in terms of the scope and depth of commitment among the sharing companies. James Staker, director of the Strategic Planning Institute's Council on Benchmarking, observes that strategic benchmarking is "using benchmarking to fundamentally change the business, not just tweak processes."[15] In this sense, strategic benchmarking is a learning process that helps to feed process reengineering. Bath Iron Works' CEO, Buzz Fitzgerald, turned to strategic benchmarking when the end of the Cold War signaled a need for a new operational strategy. "Contingency plans can be developed and implemented much faster and at a far less cost [through benchmarking] than if developed from scratch," stated William R. ("Tip") Koehler, manager of quality improvement for Bath Iron Works.[16]

A future generation of benchmarking lies in a global application where international trade, cultural, and business process distinctions among companies are bridged and their implications for business process improvement are understood. Today, only a few leading companies are systematically working these issues as part of their strategic planning process. Across the span of these generations of benchmarking, a fundamental shift has occurred in the model for competition among businesses.

A MODEL FOR COMPETITION

What do companies need in order to successfully compete? The answer to this profit-oriented question is a threefold emphasis: quality *beyond* competitors', technology *before* competitors', and costs *below* competitors'. The quality movement has shown that customer satisfaction is the key to capturing and maintaining market share. General Electric Corporation's strategic planning specialist, Sidney Schoeffler, developed the underlying concepts of studying various market influences that affect the profitability of the firm. This work migrated to the Strategic Planning Institute and became known as the Profit Impact of Market Strategy (PIMS) Program. Study of the PIMS data is essential in order to understand the influence of quality on the business success of an organization. The PIMS data base, consisting of over 450 companies and 3,000 business units, provides an exceptional opportunity for studying the influence of various hypotheses for the business factors that most greatly influence profitability. The study that linked perceived quality, market share, and profitability was Robert D. Buzzell and Bradley T. Gale's book *The PIMS Principles: Linking Strategy to Performance*.[17]

Buzzell and Gale showed that one factor drives market share: relative perceived quality. When relative perceived quality and relative market share are both high (see Figure 1–3), profitability is virtually assured.[18] The higher profits realized by those businesses with higher perceived quality were attributed by the PIMS researchers to the businesses' ability to command higher prices while achieving comparable or more favorable cost structures. They observed also that customers make their judgments relative to value or the relationship between quality and price. The perceived relative value of the total offering of product and services influences the purchasing behavior of the customer. Relative perceived quality is not the same as product quality or conformance to the design specifications. Relative perceived quality is quality from the customer's perspective, relative to alternative competitive offerings in the market; the perception results in greater satisfaction of the customer's requirements from the product or service than would be received from the competing products or services. Subsequent studies of excellent companies have shown that this measure of customer satisfaction is enabled by: strong

Relative Market Share	Relative Perceived Quality		
High	21%	27%	38%
Equal	14%	20%	29%
Low	7%	13%	20%
	Low	Equal	High

Relative Perceived Quality

Figure 1–3. Profitability as a Function of Market Share and Quality

product quality; tight cost management, which in turn enables better value chain management; innovative technology targeted to customer needs; responsive delivery of service; and the rapid resolution of issues whenever problems occur. How can a company drive for increased competitiveness using this knowledge of customer behavior?

Noriaki Kano, a senior member of the Union of Japanese Scientists and Engineers (JUSE), has developed a model that links competitive behaviors with customer satisfaction and product design innovation. Kano's model indicates that companies exhibit three types of performance as they design their products for customers. As represented by the three curves in Figure 1–4,[19] they are: innovative performance, competitive performance, and basic performance.

The first behavior pattern delivers innovative product features or performance. The product excites and delights the customers because the engineers designing the products have scratched an itch that customers couldn't reach; they have fulfilled the customers' unspoken need. John Doyle, a former senior vice president at Hewlett-Packard, has observed that customers don't always know what they want or need. "It is the job of engineering to deliver products to the marketplace that meet an imaginative understanding of the user's needs."[20] The very fact that these features are in the product satisfies a customer, even if the engineering is not executed to the best degree possible. However, customer satisfaction continues to increase as the

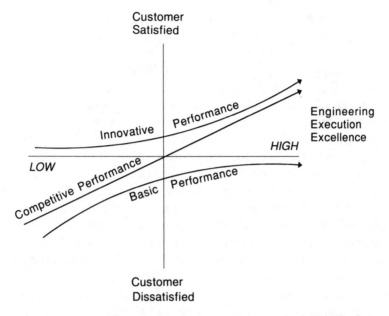

Figure 1-4. Customer Satisfaction and Execution Excellence

product design or feature capability improves. An example of this type of behavior is the coffee-cup holder that was designed for the Ford Taurus.

Prior to creation of the Ford Taurus model, plastic coffee-cup holders were after-market additions purchased at supermarkets and convenience stores. Car owners did not hold the designers of their cars responsible for providing them with coffee-cup holders. The engineers of Team Taurus, however, saw things differently. They installed a coffee-cup holder as an integral part of the automobile. Avid coffee drinkers no longer had to choose between driving their car safely and spilling coffee on their clothing or upholstery. The Taurus was even lauded for the coffee-cup holder when it was named the car of the year by *Motor Trend* magazine!

In the second behavior pattern, competitive performance, there is a direct relationship between how well the product is designed and how satisfied the customer becomes. Competition is based on the direct comparison of features among product alternatives. This type of competitive behavior is focused on meeting recognized customer requirements by delivering a better design than those found in alternative products. It is enabled by competitive product analysis and reverse engineering efforts.

What happened, predictably, after Ford introduced the coffee-carrying Taurus? All of the automotive companies lined up to deliver a more excellent coffee-cup holder with a broader range of applications. Ford's original design carried an eight-ounce plastic foam cup; Toyota's can accommodate a larger cup and Chevrolet's allows for a handled mug. The basis for competition changed from delivery of an innovative feature to excellence in the design of the feature, relative to the options available from other products.

The third behavior pattern is basic performance—the unexciting world of safety standards, basic product functionality, and other product performance aspects that customers expect will be delivered. When asked, customers do not tend to articulate these expectations; they are so basic to the products that their presence is understood. For example, it would be ludicrous to advertise that an electronic product complies with the UL code for safety, because that is an expected feature and not a competitive feature. For these fundamental features, competition is based more on a checklist (Do you have it or not?) rather than on excellence of execution. Only if the expected product features are missing will customers become dissatisfied, and no degree of engineering excellence will make up for their absence.

Where does the coffee-cup holder stand now? One engineer told me that he and his wife had decided to upgrade their selection of an automobile, at a higher cost to them than the after-market coffee-cup holder, because their desired car model did not have a coffee-cup holder. This purchasing behavior is characteristic of buyers' response to the absence of a basic feature.

Kano's model allows for a natural progression from the innovative or exciting level of satisfaction toward the basic performance level. Kano calls this the natural effect of gravity pulling down the innovative performance first into the competitive area of performance and then into the basic area of performance. The laws of entropy apply: all levels of excellence degrade naturally over time, and only an unnatural act reverses this trend. Craig Walter, director of corporate quality at Hewlett-Packard, has called quality an "unnatural act" in recognition of this relationship. Continuing product excellence is achieved by "re-creation" or by continually seeking to understand and fulfill the spoken and unspoken desires of the current and potential customers and delivering products with features that provide innovative performance.[21]

The migration of the portable computer provides an excellent example of a performance trend that can be interpreted using the Kano model. When Compaq Computer Corporation introduced its first product in 1983, the portable computer weighed 17 pounds (a disadvantage), but it ran the standard IBM PC software, an advantage that provided strong customer satisfaction. The product was exceptionally reliable, which satisfied its customers, but its heavy weight led them to refer to this product, affectionately, as "the luggable." Compaq was right on target in its initial focus on standard software and product reliability. While its competitors were trying to comprehend the effect of this design thrust, Compaq went to work on another area of focus—making the product smaller, lighter, and more capable. The company added more capacity for memory, processing, and display, as well as linkages to other systems through modems—all while reducing the overall weight and size of the portable computer. The weight kept coming down. Today, its competitive product, in the five- to seven-pound range, is as capable as the last generation of desktop computers. Innovative performance is now illustrated by the "palmtop" computers whose weight is less than two pounds. Where does the original Compaq product fit in? Reliability and standard or "open architecture" software are so basic that all products must meet these requirements in order to be successful in the field. The formerly "innovative" features now represent basic performance. What did its mastery of customer requirements do for Compaq? Its dynamic product development allowed Compaq to grow to a $4 billion corporation from a start-up company, in just 10 years.

The Kano model comprehends the effect of product technology in driving a company's competitiveness, but it is also possible to drive competitiveness with process technology. In fact, because most companies don't consider their process technology as a competitive dimension, they don't fully understand the interaction of these two drivers of competitiveness. Unless they define competitiveness using both of these dimensions, companies tend to have a reduced understanding of their inherent competitiveness (see Figure 1–5).[22]

A company can map its innovation relative to its competitors as a function of these two dimensions, to understand where it needs to

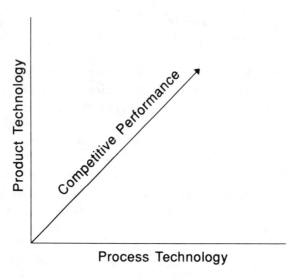

Figure 1–5. The Contribution of Product and Process Technology to Competitiveness

develop additional capabilities and enhance its core competence. The primary source of competitiveness is product technology. This is so elementary that it may be used as a reference to understand the second dimension, process technology. Process technology's importance to competitiveness is not as widely accepted. The following example will help to illustrate the significance of the relationship between product and process technology.

The Honda–Yamaha wars were waged in the 1980s.[23] In 1981, Yamaha positioned itself to attack Honda as the leader in product variety in the motorcycle business. Honda responded after observing several years of market share gain by Yamaha. In one 18-month period, Honda introduced 113 product models while Yamaha made 37 changes in its product line. Honda was able to achieve this superiority in the marketplace through excellent technology in the product development process. Honda had a better understanding of how to introduce new products efficiently than did Yamaha. Other examples of process technology's contribution to companies' market competitiveness are observable in every industry where time-based competition is a driving factor: personal computers, consumer electronics, office equipment, and automobiles, to name a few.

The significance of process technology introduces a related senior management concern with benchmarking: balancing the need for discussions with competitors and the need for protection of unique or proprietary intellectual property, which is the foundation of competitive process technology. Some managers' resistance to benchmarking is based on this issue. Benchmarking presents a paradox: the need for simultaneous cooperation and competition. This need creates an attitude of due diligence among management and reinforces the obligation to exercise prudent business judgment in directing alliances with other businesses. How can management balance competitive and cooperative directions?

A MODEL FOR BUSINESS COOPERATION

The advertising slogan "Does Macy's tell Gimbel's?" once epitomized a basic business principle: Competitors don't cooperate. This proposition has been considered fundamental to the free market approach to business competition and economics. To obtain profit, each company attacks the four Ps of Theodore Levitt's marketing model (*p*roduct performance, *p*ricing, *p*lace (or distribution), and *p*ackaging), using its own resources to establish an advantageous position with the consumer.[24] Judging by the present position of the two famous competitors—Gimbel's is gone and Macy's is struggling against continually eroding price margins—it is not clear whether the strictly competitive approach is the best long-term route for the competitors. Perhaps this is why the need for interbusiness cooperation for the purpose of improving fundamental business practices, even among competitors, is being addressed by a growing number of major companies.

As times change, many businesses are altering their relationships with competitors to include a more collaborative effort focused on common issues. Organizations such as the Computer Business Executives Management Association (CBEMA) and the Chemical Manufacturers' Association (CMA) are forging common business policy positions for their industries. Through open discussion of common issues and fundamental problems, these industries have gained a more direct approach to improving their business environment. As a corollary, they have added a fifth P to the basic marketing model: *p*rocess.

What is process and why is it important? The quality movement has taught business an important lesson over the past decade: all business is process. Process is a series of transactions that are responsive to customer requirements and expectations; process considers the entire business system—including the capability of suppliers—to be a delivery team. This lesson includes the discovery that the real job of management is business process improvement. By sharing information about business processes and process improvement techniques (rather than pricing and product), organizations seek to shortcut process development time and increase their capabilities. They learn about successes and failures in common processes from other companies. This type of direct observation is called benchmarking.

Benchmarking represents a fundamental shift in competitive business philosophy. In benchmarking, a basis for collaboration is established at the beginning, and parameters for cooperation are set. Companies that benchmark each other's common processes share process similarities that are likely to be analogous comparisons rather than directly competitive methods of operation. However, even competitors may share process improvement information on practices that are not explicitly restricted by trade sanctions such as antitrust laws.

The benefits to be gained from benchmarking for nonprocess leaders are clear, but the motivation for a process leader to participate in a benchmarking study is somewhat obfuscated. Why should business leaders want to cooperate? What motivates them to share information about the efficiency of their business operations? Doesn't benchmarking undermine the free market concept?

Benchmarking is not just about taking process ideas from other companies; it is about creating a coherent national challenge for continuous improvement. In the analysis of the factors influencing their specific competitive environments, many companies have come to recognize that their long-term success depends on two external factors: the global marketplace and the development of national productivity. Companies can no longer limit their perspective to localized or even national market boundaries. This outdated practice leads to marketplace myopia and economic downfall, as proven by the number of companies that lacked a global perspective on their potential markets and failed to counter international attacks on their existing markets. (Instances of television and VCR design and manufacture that have migrated offshore are well-known.) An organization that establishes and maintains a global outlook is better able to meet and respond to customers' ongoing and changing needs. As for the development of national productivity, only through increased innovation and quality, and the effective and responsible use of natural and human resources, will the United States strengthen and maintain its position as an economic world leader. Companies working together to increase overall efficiency of business processes will lead to greater productivity and competitiveness both at home and abroad. This is particularly true when competing against the Japanese market. Japan's Ministry of International Trade and Industry (MITI) fosters technology development through a broad program of tax credits and encourages strategic alliances among major companies. Those who still view increasing cooperation among American companies as a threat to our local free market must awaken to reality: sharing process innovations leads to the creation of more effective and efficient business systems that are capable of supporting a stronger national productivity and increasing the global competitiveness of American industries.

When global competitiveness and national productivity are kept in perspective, benchmarking emerges as a vehicle for promoting and propagating the free market concept. Sharing process improvement information helps to avoid the redundancy that can be built into the business system of a nation. When each company is left to its own resources, options for process improvement are limited to individual experiences. Companies may, through self-discovery, find ways to improve their own processes in response to specific occurrences or problems; they may imitate imperfect perceptions of the processes that other companies have followed, or they may even create and develop their own processes. None of these approaches, however, can incorporate the collective learning and process knowledge that are acquired through the shared experiences and practices of a "society of firms."

A benchmark study produces two results: (a) a measure of process performance excellence that can be used as a standard for comparison (for example, turnover rate of inventory, or the number of stockouts for hot sales items), and (b) a determination of the process enablers that helped to develop the level of performance observed (for example, information technology applications, or specific procedures used for monitoring inventory). These enablers are the key to improving the observer company's performance, and their discovery is the real goal of the benchmarking study.

Suppose you are a principal in a new venture, a start-up company that is opening a chain of bookstores to compete against B. Dalton, Waldenbooks, and Crown Bookstores. When you consider the critical success factors of your business, you discover that inventory control—specifically, the process for reordering books from trade publishers—is the critical process. You know that each company in your target market has studied this methodology and considers its own system to be the best. Yet not one of the established chains will divulge such proprietary information to a potential competitor. Using a benchmarking process, what options are available for establishing a first-class book-reordering process from the beginning?

To commence your study, you would first analyze *the process.* Every reorder system includes some similar functions: developing an inventory policy for each article, setting a level of safety stock, establishing a reorder point, monitoring outgoing sales and decremental inventory. These process steps are not peculiar to the book-selling industry. Appliances, computer software, pharmaceutical drugs, and convenience foods all need similar systems for supporting their sales and inventory. Within the book-selling industry, there may be trade associations, professional societies, publishers, or noncompeting specialty stores that would be willing to discuss particulars of their reorder systems. One strong analogy may be found in computer software sales, which have similar trends in seasonally "hot" products and consumer spending patterns. Establishing a partnership with the inventory control managers of Egghead Software or MicroAge Computer would held to provide both a technological answer to your problem and, perhaps, a potential solution using their information technology. Another option would be to "muddle through" by developing your own system and probably making the same mistakes that others made. Which approach is more likely to provide you with a competitive book-selling business within a propitious time frame?

This discussion of the reordering process study for book distributors illustrates how the power of analogy provides the ability to learn about process from both within and outside of one's own industry. Macy's may have been reluctant to talk with Gimbel's, but other organizations may be willing to discuss their business processes with you. The prime consideration in discovering which companies would be willing to discuss your process is the building of the analogy between the prospective companies and the establishment of specific selection criteria for making the final choice of participating companies.

BENCHMARKING AS A MORAL AND LEGAL CONSIDERATION

"It's a very, very hot topic now," says Kent Johnson, corporate counsel for Texas Instruments. "All these lawyers had been hearing about benchmarking from their corporate clients. Their first reaction was to say, 'My God, we've got to tell them not to do this.'" While the openness required for benchmarking is anathema to most attorneys, Johnson says that attitude is changing. "Attorneys believe their primary goal is to avoid risk, when really it's to help the company perform its mission." Benchmarking does that.[25]

Pundits of benchmarking believe it is contrary to the free market concept because it focuses on sharing rather than on competition among companies. However, closer examination reveals that their observation has a fundamental error. If companies do not compete in the marketplace, then there is no reason why they should not cooperate. Companies can even strengthen their competitive position by effectively applying lessons that have been learned, and paid for, by other companies that have faced similar situations or related problems. This is a more efficient use of "society's resources" than requiring every company to invest in relearning the lessons of the marketplace. Indeed, this approach has its foundation in the basic case study method of business, where companies learn by examining static cases of business decisions. In benchmarking, the discovery is part of a dynamic, less defined situation than the academic case study. However, having said this, it is important to note that the cooperative model does indeed extend to competitors in areas where competition is not a driving influence because of shared similar concerns for public responsibility: healthcare for employees, environmental protection, development of industry-wide strategic technologies, or legislation and regulation affecting an industry as a whole. These areas are legitimate industry concerns. However, it is appropriate to ask where to draw the line with competitors. Certain legal boundaries exist for sharing technology, trade secrets, and marketing information, and these boundaries are defined by corporate legal advisers. However, where such restrictions do not formally exist, there is a gray area for discussions with competitors.

When Xerox first disclosed the practice of benchmarking to the public, journalists likened it to "industrial espionage." Xerox was depicted as a business "spymaster" and the whole practice was viewed as sinister, unacceptable behavior.[26] This was an incorrect perception: successful benchmarking does not require either immoral or unethical behavior.

There is a fundamental distinction between competitive intelligence and benchmarking; it is identified by the degree of openness with which an organization pursues its study. The fact that a company is a target of a competitive intelligence study is itself a confidential matter. In benchmarking, however, the objective is to develop an open sharing of information directly with the target company. In this environment, any hint of "industrial espionage" is eliminated because the investigation is conducted openly rather than in secret.

Managers need to understand the direction of development for both product technology and process technology. However, when sharing information about these areas, managers have a basic concern: to fulfill the need for sharing information, are they trading off the security requirements for protecting proprietary information and trade secrets? The APQC IBC addressed this concern of top managers by cooperating in the development of a Code of Conduct for benchmarking (see Appendix A)[27] with the Strategic Planning Institute's Council on Benchmarking. This Code of Conduct is subscribed to by over 100 companies as the normative behavior for conducting benchmarking studies. The Code describes the protocol of benchmarking—the set of conventions prescribing correct etiquette and procedures to be used in conducting benchmarking studies. It provides an appropriate starting point for beginning discussions about benchmarking and for setting expectations about how teams conducting a benchmarking exchange should interact.

THE EMERGENCE OF COMPETITIVE IDEAS

Managers have been conditioned to think of their business in terms of their competitors. A key learning for management is to build broader awareness of the business world by getting outside of the company's own "competitive silos." In presentations to senior managers about benchmarking, I have observed that many of these attendees are interested in which competitors are doing benchmarking and use this information as a guide to their own company's need for involvement in benchmarking studies. The problem with this approach is that it is regressive rather than progressive. If competitors are not publicly benchmarking, there is a tendency to believe that it is not important. However, by the time a company understands the process changes that need to take place, it could be too late to benchmark. Two examples will help to illustrate this concept.

In the mid-1960s, National Cash Register (NCR) was the dominant market force in its industry.[28] From 1967 to 1976, NCR ignored the attack by Burroughs, even as the product technology shifted from electromechanical cash registers to electronic systems based on computer technology. The result was traumatic for NCR's business: market share declined from 90% in 1972 to 10% in 1976. For NCR, the process change that needed to take place was a shift to electrical engineering and computer science in the research and development (R&D) team competency. By drawing appropriate analogies to other industries, a company can remain more flexible in its ability to analyze and understand its own industry.

Some pioneering companies, such as Texas Instruments (TI) in the consumer electronics field, tend to get so locked into their success formula that they are unable to respond to changes in their basis for competition.[29] At TI, the emphasis on cost leadership in product development was so strong that cost became a fetish. TI became so locked into cost management that it was not able to introduce new technology developments, such as C-Metal Oxide Semiconductor (CMOS) with higher production yields and more cost-effective manufacturing, as quickly as their competitors. TI focused on its success strategy so strongly that it failed to see the implications for its business. An engineering analogy may help to illustrate the problem. Engineers compare signals with background noise level to understand the capability of a signal to be discerned within the noise environment; this signal-to-noise ratio provides a basis for comparative analysis. In business, the signal is the core competency of the business, and the noise level is the capability of related technologies and their innovation environment. TI lost its leadership position because its analysis was only of the business signal and did not include a comparative measurement of the noise. The industry was competing on technological introductions and time to market; TI continued to compete on cost.

These two examples illustrate the need to have, at the business strategy level, a broad environmental scanning process for both product and process technology. Some industries are leading indictors of trends for other industries. These relationships, once properly understood, can help to project shifts that will occur in both product and process technology. "No new idea springs from a void. Rather, new ideas emerge from a set of conditions in which old ideas no longer seem to work."[30] By broadening the perspective of a company's strategic analysis through the use of process benchmarking as a supplement to competitive analysis, a company increases its ability to understand those shifts that need to occur in its strategic intent and capabilities.

INFORMATION-SHARING ISSUES FOR MANAGERS

The extent of interest in benchmarking among businesses may be measured by the number of groups that are participating in sharing business process information. Xerox publicized its benchmarking efforts after it won the 1989 Malcolm Baldrige National Quality Award and Robert C. Camp authored the first book on benchmarking. Just three years ago, the Strategic Planning Institute's Council on Benchmarking represented the single meeting place for the regular discussion of benchmarking among experienced companies. About 20 companies participated regularly in benchmarking efforts, and early examples of intercompany benchmarking efforts indicate the building of a cooperative model from 1983 to 1989. Organizations such as The Conference Board and The Management Roundtable have established forums for sharing among companies. Consulting firms have rushed into the practice of benchmarking as a legitimate third-party role, and one survey indicates that over 100 consulting firms offer benchmarking services. Perhaps the most extensive benchmarking project has been the APQC IBC in Houston, Texas. APQC has gathered over 100 major businesses from various industry segments (electrical, computer, petroleum, utilities, telecommunications, and service, among others) to share in a membership-based information network for benchmark and process information sharing. The founders of this network include: AT&T, Hewlett-Packard Company, Arthur Andersen, Browning-Ferris Industries, Campbell Soup Company, DRI/McGraw-Hill, IBM Corporation, General Motors Corporation, Honeywell, Inc., Price Waterhouse, and Xerox Corporation. These companies are committed to the continuous improvement of their businesses and believe that benchmarking is a vehicle that will provide business renewal through continuous learning in cooperation with partnership organizations. The cooperative business model is being further developed through efforts such as the APQC IBC and the Strategic Planning Institute's Council on Benchmarking. These activities represent a subtle shift—from a business model where competition occurs on all dimensions, to a business model where competition is focused on differentiated market issues that are significant to the customer. Benchmarking is a business practice that will play a role in facilitating this transition.

MANAGEMENT ISSUES IN BENCHMARKING

This chapter has illustrated several aspects of benchmarking that a senior manager should not ignore and that should be subjects for executive-level review:

- The strategic choice of benchmarking topics and potential partners for benchmarking studies;
- Integration with other competitive information to provide an accurate picture of the options available for development of a company's future;
- Exposure to the potential disclosure of intellectual property that should be carefully protected; not all employees will understand the appropriate level of disclosure or the criteria for disclosure of this information to other companies;
- A need to establish reasonable goals for development of a company and to determine change implementation strategies to achieve those goals.

These considerations form the foundation for the linkage of benchmarking to business strategic planning.

Benchmarking is like democracy: it is built on sound objectives and principles, and it requires not only belief in its premise, but also diligence in its practice and patience in achieving its benefits.

2

Linking Strategic Planning with Benchmarking

WHAT IS STRATEGY?

Strategy is what generals do for a living. Strategy is what a coach does before the big game. Strategy is what a housewife does when she cleans her house, feeds her family, purchases groceries, and keeps her children amused—and still has time for herself. Strategy is also what management does at off-site meetings. Bruce D. Henderson's definition of strategy, in *Harvard Business Review,* is a starting point for a working definition:

> A deliberate search for a plan of action that will develop a business's competitive advantage and compound it. For any company the search is an iterative process that begins with a recognition of where you are and what you have now. Your most dangerous competitors are those that are most like you. The differences between you and your competitors are the basis of your advantage. If you are in business and self-supporting, you already have some kind of competitive advantage, no matter how small or subtle. Otherwise, you would have gradually lost customers faster than you gained them. The objective is to enlarge the scope of your advantage which can only happen at someone else's expense.[1]

Definitions like this one have led to the application of the warfare analogy because strategy then has definite winners and losers, and the cost of the loss is extinction. This art of business warfare was described

25

centuries ago by Sun Tzu, author of the timeless *The Art of War,* as a constantly changing set of conditions in which the general must reconsider every move of his opponent before the battle begins, to ensure a victorious outcome. "Just as water retains no constant shape, so in warfare there are no constant conditions."[2] Another Asian influence in developing a military metaphor was Miyamoto Musashi, author of *The Book of Five Rings* and a master of kendo—the Japanese art of sword fighting. Musashi believed that a well-prepared samurai knew each aspect of a particular engagement prior to ever striking the first blow. Preparation and understanding were the primary ingredients to success. "If you are thoroughly conversant with the enemy's strategy, you will recognize the enemy's intentions and thus have many opportunities to win."[3] Beyond the context of the military metaphor, it is instructive to note that the essential ingredients to success are observation, learning, and adaptation. These ingredients define success in the strategic arena, and benchmarking helps to facilitate their implementation.

One confusing aspect of any discussion centered on strategy is the loose manner in which the term is applied in business. Some of its applications mean Grand Strategy ("the Big S") and others mean simply a team's approach to problem solutions ("the Little s"). The distinctions are similar to the word usage problems surrounding quality which can mean company-wide total quality management (TQM) ("the Big Q") or, in other applications, the conformance quality of a product ("the little q"). Emphasis in this book will be on "the Big S" rather than on the more tactical applications of the term. As a formal definition of strategy, this book will use:

> The art of developing plans that deploy the focused capabilities and competencies of an organization against a recognized competitive environment in a manner that provides the maximum support for the leadership's policy and allows flexibility to permit those real-time adaptations necessary for achieving evolutionary success.

The book's working definition of strategy is: *the persistence of a vision.* Strategy is the ability to see where one wants to go, and to do those things necessary to stay on track and get there. Using this definition, strategy is both forward-looking (proactive) and side-looking (reactive). Both elements require the same support for enduring success: observation, learning, and adaptation. Without an adaptive follow-through, the best strategic plan is only that—a plan. As Dwight D. Eisenhower, architect of the Normandy invasion, once said: "Plans are nothing; planning is everything."[4]

THE MODEL FOR STRATEGIC THINKING

Strategic thinking in business is the matching of a business's opportunities with its resources in order to develop a direction or course of action that leads to success. The thought pattern involved considers a company's distinctive technical competence and the capabilities of its value chain (suppliers and distributors of its goods and services) as well as the resources available to support the decision. The allocation of resources follows the careful consideration of these factors relative to the competitors and with supporting analysis of technical and business risks associated with the various product and market development options.

This approach to strategic thinking can be communicated as a set of considerations that fits into a natural hierarchy of goals, strategy, and action. Goals (visions of the attainable future) form the top of this hierarchy and are the result of strategic direction—what the organization will commit to achieve. The strategy, the center of the structure, puts into effect the actions intended to achieve these goals; the plans for these actions are a roadmap from the present to the future. An action, part of the base of the hierarchy, is a specific set of tasks that transforms the strategy into a reality. This hierarchical structure provides a basic model for the deployment of strategy or policy direction from the top of the company, using a three-tiered approach. The top tier represents the corporate management team; the middle tier represents all intermediate levels of the business management team; the third tier represents the action of the operational teams—the individuals who are implementing the plans. In Figure 2–1, this structure is shown as a set of three overlapping circles. Interaction and communication must occur among the organizational levels, and feedback must be provided to the top level to make the strategy adaptive.[5]

The responsibilities for deployment of strategy occur in three general levels of an organization. The highest level, senior management,

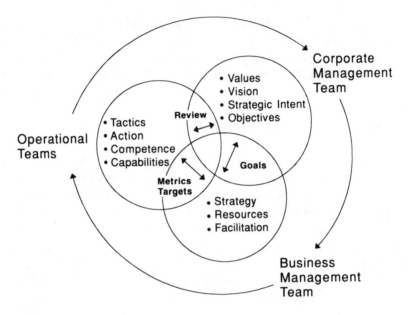

Figure 2–1.   The Deployment of Strategy in an Organization

sets the values of the organization, the vision of its future, the strategic intent for its direction, and the broad objectives for achieving that direction. Senior management then conducts a negotiated dialog with middle management on the appropriate goals for achieving their stated objectives. In Japanese planning systems, this negotiated dialog is called playing "catchball," a children's game of playing catch with a baseball. The ball (an idea or goal, in this case) is tossed around from child to child in a random fashion but with the general understanding that all in the circle will participate by both receiving the ball and passing it on to another player. Catchball builds buy-in through participation in the goal-setting process. It also builds consensus among the larger team for the appropriate level of the goal. Middle management takes the agreed on goals and develops strategies to accomplish them; it allocates resources accordingly, and serves as a facilitator, mentor, or coach of the teams that will be implementing the action. Middle management also plays catchball with the implementation teams over the selection of metrics and targets for performance that will satisfy the goals that have been set. The implementation teams develop tactics, take action, build personal and collective competence, and increase process capability as required to meet the company objectives that have cascaded to their level. The final level of communication is created when management (both middle and senior) reviews the progress of the teams—their actual performance against their targeted performance—and adjusts the expectations of the organization as a result of the learning that occurs within the teams. This closed-loop deployment of strategy developed from Peter Drucker's Management by Objectives (MBO) and is called hoshin kanri in Japan and policy deployment in the West.[6]

UNDERSTANDING THE *HBR* DIALOG ON STRATEGY

Over the past several years, a series of articles in *Harvard Business Review* has stimulated a dialog about strategic direction setting and has provided a context for understanding how strategic benchmarking fits into the strategic planning process. Three *Harvard Business Review* articles are particularly relevant here: Gary Hamel and C. K. Prahalad's articles, "Strategic Intent"[7] and "The Core Competence of the Corporation,"[8] and an article by George Stalk, Philip Evans, and Lawrence E. Shulman, "Competing on Capabilities: The New Rules of Corporate Strategy."[9]

Strategic Intent

Strategic intent is a company's ability to maintain a long-term commitment to global leadership over its current arch rival. Hamel and Prahalad identify it as "an obsession with winning at all levels of the organization" whereby companies "then [sustain] that obsession over the 10-to-20-year quest for global leadership."[10] This identification is consistent with our definition of strategy as the persistence of a vision. Strategic intent is the action that follows through on the vision that has been established. A key weakness that prevents most companies from maintaining this long-term perspective is their inability to "read the tea leaves" for their competition. As Hamel and Prahalad observed:

> Few Western companies have an enviable track record anticipating the moves of new global competitors. Why? The explanation begins with

the way most companies have approached competitor analysis. Typically, competitor analysis focuses on the existing resources (human, technical, and financial) of present competitors. The only companies seen as a threat are those with the resources to erode margins and market share in the next planning period. Resourcefulness, the pace at which new competitive advantages are being built, rarely enters in.[11]

The obvious moves in the marketplace may indicate what current competitors are doing today, but they will not indicate what latent competitors are up to. In the world of portable computers, Compaq had established an early lead. However, Compaq failed to make an early observation of Toshiba's transition into the status of a capable competitor. Toshiba was one of the first heavy equipment manufacturers to move into computer-assisted manufacturing—the use of embedded computers to set up, manage, and monitor manufacturing tasks on machine cutting tools, injection molding equipment, and sheet metal stamping presses. Toshiba transitioned its computer competence and manufacturing process capabilities, gained by automating its lines of injection molding machines and sheet metal stamping equipment, into a portable powerhouse that has the most complete line in the industry. Toshiba's initial tactical moves were evident, but it took time to see its intent to dominate this field. As Sun Tzu said: "All men can see the tactics whereby I conquer, but what none can see is the strategy out of which great victory is evolved."[12]

Strategic intent is observable in the long-term direction-setting mechanism of a company. It also implies the "stretching" of individual and corporate competence to meet technological goals and the extension of process capability to transfer the resulting technical breakthroughs into a marketplace advantage. In the late 1970s, Canon's "Beat Xerox" slogan was not taken seriously by Xerox because Canon was not one of the embedded industry competitors. However, "Beat Xerox" was the visible evidence of Canon's strategy to attack the reprographics industry at the low end of the business, where Xerox did not focus the majority of its marketing attention. Canon built new competencies in both reprographics and product distribution, to follow through on its long-term strategic intent. Canon's distribution strategy outflanked the Xerox direct-marketing approach and did not challenge Xerox directly because Canon entered a distribution channel that Xerox did not use. Canon also applied its manufacturing process capability to the production of low-cost personal copiers, to win this price-sensitive market over the long term.[13]

Core Competence

The idea of a core competence is closely tied to a company's strategic intent. "Core competencies are the collective learning in the organization, especially how to coordinate diverse production skills and integrate multiple streams of technologies."[14] The building of core competencies is not visible to other companies. Hamel and Prahalad observe that few companies will develop more than five or six core competencies. They help to make this concept more pragmatic by providing three tests for a core competence:

1. It provides potential access to a wide variety of markets;
2. It makes a significant contribution to the perceived customer benefit of the product;
3. It should be difficult for a competitor to imitate.[15]

These tests focus on a technology-driven definition of a core competence. In the case of Toshiba, its competence in ruggedized microcomputers, communications interfaces, and display technology was directly transferable from computer-controlled machines to the portable computer market. Canon's imaging and microelectronic technologies provided the competence to enter the world of reprographics and thereby challenge Xerox.[16]

Process Capabilities

The idea of a technology-driven core competence was criticized by Stalk, Evans, and Shulman, who viewed capabilities as more important than competencies. "A capability is a set of business processes strategically understood."[17] In their view, a company's strategy is built of key, cross-functional business processes that provide superior value to the customer, not of products and markets. Hamel and Prahalad see little distinction between their definition of competencies and this definition of capabilities.[18] However, the operational distinction lies in the focus of the examples used for each. Hamel and Prahalad revert to technology for their examples of competence. Their illustration of Canon's method of building the technical competence of individuals (job rotation between the camera and copier business) gets at the need to build a broad-based application of technology. Stalk, Evans, and Shulman focus on business process for their examples. It is interesting to note that both Toshiba and Canon combined their technology focus for product and market application and their manufacturing and distribution process capability, in their attacks on the market leaders— Compaq and Xerox, respectively.

An Integrated Approach

To be useful, these concepts must be integrated. Strategic intent may be observed as the combination of a management team's investment decisions for (a) development of core competencies to support new technologies and products and (b) process capability for improving functional performance. Combining these ideas creates a competitiveness map of an industry, as shown in Figure 2–2. The process and product axes share a dedication to customer satisfaction—the factor that results in the long-term success of the organization. In addition, a company can plot an assessment of its current position against that of competitors. These factors must be interpreted in the light of the movement of competitors and potential challengers, to provide a meaningful long-term direction for resource allocation and market strategy. The competitiveness map is a new approach to understanding the competitive dynamics of an industry from a balanced perspective of both product-focused (technology and market) and business process factors.

The lesson learned from identifying the need for an integrated approach to strategy parallels the need for an integrated approach to benchmarking. The bias of many beginning benchmarkers leads them to focus only on those processes which, if understood, will ensure the success of their project—for example, a manufacturing process such as printed circuit board loading, or an administrative process such as patent application. A mature company's approach to benchmarking will focus the majority of a its available resources on benchmarking key, cross-functional business processes that support the long-term strategic intent and develop process capability, or on those areas that develop core competence. The synchronization of the benchmarking

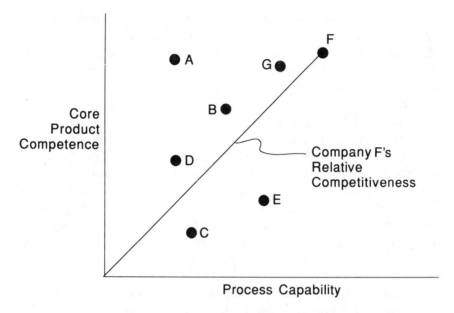

Figure 2-2. Relating Process Capability and Product Competence to Industry Competitiveness

activities and the strategic intent of a company form the fundamental principle behind strategic benchmarking.

WHAT IS STRATEGIC BENCHMARKING?

Benchmarking involves the application of process benchmarking techniques and methods to the development of an increased understanding of strategic business issues, with the cooperation of companies that participate in long-term business alliances. Bill Lehman, managing partner of the Price Waterhouse Manufacturing Management Consulting Practice, has observed that strategic benchmarking is similar, in application, to benchmarking of operational processes, but it is different in scope. "Armed with this [strategic benchmarking] information, the process of developing a vision of the changed organization can be very rich indeed."[19]

What issues are addressed by strategic benchmarking as opposed to "operational" benchmarking? Among the issues are: building core competencies that will help to sustain competitive advantage; targeting a specific shift in strategy, such as entering new markets or developing new products; developing a new line of business or making an acquisition; and creating an organization that is more capable of learning how to respond in an uncertain future because it has increased its acceptance of change.

In the mid-1980s, when Jack Welch, a forward-thinking CEO of General Electric, wanted to position his company for the coming decade, he asked his strategic planning group to study how successful companies positioned themselves for continuous improvement. The General Electric benchmarking team conducted internal interviews of leading GE divisions and visited nine companies in the United States and Japan. They found that the companies that had set aggressive goals (such as halving the product development cycle time, or tripling the level of productivity) had high levels of sustained improvement. These leading companies viewed productivity as a combined issue of customer satisfaction and competitiveness. The benchmarking team also observed a common approach to change: driven by top-down changes in the management system, the emphasis was on process rather than on programs (or, in their words, input over output). The conclusion of the study provided an operating definition of a company that is a world-class competitor:[20]

- Knows its processes better than its competitors know their processes;
- Knows the industry competitors better than its competitors know them;
- Knows its customers better than its competitors know their customers;
- Responds more rapidly to customer behavior than do competitors;
- Uses employees more effectively than do competitors;
- Competes for market share on a customer-by-customer basis.

Aside from its interesting observations, why is this particular GE study significant? Note its parallels to the earlier discussion of core competence and process capability. GE applied benchmarking in the area of strategy to address the same basic issues, and the GE results reinforce the need for an integrated approach to understanding competition, in order to satisfy customers in the long run. In its approach to benchmarking, GE observed the change in strategic direction and company culture (values and vision) over a three-year period. Each of its benchmarking partners joined the study for the long haul. They participated by allowing the GE interviewers to visit multiple facilities over the duration of the study. The study was, in effect, an extension of GE's approach to forming strategic alliances with technological partners by seeking strategic partners who could help GE learn the lessons of adaptation for the future. A final interesting observation is that the GE study was directed out of the strategic planning function, which clearly illustrates the contribution of benchmarking for developing long-range plans.

STRATEGIC BENCHMARKING AS AN ELEMENT OF PLANNING

The job of planning is to take into account the uncertainties of the future and make preparations that will carry the organization through that time, especially by setting achievable goals that will bridge to the future. How can challenging, yet achievable goals be set to direct an organization's vision of the future? One lesson that needs to be learned is that the different stakeholders in the organization—customers, stock analysts, employees, and management— have different perspectives and values for making their judgments about its goodness. All share a common perspective in wanting the organization to continue to improve and create value for them. This requires the organization to learn how to adapt to a changing environment faster and more effectively than its competitors will. In an article on performance measures, Robert S. Kaplan and David P. Norton observe that benchmarking is a technique that companies use to set goals based on external standards: "[T]he company looks to one industry to find, say the best distribution system, to another industry for the lowest cost payroll process, and then forms a composite of those best practices to set objectives for its own performance."[21] This is the essence of strategic benchmarking and the link to a company's planning process. Companies selected for benchmarking because of their key business process knowledge and performance indexes can serve as a basis for establishing challenging, yet realistic and achievable goals. When John Young was driving Hewlett-Packard toward tenfold improvement of its hardware reliability during the 1980s, he encouraged management not to think "the same old way." He deliberately chose goals to stretch the organization—to challenge it to do things differently. The goals were out of the reach of its current process capability so that it could not finesse a goal by doing things the "same old way." Change was necessary or it wouldn't be able to meet the goal.[22] Roger Milliken has observed: "Insanity is doing the same thing the same way and expecting a different result."[23]

What is the process for applying strategic benchmarking to a company's planning process? This activity tends to be a staff function, as the GE example indicated; it supports the development of objectives by the senior staff, and guides the selection of appropriate goals during the catchball with middle management. A process flow

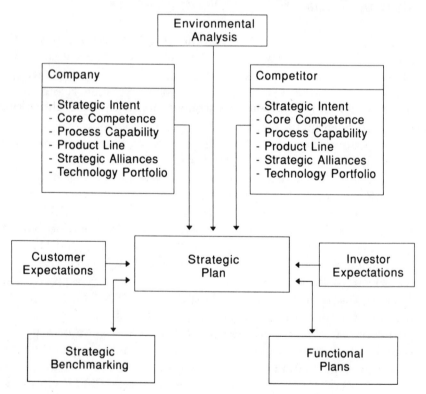

Figure 2–3.   The Application of Strategic Benchmarking

of planning considerations illustrates how strategic benchmarking fits into the development of the strategic plan (see Figure 2–3) and then flows into annual or functional plans. Note that head-to-head comparisons are made between the company's own strategy and that of the major competitor. In addition, customer expectations and investor expectations must be factored into the strategic plan along with an environmental analysis (considerations from government regulations, technology developments, economic conditions, and similar factors). Strategic benchmarking studies address particular issues in the strategic plan: development of organizational infrastructure, establishment of goals and objectives, selection of key business processes for improvement, identification of technology areas targeted for development, and so on. The scope of the strategic benchmarking study is established by the senior management team, but the method for conducting the study is the same as for all process benchmarking studies. The method will be described in depth in the following chapter.

INFLUENCING A PLAN FOR THE FUTURE

A company that is developing its strategic approach to benchmarking should consider establishing long-standing relationships with a limited number of companies that will serve as a network for sharing strategic direction and methodology. A company should consider its natural alliances as a starting point for developing a small number of strategic partners. (GE used nine companies and planned to increase it to no more than 16.) The natural alliances include those with customers (major accounts and product distribution channels, in particular), suppliers (preferred suppliers, in particular), stockholders (major institutional stockholders or companies with large interests), strategic alliances (companies in which the benchmarking company holds a significant interest, or with which it has technology, patent-sharing, manufacturing, or OEM agreements). These companies may be supplemented by others that have earned management admiration for their business performance. No matter how the initial list of companies is formed, it is important to establish a set of objective selection criteria (described in detail in Chapter 3), in order to identify the companies that have the best possible long-term contribution toward understanding of strategic alternatives. This use of networks, alliances, or even "good friends" permits the influence of a consistent external perspective in the process of developing strategic direction.

External perspective is a value normally described for external members of a company's board of directors. Strategic benchmarking studies are based on facts culled from direct observation within the context of the organization's own problem; the members of the board of directors must rely on recollections of personal experiences, and these, most probably, are restricted to conditions that are different from those facing the current management team. The external board of directors can apply seasoned judgment to a particular situation, but the strategic benchmarking study can complement this judgment with a solid factual basis, providing "fodder" for the debate on which directions to set.

The stakeholders in a company have a right to understand and influence the direction of that company. Stakeholders are stockholders, industry analysts, customers, employees, managers, and, like it or not, the government—local, state, and federal. The most active participants in the stakeholder role of advisers to management tend to be the community of investors, customers, and employees. These groups share a common trait: "Everyone is a volunteer." None of these groups has to invest its energy or resources into the organization; each has a choice of where it will invest, purchase, or work. The volunteers must be convinced that they should "re-enlist" as participants in the company's future. The bridge to the future is in the lessons that an organization learns today and in its ability to apply the lessons rapidly for growth in the future. Core competencies and process capabilities may be invisible to the external stakeholders, but their importance is fundamental to their best interests. Communicating the lessons learned from a company's overall learning strategy is essential; all stakeholders will then understand the strategic direction, and the organization can align its goals in a congruent manner. However, the ability to satisfy the various stakeholders of the company is only as great as the company's ability to internalize the lessons of benchmarking.

3

Understanding the Essentials of Process Benchmarking

I stated earlier that benchmarking is developing from an art into a science. Yet, to qualify as a *quality science,* a discipline needs to incorporate a distinct body of knowledge consisting of, at a minimum, a basic theory, a process model, and examples of demonstrated results from business applications. Many quality experts tend to focus on these minimum requirements as compartmentalized or separate issues; too few spend the time and effort required to promote a comprehensive body of knowledge that focuses on broader business issues. *The appropriate acquisition and application of quality methods, combined with the continuous pursuit of business knowledge, sets the foundation for successful benchmarking.* To put a new twist on an old adage, it's not just whether you win or lose; it's how well you *continue* to play the game.

Many quality professionals choose to implement every available quality tool by training all professional-level employees in how to use each one, but not necessarily in how each one is used to complement the others. When the International Quality Study conducted by Ernst & Young and the American Quality Foundation[1] reviewed the application of various management and quality practices—those recommended for improving productivity, quality, and profitability—it was found that many of these tools do not, in and of themselves, provide significant gains. The study also indicated that inappropriately used tools can have a negative effect leading to decreased productivity, quality, and profitability performance. No correlation was found between generic quality approaches and the level of a company's performance—an indication that there is no single, minimal solution for implementing Total Quality Management (TQM) in a company-wide application. The true implication of this finding is that companies must create their own TQM process by adapting appropriate practices from the full set of quality and management practices. Thus, the careful selection of management practices and quality tools is imperative to the design of a well-functioning organization and should be based on the particular context within which they will be applied. The same is true of benchmarking.

Companies that have failed to benefit from their benchmarking efforts tend to overlook a basic prerequisite: quality preparedness. For instance, although benchmarking is an advanced quality practice, the effectiveness of any benchmarking activity is still greatly dependent on the basic quality skills: interpersonal communications (which support team activities), problem-solving and decision-making methods, simple statistical methods for data analysis and graphical display, and business process analysis, modeling, and documentation. Although knowledge of these basic skills is, in fact, a requirement for conducting a successful benchmarking study, it is not a substantial enough basis from which to begin. The ongoing *application and development* of key quality and decision tools, both *qualitative and quantitative* practices, need to be an existing, functional part of an organization's managerial repertoire. The factors that comprise the fundamental aspect of the benchmarking team's study approach are described in the following sections.

COMPANY PARTICIPATION

When should a company actively participate in benchmarking, and at what rate should it cultivate interest in the application of this advanced quality practice?

As an advanced quality practice, benchmarking is an exciting management process to implement. It legitimizes the pure observation of well-run businesses, provides the in-depth learning needed to support process improvement, and helps to improve the career potential of team participants. These elements alone generally create an enthusiastic response to the proposed implementation of benchmarking. In fact, most business management teams have observed that benchmarking is the only quality practice that is most often accepted with little resistance.

However, an overwhelming impetus to jump on the bandwagon should be a sign to management that a need exists to contain this enthusiasm. One way to do so is by conducting a quality maturity assessment to determine an organization's readiness for benchmarking. The assessment will establish the degree of benchmarking that is appropriate to support the outstanding strategic and tactical business issues. In other words, a company must be sure it knows where it is, and where it needs to go, before it sets out on its journey. Early success in benchmarking comes from selecting appropriate initial studies—those that will "make a difference" in the operation of the business. By basing the requirement for benchmarking on immediate business objectives, management can help to ensure that the organization's involvement in benchmarking provides a near-term payoff and, hence, justifies the need for conducting the study. Management should consider providing a specific commission—including team membership and boundary levels for authority and responsibility—as well as dedicated resources, ongoing review, and consistent support for progress achieved in benchmarking studies.

BENCHMARKING AND QUALITY ASSESSMENT

What assessment of quality maturity should a management team make when considering the appropriateness of a benchmarking effort?

The implementation of benchmarking practices should complement the quality development of a business. This concept of quality maturity is based on close observation of the progress in quality movements within Hewlett-Packard, Compaq Computer, and Xerox over the past decade.

The concept of quality maturity was first introduced by Philip Crosby in *Quality Is Free*.[2] Crosby used a quality maturity grid to evaluate progress among companies in introducing his philosophy. The concept as described here differs slightly from Crosby's, but the underlying concept is similar. The quality maturity of an existing business follows a four-stage development process; it progresses as the concept of quality grows and develops. The four stages in quality development are: inspection, control, partnership, and maturity. They are defined in the following sections. The discussion of each stage indicates how the application of benchmarking should coincide with the development of a firm's overall quality maturity.

Inspection

A company that tends to concentrate on the quality of its end product or service is characteristic of a business in the early stages of quality development. Its focus is on quality assurance (QA), the quality inspection aspect of assurance. QA, as defined in *Juran's Quality Control Handbook,* is:

> The activity of providing evidence needed to establish confidence, among all concerned, that the quality function is being effectively performed.[3]

Inspection-based quality systems tend to focus on the measurement of completed products or services against a predetermined standard for both incoming materials from suppliers and outgoing products to customers. The quality methods used are dependent on measurement, standards, calibration, testing tools and methods, problem solving, and discrepant material handling.

Companies with an inspection-based quality approach soon find that inspection is an inefficient means to determine failures and keep them from reaching customers. Instead, a preventative approach, extending the QA mission into the areas of quality engineering and quality control, is required. In such cases, benchmarking is not an appropriate emphasis for the quality program, because the company has not established the prerequisites for its benchmarking studies. A company in the earliest stages of quality development should begin by focusing on developing fundamental quality capabilities; it should not de-focus its efforts by attempting to cover the world with a dazzling array of quality tools. The challenge for management will be to contain the desire of individual teams to benchmark when they should be putting their energy into their own attempt at process improvement. As an aid to management, the benchmarking process recommended in this book will eventually bring the teams back to the point where they recognize the need to focus on their own process as a necessary stage in benchmarking.

Control

The second level of quality maturity develops when a company begins to focus on prevention by emphasizing control on design engineering and manufacturing. This is accomplished by establishing product documentation and critical part parameters, as well as by monitoring manufacturing and distribution processes using statistical quality control and basic statistical tools. This level of maturity is marked by "organizational introspection," or a focus on those aspects of final product quality that can be controlled internally. Inspection is then used to complement the introduction of control methods. As maturity develops in the control systems, the inspection function is gradually transferred from an independent quality organization to the workers who actually perform the activities of production.

The control approach to quality becomes an operational function of the company in that each functional organization has a defined responsibility for delivering quality to the next functional organization throughout the product's or service's development. This hands-off phase tends to require testing (for example, a field readiness demonstration test for design engineering or pilot production for manufacturing), which provides assurance that responsibilities have been met. Meanwhile, the concept of internal customers is beginning to be realized.[4]

During the development of quality control maturity, companies tend to recognize the need for facilitated teamwork, basic statistical tools, interpersonal communication skills, and business process analysis using flow-charting techniques. The concept of internal customers can be further integrated to encourage intraorganizational cooperation and to establish the principle of participation by all employees in achieving process improvement. These elements of quality control help to improve productivity by establishing an analytical approach that can be used in problem solving by functional teams.

In this control phase, a company develops its capability in applying the appropriate quality tools and documenting their processes, often to the ISO 9000 standard.[5] The company may even take on selected advanced quality practices that enhance particular functional areas, such as design of experiments and quality function deployment for engineering; statistical process control in manufacturing; or customer satisfaction surveying in marketing. At this point, a firm may be prepared to consider applying benchmarking as a business practice.

Initial interest in benchmarking at this stage may follow one of two tracks. The first is participation in an industry-specific study of, perhaps, one of the company's key business practices. For example, a chemical manufacturer may study environmental waste management, or a computer manufacturer may study common distribution systems. The second type of participation that can occur is a sponsored study that is of strategic significance to the business, conducted by an external organization such as a trade association or consulting firm. Both of these types of study should be carefully controlled by management. Management-directed studies will help to initiate the application of benchmarking in a limited context, and will provide an opportunity for management to learn how to use this practice in the future. If this learning opportunity is not captured, then implementation of benchmarking as a general practice may be suboptimized and not linked into the strategic direction of the business.

Partnership

The third level of quality maturity naturally follows as businesses observe the need for greater internal cooperation or partnership among their various functional organizations. For functional organizations to operate internally at their most efficient levels, they need to develop cross-functional perspectives and relationships. The seams of an organization are most strained where the transference of knowledge is hindered by professional distinctions among its organizational functions. Typically, each functional organization speaks its own language and applies its own methods to achieve specific goals. Only with practice and experience can individuals effectively translate information coming across "foreign" boundaries.

Part of management's job is to help move cross-functional processes beyond these intraorganizational boundaries. The key focus in this phase of internal development is on overall business process; simultaneously, relationships are developed through improved interpersonal communication skills. In this level of development, the meaning of internal customers is extended from one's own internal work group to the concept of "associates"—the individuals who are working together as a larger team to deliver the needs, expectations, and requirements of the ultimate customer, the external consumer of the firm's products and services.

The partnership level of quality maturity also recognizes the broader partnerships that occur with suppliers and with external customers. Suppliers contribute to the final quality of the product or service delivered to the customer and they share in the desire to achieve the lowest possible cost and highest quality. In addition, soliciting customer participation early in the design and production processes has been demonstrated by many leading companies to improve the quality and reduce the cycle time of the product development process. Gaining customer involvement in product development has also been shown to have a favorable effect on the final market acceptance of the product.

Partnerships may take the form of strategic alliances for technology development or cross-licensing of patents, manufacturing, distribution, or service. Companies involved in these external partnership activities have reached mature levels of quality. They are prepared for a strategic approach to benchmarking that supports the improvement of management-selected key business processes (as described in Chapter 2).

Maturity

The fourth level of quality maturity is characterized by the seemingly automatic consideration of quality issues in all areas within the business system: the underlying attitude of teamwork in all areas of operations; the use of data to drive all decision processes, and the elevation of the customer's satisfaction to the forefront of all business decisions. This maturity level is utopian. Naturally, they benchmark.

THE THEORY BEHIND BENCHMARKING

Benchmarking is a management practice that facilitates the continuous input of new information to an organization. As defined earlier, it is a "systematic and continuous measurement process." Robert C.

Camp, manager of benchmarking competency at Xerox Corporation, has offered a simplified description of benchmarking as:

> A positive, proactive process by which a company examines how another company performs a specific function in order to improve how it performs the same, or similar function.[6]

Benchmarking seeks two types of information: measures that indicate process excellence, and enabling activities that have produced the observed exceptional results. The benchmarking process, therefore, serves as a venue where organizational learning progresses and where external opportunities for further learning and development are discovered. James H. Trask, director of international competitive analysis at General Motors Corporation, described the purpose of benchmarking as twofold: "To learn and improve."[7] The objective of benchmarking, as described by Carla O'Dell, senior vice president at APQC and director of the International Benchmarking Clearinghouse, is to "accelerate the process of business change that leads to both breakthrough and continuous improvements in products, services, and processes—that results in total customer satisfaction and competitive advantage—by adapting business process improvements and best practices of organizations who are recognized for excellence in execution."[8]

Learning occurs because a gap in performance is observed and the root causes of that performance gap are identified. The gap between a company's observed internal practices and observed external practices creates the need for managed change. An understanding of an industry's best practices identifies what must be changed internally, the externally benchmarked practices provide a picture of the potential results from implementing these changes.

To introduce the theory of benchmarking, the chapter builds on these definitions and objectives to present the basic principles and code of conduct. It then moves on to the questions for which benchmarking teams seek answers, and it concludes with a description of the process model for benchmarking. These considerations will provide a background for study of the applications of benchmarking made by various businesses to help improve their operations. The next section begins this journey by describing the essence of a benchmarking process in terms of four principles which, when followed, will result in a successful study. These principles are: reciprocity, analogy, measurement, and validity.

THE PRINCIPLES OF BENCHMARKING

Reciprocity

The key to successful benchmarking is the principle of reciprocity. Benchmarking is a practice based on reciprocal relationships, as reflected in the popular phrase "creating a win–win situation." All participants are winners as a result of the information shared and exchanged between the companies. Reciprocity, however, does not happen blindly. Information boundaries and data exchanges must be negotiated up front, along with the logistical considerations of conducting the study. Each benchmarking partner must be assured of each other's intention. A "win–win" will not result if there is fear of intrusion or misappropriation, as can occur when benchmarking objectives have not been clearly defined. Creating a "win–lose" or "lose–lose" situation—regardless of intention—is a reflection of how well each participant plays the game. When seeking a benchmarking partner, a company should always consider that any motivation to participate in the study will be precipitated by the other company's silent (usually) perception of: What's in it for us? A company must be able to deliver what has been negotiated and agreed to up front.

Analogy

Benchmarking a company with a nonanalogous process is like going to a vegetarian barbecue. An enjoyable experience, but where's the beef? Even if the food is tasty, the menu cannot satisfy a meat lover.

Operational processes must be comparative or analogous if the highest degree of knowledge transfer between benchmarking partners is to be achieved. Any work process from any company may be evaluated, as long as the team conducting the study is able to translate the other organization's cultural, structural, and business context into its own. In short, when teams return to their own companies, they must be able to demonstrate how to adapt and implement the lessons learned. Building this analogy and understanding the explicit criteria for selection of benchmarking partners will, ultimately, determine a company's success in discovering business process improvement opportunities.

Measurement

Benchmarking is a measured performance comparison between two companies; the objective is to understand why the varying degrees of performance exist and how the higher degree of performance was obtained. The why and how of process performance are called process enablers. In other words, identifying the specific key aspects of a process that lead to increased performance is tantamount to trying to understand how a whole process fits together. Careful measurement and observation of analogous processes ultimately enable companies to adapt identified process enablers to their own processes.

The measurement systems and tools used in process analysis are dependent on the factors being measured. The same systems and tools should be used for process analysis by each benchmarking partner. Here again, knowledge of and experience with basic quality tools application are essential.

A measurement system in this context refers to the extent of the measurement history. This includes baseline measures and monitored measures over time, as well as a description of controlled variables and an indication of any existing uncontrolled variables. When interpreting data and measured results, it's important to stay within the established process context. A tendency to seek only "the good" may result in an oversight of obfuscated weaknesses, especially when the context is ignored. This occurs most often when the scope of the measurement context is either too narrow or too broad. A keen eye is needed to spot "false" enablers or performance results. However, asking the following questions can help clarify this issue:

- What is the extent of time over which the process was measured?
- Was there any change in the measurement system, such as the measurement tools used?
- How much of the measurement system relies on human observation or correlation, versus true data analysis?
- How are these correlations substantiated?

- How often or at what intervals were measures taken?
- What is the estimated margin for error?
- Are all controlled variables accounted for?
- Are there any uncontrolled variables, and have adjustments been made for them?
- Are the measures verifiable, auditable, or repeatable?

Experienced benchmarkers recognize that it is often necessary to make estimates of performance, but they are primarily driven by a desire to estimate performance using the best data available and deriving any "missing" data, whenever possible, from other data sources using accepted practices.

Validity

Most companies willing to partner in benchmarking have no problem sharing their own measures or encouraging their partners to measure a representative sample of their process through inspection and observation. To ensure accurate representation, sample measures—measures of occurrences over time or place—need to correspond to the measurement system used. One reason for a company's wanting to complete its own sample measurement is to check for reliability. Because reliability can be validated, process measurement validation should be an objective for all process owners.

In order to observe and correlate process enablers (the specific practices that caused increased performance) with the process performance measures, valid facts and data must be collected and used for process comparisons. Relying on intuition, opinion, or assumption only leads to "guesstimates" that cannot ensure validity or reliability. At the risk of overstatement, these two factors are essential to an effective process. A benchmarking process must follow a "management-by-fact," data-driven approach to business process analysis rather than a "management-by-gut," intuition-based approach.[9] At this point, according to Noriaki Kano of the Union of Japanese Scientists and Engineers (JUSE), a team must learn to "sweat" in order to achieve quality. The problem with too many companies is that they are 90 percent aspiration and only 10 percent perspiration when it comes to exercising the quality tools to conduct root-cause problem analysis using process measurement data. A characteristic of more mature companies in quality execution is a natural propensity for data-driven decision making and problem solving.

These four principles of benchmarking form the methodological basis for conducting a study; the Benchmarking Code of Conduct (see Appendix A) provides the protocol. The Code is, in reality, an extension of basic business ethics. It was developed to serve as a reminder of the specific principles that should govern the relationships among benchmarking partners.[10]

THE BENCHMARKING CODE OF CONDUCT

One sign of the development of a professional body of knowledge is an accepted standard or code of behavior. Such a code of behavior has been developed jointly by the American Productivity & Quality Center's International Benchmarking Clearinghouse (APQC IBC) and the Strategic Planning Institute (SPI) Council on Benchmarking.[11] It summarizes the protocol of benchmarking—the set of conventions prescribing correct etiquette and procedures to be used in conducting benchmarking studies. The Benchmarking Code of Conduct has been signed by each of the members of the APQC IBC and has been adopted by the membership of the SPI Council on Benchmarking. It presents a good definition of the collaborative efforts that mark the behavioral interactions between benchmarking partners. A brief discussion of the nine principles within the Benchmarking Code of Conduct follows; the complete text is reproduced as Appendix A.

Principle of Legality

Essentially, this principle deals with refraining from any discussion or actions that may imply a restraint of trade, market and customer allocation schemes, price fixing, dealing arrangements, bid rigging or bribery, acquisition of trade secrets, or disclosure of proprietary information. Before proprietary information can be shared, the consulting lawyers may require both companies to execute nondisclosure agreements prior to the study. Stated simply and succinctly: if in doubt, don't; if there's a question, seek legal counsel.

Principle of Exchange

Benchmarking has always assumed a quid pro quo, with each organization realizing an ability to make process improvement as a result of its interaction. The real need is to be sure that each organization gets something of value from the investment of its time in the study. The Golden Rule applies here. Never ask for any type of information or data that your own company would be reluctant to share with another. Xerox benchmarkers explicitly state that they do not want their partners to share information that would be considered proprietary by their partners' management. To alleviate concerns about equitable exchanges, it is important to clarify expectations and objectives, and to set informational parameters up front, before engaging in any benchmarking activities. Complete, open, and honest communication in the initial stages of establishing the benchmarking relationship can help each partner understand the value of the exchange to be made. The exchange may be as simple as receiving a copy of the trip report that documents the benchmarking team's observations of the process at the partner company or a copy of their final report (with other participants' information "blinded," to prevent inadvertent disclosure of information). The exchange may also be an agreement to conduct a reciprocal benchmarking study that has more relevance to the partner company.

Principle of Confidentiality

Treat all information gained from any benchmarking partner as proprietary and confidential. Never disclose anything learned about a benchmarking partner to another company without the benchmarking partner's expressed permission. Benchmarking study findings should not be extended to another company without getting the benchmarking partner's agreement to do so beforehand.

Principle of Use

Information gained from any benchmarking study is for the sole purpose of improving operational processes within a company. Never use benchmarking as a means for advertising, marketing, or selling.

Principle of First-Party Contact

Always initiate benchmarking contacts with the partner's process owners through the designated benchmarking contact at the specific company. If such a designation or person is not known to you, try contacting the appropriate senior manager, quality manager, or human resources manager for assistance. The most appropriate venue for making contact is one that is respectful of the other company's corporate culture. Always obtain agreement with the benchmarking contact (whether designated or eventual) regarding any hand-off communication and fulfillment of responsibility among the benchmarking team participants.

Principle of Third-Party Contact

Do not share the names of company's benchmarking participants with other companies requesting contacts, without first gaining permission to do so from those persons as well as from the benchmarking contact person.

Principle of Preparation

Complete all preparatory work prior to contacting a prospective benchmarking partner. This includes assessing and being aware of your company's quality maturity level. Know where your own process strengths and weaknesses lie: complete internal studies and comparisons, measurements, validation, and so on, before seeking outside analogies. Use a benchmarking process model to guide and formalize your approach to the benchmarking study. This model should be understood by all parties as a means to set expectations about the degree of detail to be used in the study and to establish agreement about the logistics of conducting the study. Determine what information you are willing to share, and have it prepared in a presentable and complete manner. Provide any type of interview guide, questionnaire, or other appropriate documentation to your prospective benchmarking partner. Let the partner know specifically what you are looking for. Finally, when working with a benchmarking partner, make the time together valuable to both parties.

Principle of Completion

Do not make any commitment to a benchmarking partner if you are not certain you will be able to follow through in a timely and propitious manner. Be sure that the completion of each benchmarking study has reached a satisfactory and agreeable conclusion for all parties.

Principle of Understanding and Action

Before starting a benchmarking study, gain explicit understanding and agreement as to how both your company and your partner company would like to have information treated and handled. Adhere to that agreement. Always honor the protocol and guidelines for interaction of any benchmarking partner.

These nine principles are not to be taken lightly, nor are they to be viewed as separate items. These principles should be seen and interpreted as complete, structured guidelines for appropriate behavior in benchmarking.

The Benchmarking Code of Conduct is not, however, intended as a substitute for the advice of legal counsel whenever doubts exist as to the propriety of sharing information among companies. Indeed, different industries, because of their historical development, are much more susceptible to concern about information sharing and antitrust violations than others may be. Much of American industry is still hampered by earlier antitrust legislation—the Sherman Act of 1890, the Clayton Act of 1914, the Federal Trade Commission Act of 1914, and the Robinson–Patman Act of 1936. These Acts, written generations ago, in a different business environment, were intended to protect trade and commerce from unlawful restraints, price discrimination, price fixing, and monopolies. In today's global marketplace, they hamstring discussions among many American companies that must compete against international and multinational organizations not restricted by these laws. If these laws applied in Japan, for example, as they do in the United States, their continued existence would be of value. Because this is not the case, laws of this nature are proving to be more and more antiquated; they reflect the antithesis of

American productivity and quality progress. As business moves more toward a more cooperative model and differentiates its competitive focus more sharply, the need for further dialogue on common issues becomes stronger. National competitiveness can only be achieved when the businesses of a nation can be free to discuss their common issues without fear of reprisal from their government.

THE QUESTIONS OF BENCHMARKING

Perhaps the most straightforward approach to understanding the process model for benchmarking is to consider the questions that are often asked by teams conducting benchmarking studies. Teams tend to follow a two-dimensional discovery process in benchmarking. The first dimension is internal performance, which includes determining what operational process to study and developing the internal measures of performance for that process. The second dimension is external performance, which includes identifying external companies as benchmark candidates and learning from them by determining their performance measures and gaining knowledge about their process capability.

These two dimensions permit analysis of the existing performance gap between the two companies. This gap can be identified by first establishing and comparing the measurements of the relative process capabilities, and then identifying and recognizing the set of activities or enablers applied by the best practice company to achieve its performance. These enablers provide a cornucopia of ideas on how the internal processes can be improved. In simple, common-sense terms, benchmarking means:

- Determining what operational process to study;
- Discovering the performance level of excellence in that process relative to one's own firm's process performance;
- Deciding how to make the changes that will result in improvement in one's own company.

As teams conduct their study of these internal and external dimensions, they tend to ask themselves four questions:

1. What should *we* benchmark?
2. Whom should *we* benchmark?
3. How do *we* perform the process?
4. How do *they* perform the process?

These four questions form the basis of a benchmarking process template developed jointly by Boeing, Digital Equipment Company, Motorola, and Xerox, to help facilitate their communications on benchmarking projects. Each of these companies used its own process model to conduct its benchmarking studies; however, agreement on the general approach to benchmarking was obtained by developing the template illustrated in Figure 3–1.[12]

What Should WE Benchmark?

Decisions on what to benchmark are based on a company's business objectives, as well as its quality maturity level. Management's task is to gain consensus on which processes should be selected for study.

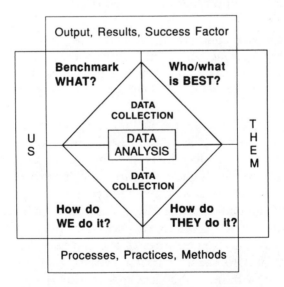

Figure 3–1. The Benchmarking Template

This is a key leverage point for management because it allows for the alignment of the company's strategic direction with the major team activities that are ongoing in the company. By specifically chartering benchmarking teams to study those processes that most greatly influence business performance, management also implies support for the implementation of team discoveries. This alone can increase team motivation.

APQC's 1991 survey of benchmarking in major companies indicated that the cost of a benchmarking study can range from $5,000 to well over $100,000, depending on the need for external consultants, research support, and travel.[13] A robust benchmarking study, even conducted by internal people, may consume around $60,000. Because most companies have limited resources to devote to benchmarking studies, prudent managers should focus benchmarking teams on key business processes—those that will provide significant payoffs and will justify the time and effort extended.

How does one determine key business processes? *Business processes* are logical combinations of people, equipment, materials, and methods organized into work activities that produce desired outputs.[14] In a speech to senior executives at Chevron, John Young, CEO of Hewlett-Packard, described all business activity as "process":

> We have come to recognize that all activities are essentially process. If we focus on improving our processes, then we can achieve gains in productivity, cost reduction, and quality by eliminating those problems areas where we don't do the process right the first time.[15]

The basic lesson learned in the quality movement relates to process and the Pareto principle (the 80/20 rule, or 20 percent of all activity affects 80 percent of results): focus should be on those "critical few" processes that have the highest potential for "return on attention." These are the *key business processes;* they produce outputs that contribute directly and materially to the operation of the business. These processes represent the core, cross-functional efforts that influence the external customer's perception of the company. They are prime process candidates for benchmarking because they have a broader scope than specific business practices and are essential to achieving the critical success factors of an organization. Some examples of key business processes that may be candidates for benchmarking consideration include: product or service definition and development, customer service performance, product pricing, production control, inventory management, and purchasing. The degree to which any of these processes is a "key business process" depends on the specific factors that drive a particular business.[16]

Business practices are those methods or approaches that facilitate the execution of a business process. Examples include presidential reviews, management bonus systems, organizational structure for product development, training and development of employees, and the application of specific analytic tools, such as design of experiments, quality function deployment, or benchmarking. Both business practices and critical success factors may be enablers of benchmark performance in business processes.

Critical success factors (CSFs) are those characteristics, conditions, or variables that have direct influence on customers' satisfaction with the output—product or service or both—of specific business processes and, hence, are critical to the success of the entire business. These factors represent measurable or observable aspects of business processes, which, when performed well, result in the continuing growth and success of a business. In short, they are the critical few factors that have the most impact across the entire business system. Examples of critical success factors include: cost management, perceived product quality, product design features, and company image. To determine its critical success factors, a company must identify those process performance measures that indicate the quantitative level of performance for a key business process.[17] Because identifying key process enablers through the discovery process of benchmarking is the true objective of a benchmarking study, the initial focus is usually based on the need for either a reactive or a preventive initiative. Examples are: an identified problem area (reactive), a strategic change initiative or business process reengineering project (preventive), or a continuous process improvement effort (preventive). Once the initial focus of a benchmarking study has been determined and the key business process has been identified, an operational definition needs to be completed.

An *operational definition* is one that describes the critical success factor—in terms of observable characteristics or measurements—of the process being defined. In other words, it is used to clarify, in specific terms that everyone involved can understand, the critical success factor that a company is going to benchmark. The definition's objective is to gain understanding; whether everyone agrees with the definition should not be allowed to become an issue.

Creating an operational definition begins with a statement, in exact terms, of the objective one wants to achieve. This is called a "benchmark goal statement." For example, suppose the key business process to be benchmarked is "filling customer orders." The study is being conducted to identify enablers that will help to reduce distribution time and costs. Given this objective, the benchmark goal statement may read: "Prompt customer delivery at a minimal distribution cost."

This statement is straightforward, but does it completely specify what the company needs to know? Could its team thoroughly discuss this objective with a benchmarking partner? For instance, does it indicate what the objective will "look like," once it has been achieved? How will participants know it when they see it? What does prompt mean? How is it measured? Who is the customer? Where and how is the product delivered, and to whom? How is "minimal" measured? What does distribution entail? How is cost established?

The next step in completing an operational definition is to define each of the operative terms within the benchmark goal statement. Figure 3–2 is an example of what an operational definition based on this scenario might look like.[18]

Once the operational definition has been completed and agreed on, key measures and methods of data display need to be selected. For instance, what is the company going to measure: dollars, units, sales, shipments; percent of customers per locale, percent of shipments per locale, percent of sales per locale; some of the above; or all of the above? How will the company illustrate the measurement results obtained? In making this determination, the following questions should be considered:

- What measure or measures will give us the best picture of reality in terms of what we want to know?

- Do we have the information or data needed for these measures?

- Is the information available in a measure that will meet our needs?

Operative Term:	Operative Definition:
Prompt	Within 48 hours regardless of destination or size of order/shipment.
Customer	External: Users of our educational products; sales centers. Internal: Market reps; consultants.
Delivery	Means: U.S. mail, UPS, or Federal Express, depending on customer locale or delivery destination. Point of origin: Centralized distribution center.
Minimal	Not to exceed 3% of sales price per unit.
Cost	Dollars per shipment.

Figure 3–2.   Example of an Operational Definition

- Is the measure common enough among industry or business representatives that comparable measures can be found?
- Can these measures be charted for making comparisons?
- How likely is it that another company will have comparable data?
- How likely is it that another company will give us this information?
- Would we give it to another company that may or may not be a competitor?

Whom Should We Benchmark?

Many companies focus on seeking the "best of the breed" or the "best of the best" as a benchmarking partner for a particular process. However, if there is only one known "best," that company will soon be overwhelmed by requests for benchmarking studies. Moreover, "the best" may be a Fortune 50 company, which may be analogous to another Fortune 50 company or to a Fortune 500 company, but not to a Fortune 5000 company. Additionally, "the best" may reflect only some particular activities, not an overall process. Thus, compiling a final set of adaptable enablers may result only after observing the "best" among several companies. This approach may prove to be costly, time-consuming, and frustrating.

A more careful approach to determining "whom we should benchmark" is to first examine the specific criteria outlined in the operational definition. Rather than seeking the "best of the best," it may be more advantageous to seek a partner that is considered to be an example of "performance success" in an analogous process.

These criteria can also help to ensure that "political acceptability" issues do not drive the selection process. Given the existence of personal biases, the potential for learning can be influenced by the degree of admiration held for a particular company. This aspect is often overlooked when teams are left to select partners without management participation. Therefore, management should be involved in helping the team to stay focused on the defined criteria, or in helping them to develop any additional criteria that may be required for partner selection. For instance, one company, concerned about the cost of travel for conducting a benchmarking study, limited its teams to making direct observations at companies within a 50-mile radius of its plant. Because this company's "local benchmarking" partners provided enough creative substance to stimulate process improvements, any residual or subsequent argument for visiting the "best" became moot. The concept of "selection criteria" is discussed in more detail later in the chapter.

Management may also be helpful in assisting the benchmarking team's examination of existing intercompany relationships. This is done to determine whether any natural company alliances (long-term suppliers, technology sharing agreements, manufacturing alliances, distribution channels, major accounts, and so on) meet the criteria for both analogy and success, and are willing and available to participate.

How Do WE Perform the Process?

Because this activity tends to be conducted by the team participating in the process being evaluated, competency in teamwork and interpersonal skills are needed to achieve effective performance. This is why knowing the basic quality tools and developing basic quality skills are considered prerequisites to benchmarking. A company's ability to answer this question is dependent on its own process knowledge and its ability to apply the basic quality tools.

Finding out "how WE do it" means assessing one's own process. It involves careful self-study and examination of the critical factors that influence a process's performance. The company must document its process and identify the process inputs and output, as well as the requirements and expectations of customers for that output. Self-assessment also includes collecting, measuring, and analyzing data that characterize the performance capability of the process. These process capability measures indicate the process's quality, cost, and deliverability.

Three indicators of process capability are fundamental TQM metrics and tend to be common industry measures: first-pass yield, value-to-cost ratio, and cycle time. The level of process performance and the trends revealed by these measures are used to establish an internal baseline for comparison with external processes.[19]

First-pass yield is a measure of effectiveness: How well does a process perform its function, without defects, the first time? *Value-to-cost ratio* is a measure of process economy: What is the process's ability to produce a higher value of output with lower levels of cost? This measure of economy is supported by activity-based cost-management methods. *Cycle time* is a measure of process efficiency: What amount of time is consumed for each functional transaction?[20]

There may also be measures pertaining to the particular process being assessed, or reflecting specific information that the benchmarking team desires to know. For the benchmarking objective stated earlier—"Prompt customer delivery at a minimal distribution cost"— specific measures might include "Percent of delivery success ± the industry average," or "Mean average of delivery success for comparable sales and distribution," or "Percent of delivery success for decentralized distribution ± the industry average." These measures are used to establish a process profile that indicates the current capability and performance trend of a process, as shown in Figure 3–3.[21]

These performance metrics and a process map or flow chart will indicate how a process is functioning. The process map shown in Figure 3–4 illustrates the customer relationships among various internal organizations as they deliver their process outputs to achieve an order shipment.[22] This type of process map is essential to the comparison of

PROCESS INPUT	INPUT	SUPPLIER
	_____	_____
	_____	_____
	_____	_____
PROCESS OUTPUT	OUTPUT	CUSTOMER
	_____	_____
	_____	_____
	_____	_____

PROCESS PERFORMANCE MEASURES	CURRENT LEVEL	TREND
QUALITY		
FIRST-PASS YIELD	_____	_____
CUSTOMER RETURNS	_____	_____
COMPLETION/PLAN RATIO	_____	_____
COST		
WORK-IN-PROCESS INVENTORY	_____	_____
PROCESS COST	_____	_____
PROCESS VALUE-ADD	_____	_____
VALUE-TO-COST RATIO	_____	_____
CYCLE TIME		
PROCESS CYCLE TIME	_____	_____
PROCESS CHANGE OVER TIME	_____	_____
PROCESS DOWNTIME	_____	_____

PROCESS PERFORMANCE GOALS	SHORT TERM/LONG TERM	
FIRST-PASS YIELD	_____	_____
VALUE-TO-COST RATIO	_____	_____
CYCLE TIME	_____	_____

Figure 3–3. Sample Process Performance Profile

another company's process because it allows for observation of process flow. It is used to illustrate the steps that are taken to deliver value to the product as it passes through the organization's product delivery process.

How Do THEY Perform the Process?

To study the performance of an analogous process, the same process for measurement and analysis should be followed at both companies.

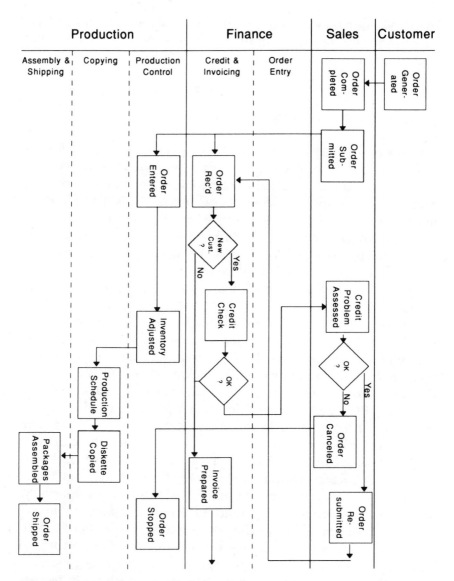

Figure 3-4. Process Mapping Example

This duplication provides a consistent analytical capability for evaluating performance gaps and identifying areas of business practice that enable performance improvement.

THE PROCESS FOR BENCHMARKING

If quality professionals seem to have a passion for flow charts, it's because they view all business operations at processes. As was just observed, one of the most effective ways to illustrate an operation is to create a flow chart of its process. One weakness of this type of process model, however, is the extent of variability inherent in process interpretation, which often results in different models—created by different individuals—of the same process. Perhaps nowhere is this more evident than in the quality literature regarding benchmarking. Every company seems to have its own unique model of the benchmarking process.

Companies taking the first step in developing a benchmarking program tend to want to create a new benchmarking process model—complete with accompanying flow chart—to represent how they intend to benchmark. Yet, when 42 benchmarking models were studied and evaluated by the APQC International Benchmarking Clearinghouse (IBC), each contained relatively the same ingredients. One reason for this imitation is that those creating the models were strongly influenced by early published examples shared through quality networks created by Alcoa, AT&T, Florida Power & Light, GOAL/QPC, Kaiser Associates, Motorola, Westinghouse, and Xerox. Another reason is that the early models worked. Not surprisingly, companies that received the Malcolm Baldrige National Quality Award and shared their benchmarking process—specifically, Motorola, Westinghouse, and Xerox—became the models for others to benchmark. The APQC study resulted in recognition of four basic steps in the benchmarking process. These steps, which track the four steps of the Deming cycle for process management (Plan-Do-Check-Act), are:[23]

1. Planning the benchmarking project;
2. Collecting the necessary data;

3. Analyzing the data for performance gaps and enablers;

4. Improving by adapting process enablers.

The overwhelming conclusion of the APQC study was that a successful benchmarking project needs to follow a rigorous process model in order to provide an integrated, systematic, measured approach to completing a benchmarking study. Because most of the company models followed essentially these same steps, companies should not spend a lot of time creating new benchmarking process models when they could be putting their efforts into the benchmarking project itself.[24]

It's important to understand that each benchmarking study does not have to complete the entire sequence of steps proposed in the process model. The model should be viewed as a guide to learning, which in itself is a guide to the discovery process. Figure 3–5 provides an illustration of how the four steps listed above are integrated into an ongoing, benchmarking process model.

Each of the four steps contributes to the development of a "gap analysis," which is used to indicate the degree of the performance

Figure 3–5. The Benchmarking Process Model

differential between the leading company and the benchmarking company. Gap analysis is key to identifying companies for business-practice emulation. Figure 3–6 shows how a gap analysis chart is constructed from the output of each of the four steps in the benchmarking process.

The first step in gap analysis identifies the process performance measure. The second step identifies both one's own company's performance and the performance of the benchmarking partner involved in the study. (Figure 3–6 is simplified to show only a two-company comparison; up to three, four, or five companies can be involved in a study.) The third step indicates the magnitude of the performance gap between one's own company and the leading company at the current time, as well as the performance trend of the leading company as projected to the planning horizon of one's own company. The fourth step contributes the goal that a company sets for improvement of the process out to its planning horizon, and, thus, the magnitude of improvement that the company has selected toward becoming the "benchmark" for this process relative to its partner company.

Each of the four steps of the benchmarking process model is further illustrated in the following sections. The discussion is intended as an executive overview rather than as a teaching model for conducting a benchmarking study. *The Benchmarking Workbook: Adapting Best*

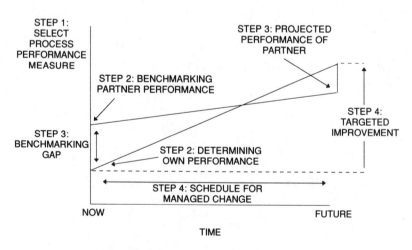

Figure 3–6. Process Contributions to Developing and Closing the Gap

Practice for Performance Improvement is recommended to teach teams how to progress through a simplified benchmarking process.[25]

Step 1. Planning the Benchmarking Project

When first introduced to benchmarking, some people feel that it is really nothing more than applying common sense to a rigorous sequence of events. For the most part, they're right. The sequence of events in the planning step, however, is introspective, and therefore requires great effort toward achieving objectivity. The outcome of these events is what enables a company to assess a direction for the subsequent external focus.

There are three phases to the planning step in the benchmarking process model:

1. The company must identify its strategic intent, core competencies, capability maps, key business processes, and critical success factors. This phase applies the considerations described in Chapter 2; process performance discovery and external learning can help provide a "wakeup call" for the management team.

2. The particular process to be benchmarked must be documented and characterized, to determine its inherent capability. This phase applies basic quality tools to business process analysis.

3. Requirements must be established for selecting benchmarking partners, given the benchmarking objective, or for characterizing the degree of relevance that any particular company may have as a potential benchmarking partner.

These criteria should be established and blessed by management before engaging a management team in discussions of the "political acceptability" of any particular candidate-partners.

Selection criteria are used to establish the appropriate "learning environment" for observing process analogies, which should be taken into consideration in selecting benchmarking partners. Selecting a benchmarking partner that is "misaligned" in its own company culture, organizational structure, or decision-making process can result in ineffective implementation of factors discovered during benchmarking. Thus, the criteria for consideration and selection of potential benchmarking partners should be tied to the understanding of data collection requirements, and should be used as a basis for creating a preliminary benchmarking study questionnaire.

A benchmarking questionnaire is used to help drive the data collection process and ensure that all required information is collected. The following list provides a set of conditions that may be considered in developing a specific set of criteria for a benchmarking study:

- Type of business;
- Company culture;
- Organizational structure;
- Employee profile (including teamwork and empowerment);
- Company demographics (size, stability, and brand reputation);
- Multinational facility or geographic representation (includes diversity of work force and union representation);
- Product size or complexity;
- Product technology;
- Process technology;
- Key financial performance indicators (gross revenue, cost of sales, R&D investment, manufacturing overhead, debt–equity ratio, inventory management, and so on);
- Distribution channels;
- Manufacturing approach and volume;
- Decision-making style of management.

These criteria provide a more complete, rational basis for selecting companies to benchmark, which also helps to keep the emotional ("I like the way that John Young manages H-P") or the publicity-driven ("I just read in *Fortune* that Rubbermaid was considered to be best at time-to-market") considerations from overly influencing the selection of target companies for benchmarking.

The logical sequence or flow of the planning phase is shown in Figure 3–7.

The specific activities followed during the planning step of a benchmarking study are:

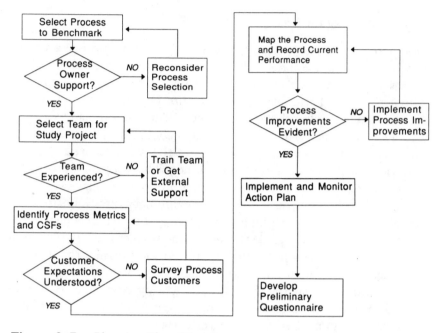

Figure 3–7.   Planning Flow Diagram

- Identify business strategic intent and core competencies, and map company capabilities;
- Select key business processes for consideration to benchmark;
- Select the specific process to benchmark;
- Gain participation of the process owner;
- Select a benchmarking team leader and participants;
- Identify the customer profiles and expectations;
- Analyze process flow and performance measures;
- Define process inputs and outputs;
- Document and flow chart the process;
- Understand and measure critical success factors;
- Select critical success factors to benchmark;
- Develop the company selection criteria;
- Establish the data collection method;
- Develop a preliminary questionnaire.

Step 2. Collecting the Necessary Data

Compared to the sequence of events in the planning process step of the benchmarking model, which is introspective, the sequence of events in the data collection step is more externally focused. The completion of a preliminary questionnaire provides a bridge to this second step in the benchmarking process. The questionnaire serves as a tool that organizes the team's thoughts about its data search, and it does so by directing the responses of the survey participants to specific topics, using a common reference. This tool then provides a basis of comparison for selection among different companies.

The subject matter outlined in the preliminary questionnaire must be agreed on, prior to beginning any activity, by partners engaging in the benchmarking study. Consensus on the subject matter "puts meat on the bones" of the operational definition and provides the specifics for exactly what data are desired. A later refinement of the questionnaire becomes the survey that all participating companies will complete as part of the data collection process; it may also be executed as a phone survey, mail survey, or face-to-face interview. It cannot be overemphasized that the survey should be piloted before attempting to use it for data collection. The clarity and validity of the survey must be verified by an independent respondent, to ensure that the instructions, questions, and analysis approach yield the data that are desired.

The second step of the benchmarking process model, which concentrates on data collection, contains three phases; internal data collection (application of quality tools), secondary research, and external primary research/data collection (using the same approach as for internal data collection). The first and third phases are almost identical. They consist of answering the questions: "How do WE do it?" and "How do THEY do it?" The same degree of process detail is collected for the company's own processes and for the partner's processes, using the same data collection approach and metrics.

In the second phase of the data collection step, secondary research is conducted. Secondary research is the practice of searching for information about a particular subject, using indirect sources. It prevents any reinventing of the wheel and saves team effort by focusing the face-to-face interactions on those areas where the information is new and has not been disclosed publicly. It can provide company background information and public disclosures of process knowledge, while establishing an external perspective of the "process excellence" of potential benchmarking partners. It provides historical perspectives to the benchmarking study, and it helps to develop an independent standard for comparison of the potential benchmarking partner's progress in process improvement over time.

Secondary research follows a basic approach and requires either computer literacy on the part of the researcher or access to a research librarian (perhaps from a local college or university). The process begins by first determining "key words"—topics that relate to the benchmarking study objective or to how the process being studied is characterized. For instance, key words for beginning secondary research on "computer programming decision support tools" include: software engineering, structured analysis, quality function deployment, software productivity, computer programming, and the specific names of targeted companies. Key words are used to query data bases through DIALOG, an information service, to discover what companies are doing in these areas. Key words are not always specific in their interpretation, so an iterative approach is usually necessary. Employing the help of a research professional who is familiar with the key-word thesauruses of several data bases can be extremely beneficial.

Once the data are collected from a variety of sources, they are sorted into common themes and categories. It's usually the task of the process specialists on the benchmarking team to make relative sense of the information obtained. They accomplish this by comparing the information to metrics and data of their own particular process being studied.

Secondary research is a key element in a professional's approach to benchmarking. Coupled with the use of questionnaires, secondary research represents the "sweat element" in benchmarking. Making progress takes time and requires dedicated plodding, but a large payoff is available. Some benchmarking studies have been completed by secondary research alone, because the needed information had already been disclosed in available publications. Appendix B provides a basic list of secondary sources for benchmarking information.

Three other means of conducting research and data collection were mentioned earlier: telephone surveys, mail surveys, and face-to-face interviews. Telephone surveys are used to screen and sort potential

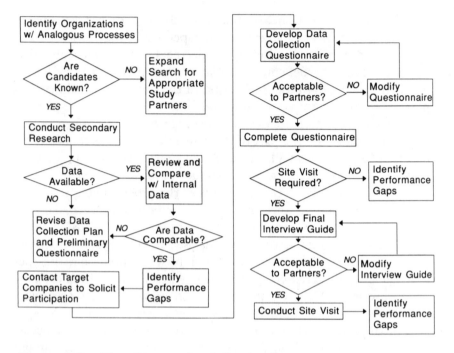

Figure 3–8. Flow Diagram for Collecting Data

benchmarking partners by determining interest in the topic. Mail surveys are used to gain more detailed information about the specific process measures and kinds of data used by other companies. Face-to-face-interview visits are used as a means to clarify and verify information collected previously.

One final way of collecting data is a site visit. It will provide a first-hand look at the rationale for process-related decisions, and will offer an opportunity to observe the behavioral aspects of process performance. These observations are usually documented in a trip report by the visiting team.

The logical sequence of the data-collecting process is shown in Figure 3–8.

Like the first step of the benchmarking process model, the second step can be described as a set of specific activities. The specific activities followed during the collection step of a benchmarking study are:

- Collect internal process data;
- Identify potential benchmarking partners;
- Research companies for appropriate comparisons;
- Conduct secondary research;
- Select whom to benchmark and establish partnership sharing conditions;
- Gain cooperation and participation of the targeted partners;
- Plan the data collection;
- Develop a final survey or interview guide;
- Conduct primary research (telephone survey, mail survey, or individual interviews);
- Monitor process performance and analyze performance gaps;
- Make on-site observations to clarify and verify previous observations;
- Conduct a post-site-visit debriefing with team members, to record observations;
- Synthesize on-site observations into a documented trip report.

Step 3. Analyzing the Data for Performance Gaps and Enablers

The analysis step in the benchmarking process model consists of five phases: data analysis, data presentation, root cause analysis, results projection, and enabler identification. The goal of this step is to identify adaptable process enablers that are candidates for implementation.

Process measures are used to identify—by the magnitude of the relative performance gap between one's own company and the process leader—which of the particular processes or process activities serve as performance enablers and, therefore, should be further investigated. (This phase of the benchmarking process follows the analytical methods used in *The Benchmarking Workbook: Adapting Best Practice for Performance Improvement,* and is an extension of basic analysis methods used in problem solving.) This approach, which consists of a thorough step-by-step application of analytical tools to sort and evaluate the data collected, has been a frequent topic in quality books and is well-documented in many available sources. However, the logical sequence of the activities involved is briefly reviewed, following the analysis process illustrated in Figure 3–9.

The specific activities are:

- Organize and graphically present the data for identification of performance gaps;
- Normalize performance to a common measurement base;
- Compare current performance against the benchmark;
- Identify performance gaps and determine their root causes;
- Project the performance three to five years into the future;
- Develop "best practices" case studies;
- Isolate process enablers that correlate to process improvements;
- Evaluate the nature of the process enablers to determine their adaptability to the company culture.

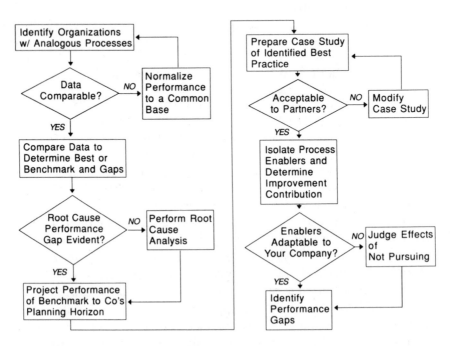

Figure 3–9.   Analyzing Flow Diagram

Step 4. Improving by Adapting Process Enablers

The final step in the benchmarking process provides the bias for action that actualizes benchmarking as a strategic change management process. The purpose of this step is to drive selected improvements into the organization by applying the knowledge learned during the benchmarking study. The step may be divided into the following phases: select improvement projects, set goals for improvement, develop action plans, approve action plans, implement action plans, recognize individual and team contributions, and monitor benchmarking requirements.

In this final step of the four-step benchmarking model, the study effort is converted into "action for business process improvement." Neglecting to take action will render the study useless, except as a purely academic exercise. Only through the proper selection of goals and the implementation of whatever is needed to achieve the determined goals can a company be stimulated toward change. As John Young of Hewlett-Packard once said: "I firmly believe in stretch goals. Without them we would do things the same old way and would never obtain degrees of improvement beyond small, incremental changes."[26]

Having the ability to set the kinds of goals that realistically challenge an organization offers an opportunity for improvement. In fact, these kinds of goals are often determined by existing benchmarks or when new ones are established. Benchmarks can be used to designate the direction of a goal, the magnitude of a goal, and the relative priority for resource allocation when faced with several processes that need improvement. Therefore, goals should be based on the factual data of the best performance observed during the benchmarking study. Proven performance of a benchmarking partner provides a realistic end vision of what change could be like when implemented within another company.

Various types of goals can serve to help a company through its improvement process. Figure 3–10 illustrates how some of these specific goals can be structured from the gap analysis. A *short-term goal* for improvement can be established by gaining the advantages of implementing entitlements—improvements that presented themselves during the course of self-inspection of the company's process. A *parity goal* can be established by applying the observations from the benchmarking partner's enablers. A *leadership goal* is a stretch

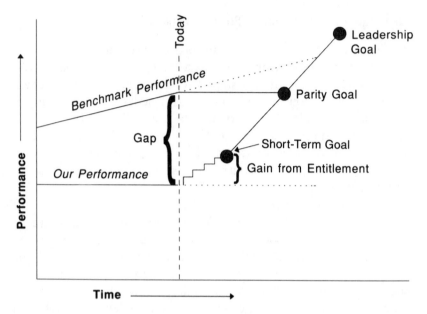

Figure 3–10. Benchmarking Gap Closure

goal that requires improvement beyond that observed at other companies. This type of goal becomes possible by integrating lessons from several companies and seeking to apply these lessons synergistically, in order to create a process that goes beyond the processes observed at other companies.

A note of caution, however, about goals. Not every process needs to be world-class. The capability of a business system should be balanced: one process should not shine at the expense of the entire system. What good would it do to have a real-time financial analysis and reporting system if the sales process is out of control? The responsibility of management is to manage the business as a complete system. Processes that are broken should be provided with sufficient resources to bring them back into balance with the business system. If a process provides a strategic competitive advantage, resources should be reallocated to permit that process to improve to its competitive domain.

Goals help to drive the implementation of improvement activities, but another aspect of closure should be accomplished at the end of a study project: the need to celebrate the contribution of the team and individuals with appropriate recognition. By providing recognition of their efforts to complete the study, management provides an open endorsement of benchmarking as a viable business activity and motivates employees to participate in other benchmarking studies when they are sponsored in the future.

Recognition as a Quality Tool

The term *recognition* is composed of the prefix *re,* meaning "again," and the noun *cognition,* meaning "the act or process of knowing including both awareness and judgment"[27]—or, more simply, "to think." Thus, recognition means "to think again." Recognition of what went right about a particular event or occurrence reinforces those particular human behaviors that management desires to support and develop as culturally accepted behavior patterns, and therefore, is a fundamental TQM practice.

To apply recognition as a reinforcer of desired behavior, managers must first seek individuals whose performance of the desired behavior is worthy of emulation, then publicize and promote their accomplishments using special rewards or awards and widespread communication. Signaling management's visible support of such behavior results in the creation of both a role model and an inspiration to those interested in personal success and continuous improvement. It also operationally defines what management considers to be appropriate behavior, and causes people "to think again" about their performance in similar or analogous situations. Providing further support through accessible training, career path counseling, and mentoring programs can help to ensure that needed skills are acquired and that the desirable behavioral changes take place.

The recognition of a concrete example of "best practice" in behavior helps to accelerate the process of behavioral adaptation faster than any other management action. The APQC's International Benchmarking Clearinghouse has developed a recognition system for benchmarking and offers awards for academic research, team study, and company programs. (See Appendix C for a description of these award criteria.) These award criteria may be used as a model for company-sponsored benchmarking recognition.

The activities of the improvement step of the benchmarking model can be described as a flow-charted sequence, as shown in Figure 3–11.

The specific activities during the improvement step of a benchmarking study are:

- Set goals to close, meet, and then exceed the performance gap;
- Select best practices and enablers for consideration;
- Modify process enablers to match the company culture and organizational structure;
- Enhance these enablers based on team observations for integrating process improvements;
- Develop a formal action plan for implementing improvements;
- Get management endorsement;
- Commit the resources required for implementation;
- Gain acceptance, support, commitment, and ownership for required changes;

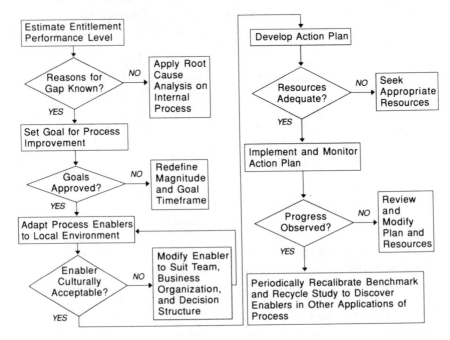

Figure 3–11.   Improving Flow Diagram

- Implement the plan;
- Celebrate the results of the benchmarking project;
- Monitor and report improvement progress;
- Identify opportunities for future benchmarking;
- Recalibrate the measure regularly and seek understanding when change is observed.

CONCLUDING COMMENTS

The purpose of strategic benchmarking is to sustain the long-term improvement of key business processes that provide continuing competitive advantage for a company. The process used for strategic benchmarking is the same as that used for a process benchmarking study; what differs is the strategic business nature of the process studied. Applying the Pareto principle and selecting those "critical few" processes that make a business difference are management's first responsibilities for developing an effective benchmarking process. Effective strategic benchmarking continues to engage management in the support, review, and implementation of the benchmarking team's study. Finally, management needs to exercise due diligence by ensuring that duplicative studies are not performed and that the results of a study are communicated to all areas of the company. The communication and preservation of the "corporate knowledge" obtained through benchmarking is the subject of the next chapter.

4

Applying Benchmarking Results for Maximum Utility

WHAT IS LEARNING?

The future business world is predicted to be filled with chaos—technological, economic, environmental, and political changes will be life-threatening pollutants in a company's business atmosphere. Old theories of management, based on tight adherence of the business system to established standards, with no anticipation of the need for rapid change, have become outdated. Because benchmarking promises to facilitate the required transition from a control-based management system to a learning-based management system, its popularity has soared. As Shoshanna Zuboff, author of *In the Age of the Smart Machine,* has postulated: "The 21st-century company has to promote and nurture the capacity to improve and to innovate. That idea has radical implications. It means learning becomes the axial principle of organizations. It replaces control as the fundamental job of management."[1]

Organizations must learn to become adaptable to changing environments and be continuously monitoring and responding to changes in their environment. Peter Senge, author of *The Fifth Discipline: The Art and Practice of the Learning Organization,* calls this response a *learning organization,* which he defines as "an organization that is continuously expanding its capacity to create its future."[2] Because benchmarking is a quality practice that does not require great mathematical sophistication and can be used by anyone who has been indoctrinated to the basic quality tools, its application can be widespread. It can provide an external stimulus to encourage a reflective environment of continuous learning.

Benchmarking facilitates learning. It involves networking—organizations with resources (knowledge) in one area meeting with organizations with needs (problems or issues). In essence, it is an application of the concept of mentoring to the interorganizational level. The premise for benchmarking is: a company that benchmarks will learn about improvements that can be applied to its own organization.

How is learning captured and what is the best way to apply the knowledge gained during benchmarking? How can an organization translate the knowledge that it gains into action? We have previously observed that benchmarking is not just about conducting a study or making a measurement; it implies a bias for action, which is also fundamental to a learning organization. The lessons of benchmarking tell the team a succinct story:

Here's where you are.

Here's where you want to be.

Here's an example of how you can get there.

NOW GO AND DO IT!

This translation to action has been a problem for many Western companies. Conducting a study is an acceptable thing to do; the difficulty seems to be in translating the study into corrective action. This observation by Senge may help to clarify how learning should be applied:

> A fundamental misunderstanding that permeates Western society is that learning or knowledge does not need to be related to action. In Japan, they say that you learn when you know it in your body—literally. There you do not say "I know it" because you heard it, but because you know it is in you. Therefore learning or knowledge has a cognitive or intellectual dimension and an action dimension, both of which are intricately intertwined and assessed relative to the needs for action. This view goes back to John Dewey, who said, "All learning is a continual process of discovering insights, inventing new possibilities for action, producing the actions, and observing the consequences leading to insights."[3]

The most effective learning comes from real-world lessons that are mastered in real time as an individual or team struggles with an immediate issue. Senge noted the similarity of Dewey's learning theory to Deming's Plan-Do-Check-Act (PDCA) continuous improvement cycle (see Figure 4–1). The alignment between Dewey's four phases and the steps in Deming's cycle is striking:

1. Discovering new insights

   Plan a course of action based on a data-defined problem statement.

2. Inventing new possibilities

   Do a test to determine the results of the hypothesis.

3. Producing the action

   Check to study the results on a trial implementation.

4. Observing the consequences

   Act, or adjust the process based on the trial observations.

These parallels between continuous learning and continuous improvement are so strong that it is almost impossible to differentiate

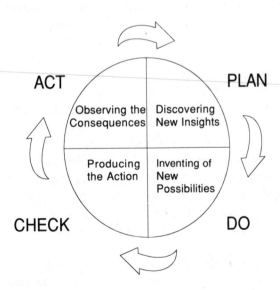

Figure 4–1.   PDCA and Dewey's Learning Theory

between the two. Perhaps, as Senge suggests, Deming's PDCA has its roots in Dewey's learning theory.

Both Dewey and Deming explained continuous improvement as an action-based cycle and relied on the creative abilities of the improvement implementors. Quality improvement, creativity, and innovation are all linked in the need to continuously rejuvenate an organization's structure, systems, and strategies in order to remain in a leadership position with customers and to outflank competitors. Learning is only an intellectual exercise unless it is targeted to a better understanding of the customers' needs and expectations. Customer-focused targeting produces true knowledge that must be applied to achieve competitive advantage. Thus, management may continuously "recreate" the company's business case from the perspective of the customer, to track the changing business environment. This continuous refreshing or renewal cycle is only possible when an organization is responding to external stimuli and has the fortitude to continuously reexamine the current application of its historical success formula.[4]

In the early 1980s, the Eagle team at Data General experienced a need to reexamine its success formula. Tom West, the Eagle team leader, conducted what he later described as his "knock-off copy work" by inspecting the installation of a new generation DEC VAX computer. He was there to understand the competitor's application of technology and how to apply this knowledge to his own project. "I'd been living in fear of VAX for a year. I wasn't really into G-Two. VAX was in the public domain and I wanted to see how bad the damage was. I think I got a high when I looked at it and saw how complex and expensive it was. It made me feel good about some of the decisions we've made."[5]

From a product development viewpoint, Aristotle was right when he decreed that the unexamined life (product design) is not worth living (launching into the market). By examining both technological capability and the competitor's moves in product design, West entered a learning environment that assured him of his team's winning design for Data General. Senge described West's situation this way:

> Learning concerns the enhancement of the capacity to create. Real learning occurs when people are trying to do something that they want to do . . . [it is an] intrinsic drive to create something that they have never done before that leads to learning. It is always related to *doing* something.[6]

In addition to the competition from DEC, West's team was competing against another, better-funded internal project. The team was focused on extending the capability of the current computer technology and delivering value to customers who had been loyal Data General supporters for years. In short, the Eagle team was doing something that provided them with a strong sense of value and accomplishment. In this environment, learning could occur from all sources, from the internal creative instinct to the competitive product that had been recently fielded. The emphasis was on delivering the best, according to the customers' definition, and it didn't matter what source of knowledge was needed to create the final deliverable.

How Long Do Organizations Take to Learn?

Work is the act of doing something that creates a product of that effort. Work tends to fall into repetitive patterns; we can identify them as processes. This definition fits a competitive model that combines both product and process technology. (This model was developed in Chapter 2.) Hamel and Prahalad have stated that:

> Competitive innovation works on the premise that a successful competitor is likely to be wedded to a "recipe" for success. That's why the most effective weapon new competitors possess is probably a clean sheet of paper. And why an incumbent's greatest vulnerability is its belief in accepted practice.[7]

Companies tend to recreate their past successes, and those that develop "entrenched success" have difficulty in breaking away from their formula for success. Part of the reason for this hesitancy to break away is the learning and reinforcement process that the company experiences as a result of its success. In fact, the learning may be so significant that it becomes the core competency of the organization; it becomes successfully integrated into the organization's fabric during the process of product development. As Prahalad and Hamel state: "Core competencies are the collective learning in the organization, especially how to coordinate diverse production skills and integrate multiple streams of technologies."[8]

The ability to learn is itself a competitive advantage. Arie P. de Geus has observed:

The ability to learn faster than your competitors may be the only sustainable competitive advantage. So the companies that succeed will be those that continually nudge their managers toward revising their views of the world.[9]

Change does not occur with a quick response, even if the stimulus is noticed. De Geus noted that: "It will likely take 12 to 18 months from the moment a signal is received until it is acted on. The issue is not whether a company will learn, therefore, but whether it will learn fast and early. The critical question becomes, 'Can we accelerate institutional learning?'"[10] Hewlett-Packard's John Young observed this conundrum firsthand when he launched his ten-year-long "10X" reliability–improvement stretch goal. No statistically significant changes were observed in the reliability performance metric for the first 18 months. The traditional decision options that Young faced were: canceling the change program, changing the performance metric or goal, or "applying management pressure" to make the results happen.[11] He chose none of these. Instead, he waited. The results began to show by the end of the second year. It appeared that the first 18 months of this strategic change effort had been an incubation period during which not much showed externally, but, internally, conditions for the change began to occur. For Young, this was probably very frustrating but acceptable in the long run, because the change was not driven by external crisis or changes in the competitive environment.[12] Others may not find themselves in Young's position and will need to find ways to accelerate their actions. De Geus states: "The challenge is to react to environmental change before it becomes a crisis."[13]

How Can We Preserve Corporate Learning?

When a lesson is first observed, how can it be internalized? This is an important next step in the learning process. Several leading companies provide examples of different ways to share or communicate acquired knowledge. Merck's program managers record the best and worst of their project development experiences in a "Book of Knowledge," which is required reading for new program managers. IBM operates a computer network for recording and sharing information about benchmarking study results. Xerox Corporation has a BEST Practices information network for filing study trip reports and final results. Xerox also has a human network of benchmarking practitioners who meet on a regular schedule to encourage group learning. In each of these "learning preservation" applications, these companies are giving information technology an important role in ensuring the widest dissemination of their acquired knowledge. They have discovered what many schoolteachers already knew: Preserving knowledge, or developing a corporate body of knowledge, is really a synonym for communicating.

ALTERNATIVE APPROACHES TO COMPETITIVE COMPARISONS

What's in a name? As Shakespeare observed, it doesn't change the fragrance of a rose; however, it does set an expectation. The use of the term "benchmarking" has been linked with various types of benchmarking: internal, competitive, functional, generic, process, global, cost, performance, customer, strategic, and operational. The loose use of these words can easily confuse a newcomer to benchmarking. Some of the confusion can be eliminated by dividing the terms into two categories—one describing where the benchmarking study is directed, and the second describing what type of study is performed. The sources of benchmarking data are described by the internal, competitive, functional, and generic labels linked to benchmarking. The remaining labels describe the type of study performed. Because this is a rule, it can traditionally have an exception: competitive benchmarking fits both categories.

To make matters worse, some practices that are referred to as benchmarking do not follow the standard benchmarking approach: they are not measures in search of enablers. Performance benchmarking, for example, is the practice of comparing products' performance on a specific test, such as the speed of computer processing of a standard mathematical problem. Cost benchmarking is another practice that falls into this category. The result of a study is a comparative number; it does not include an analysis of the operations that enabled the achievement of that level of performance. Towers & Perrin, a consulting firm, has suggested that the measurement of customer satisfaction relative to competitors is customer benchmarking. This also fails the test; it produces only a measurement, without comparative process enablers. Benchmarking is more than just comparative analysis, which has been done for years. The contribution of benchmarking to comparative analysis is that "lessons are learned." The enabling performance is observed and the enablers are then used as a model for change in the learning organization.

Companies may pursue "competitive something" practices to assess their standing relative to their competitors. Figure 4–2 illustrates a model for relating the various competitive analysis practices. These competitive analysis practices benchmark customer perceptions relative to the competition. They are conducted at two levels, using strategic or tactical perspectives, and may have four different types of applications: markets, customers, products, and processes. Global benchmarking, strategic benchmarking, and operational benchmarking are all types of process benchmarking. These practices all follow the same basic method and seek both measures of benchmark performance and enablers of benchmark performance. They differ in the application of the study (which describes the type of study). A global benchmarking study refers to a benchmarking study of best practice on a global perspective. Thus, the participants could potentially include companies from North America, Europe, Asia-Pacific, Africa, and South America. Strategic benchmarking is the application of

	Markets	Customers	Products	Processes
Strategic Perspective	Market Research Industry Analysis Competitive Intelligence	Customer Satisfaction Measurement	Reverse Engineering	Global Benchmarking Strategic Benchmarking
Tactical Perspective	Product Positioning	Customer Complaint Handling	Competitive Product Analysis Mystery Shopping Performance Benchmarking	Operational Benchmarking

Figure 4–2. The Relationship among Competitive Practices

process benchmarking to issues of strategic importance to the company. Operational benchmarking is the application of process benchmarking to a company's business processes.[14]

WHERE DO WE FIND KNOWLEDGE?

Benchmarking did not begin as *benchmarking*. It began with a need for information and a desire to learn quickly how to correct a business problem. Some of my personal experiences in benchmarking may help to provide some insights into how to develop benchmarking partners. These examples were chosen to illustrate the four basic types of studies: internal, competitive, functional, and generic.

In my initial benchmarking experiences, I didn't think of it as a quality method; to me it was applied common sense. One asked successful companies how they succeeded and then tried to emulate them as best one could. It seemed to be a logical approach to process improvement.

Internal Benchmarking

One of my most enjoyable benchmarking studies was conducted with a team of Hewlett-Packard (H-P) managers and involved the production planning process used by the high-volume manufacturing divisions within H-P: San Diego (plotters), Greeley (disk drives and scanners), Roseville (terminals and printed circuit boards), Loveland (instruments), Boise (printers), Vancouver (printers), Cupertino (personal computers and work stations), and Lake Stevens (instruments). This study was functionally oriented, but it is classified as an internal benchmarking study because the targeted partners were all within the same corporation. The clarity of the study was exceptional because there were few borders to cross to obtain cooperation and establish a "need to know."

Competitive Benchmarking

While I was working in a Hewlett-Packard R&D laboratory, I was involved in conducting competitive benchmarking studies in which H-P purchased products from competitors and evaluated them for their performance, manufacturability, technology, operability, safety, and support. Like Xerox, H-P determined materials cost by a tear-down of the products and estimated the manufacturing cost based on the materials cost, with H-P's own multipliers added for processing costs.

Functional Benchmarking

My first benchmarking study was in 1984 with Hewlett-Packard's San Diego Division, where I had been asked to work with several senior managers to develop an approach for supplier certification. The purpose of this project was to improve the management of the supplier base at the source—new product development required the selection of companies capable of meeting the demands of a just-in-time manufacturing environment. The approach to this study—a visit to Xerox—was fortuitous for me—Xerox had just won the Purchasing Medal from *Purchasing World* magazine and was cited for its supplier management efforts. Visiting Xerox helped me to establish a process for benchmarking, and the entire study set the framework for my approach to benchmarking. After it was completed and documentation for the division management had been provided, this study was one of several inputs used to develop Hewlett-Packard's corporatewide materials quality program. This type of study is an example of a functional benchmarking study that focuses investigation on a particular operating activity or function. It may also be called a generic study in that these lessons could be learned from any company that exercises that particular function. The follow-up to this study was a supplier quality assessment: companies from the same industry were evaluated against the same set of criteria to determine which were "best in class" and worthy of the business. This set of studies resulted in the analysis, in just 18 months, of some 200 companies representing a wide variety of industries: injection molding, sheet metal, die casting, tool and die makers, machining, printed circuit board, application-specific integrated circuits, power supply, and fan manufacturers. The primary lesson gained from these studies was the need to establish a set of evaluation criteria up-front so that these assessments could be "fact-based" rather than "judgment-based." These studies were also functional benchmarking studies.

Together, these studies resulted in a streamlining of the supplier base and in improved supplier management.

Generic Benchmarking

Another study that I conducted was of the training and education approaches used by several companies that are known for their excellent programs: Westinghouse, General Electric, Xerox, Motorola, IBM, Texas Instruments, and Digital Equipment Corporation. The study transcended competitive boundaries and was focused on companies that are principally in the electronics industry. Because the topic of this particular study did not involve an aspect of competitive advantage, this study could be construed as an electronics industry-targeted (generic) benchmarking study.

The distinctions among these four types of benchmarking studies are based on the source of the data and the types of partnership. Benchmarking studies may be characterized as either internal or external, depending on whether the participants are from one's own company or other companies. External benchmarking studies are divided into competitive studies and noncompetitive studies, and noncompetitive studies may be either functional or generic.

The case studies presented in the following chapters describe internal, competitive, functional, and generic benchmarking, as these practices developed at some leading companies during the formative years of "benchmarking"—before the popularization of this practice in 1989 by the publication of Camp's book and the Xerox publication of the enablers for its winning the Malcolm Baldrige National Quality Award.

5

Doing an Internal
Benchmarking Study

INTERNAL BENCHMARKING

Some of the best lessons we learn are taught at home. Internal bench-marking is an approach to process benchmarking in which organizations learn from sister companies, divisions, or operating units. These internal studies compare similar operations within different units and, typically, provide the most detailed information about process improvement potential because intercompany barriers to cooperation are not present. This matchup simplifies implementation and data access, but it yields the lowest potential for significant breakthroughs. Related units tend to be bound by similar cultural and organizational norms or biases and thus have developed in parallel ways. The following case study illustrates how Hewlett-Packard (H-P) was able to use its diverse R&D organization to develop companywide changes.

BEST SCHEDULING PRACTICE AT HEWLETT-PACKARD

In 1983, Donald G. Reinertsen, a consultant to McKinsey & Co., worked on a study of product development indicating that, for high-tech products, time-to-market was a critical factor in commercial success. R&D labs and product development teams have always labored under two critical constraints: budget and schedule. Budget control is usually a hot button for controllers and corporate managers of R&D, and marketers stay up late thinking about product introduction delays and how their inevitable occurrence will make their lives unlivable.

Reinertsen's conclusions were crystal-clear: high-tech products that come in on budget but six months behind schedule sacrifice 33 percent of their potential profits over their first five years in the market. Thus, being on-time with a new product was vitally important. To the chagrin of bean counters everywhere, the study pointed out that on-time projects that were 50 percent over budget lost only 4 percent of profits over the same period.[1]

The McKinsey study had tremendous implications for companies whose revenues streams were highly dependent on the regular introduction of new or invigorated products. Still, the idea of time-based competition did not make the rounds of American business for another few years. The first popular (and award-winning) article on the subject, by George Stalk, appeared in July 1988, in *Harvard Business Review*. The new time-based approach was quickly hailed as the "strategy of the 1990s." In a book that he authored with Thomas Hout in 1990, Stalk commented on the time-based approach to business revitalization, and its progress in American industry:

> Downsizing reduces overhead costs but does not fundamentally make the organization flexible or fast. This step has been or is being accomplished by many U.S. companies. . . . The second step is time compression, which is more difficult and takes longer. Time compression means that the basic structure of work in critical processes of the organization is altered to minimize the unproductive consumption of time. Only a few large American firms—Ford, Hewlett-Packard, Xerox, and parts of General Electric—have progressed beyond downsizing to time compression. Time compression allows an organization to improve on all dimensions: cost, variety, speed, and innovation.[2]
>
> . . . Time-based competitors are more productive in their use of asset than are slower competitors . . . they need 45 percent less cash to grow at the same pace as before [and] can grow 80 percent faster than a competitor with the old net asset productivity.[3]

Although the McKinsey study was not widely circulated during the mid-1980s, its importance was not lost on Hewlett-Packard CEO John Young, whose own keen interests in ground-breaking business practices led him to help found the President's Council on

Competitiveness. H-P had a wide range of product projects churning through its more than 50 R&D labs, and each of these projects was subject to presidential review on an annual basis. Young recognized that there was a high level of variation in project slippage rates and wanted to get to the root cause. If the cause could be identified, perhaps it could be eliminated. If schedule slippage was eliminated, the time-to-market benefits cited by the McKinsey study would accrue to Hewlett-Packard and its shareholders.

FROM *FANTASIA* TO HOT LIPS

Hewlett-Packard had gotten its start in the late 1930s as a small producer of electronic equipment. Its first products were video oscillators, ten of which were sold to Walt Disney for use in creating the animated film classic, *Fantasia*. During World War II, the firm developed a number of technical and analytical instruments for the War Department.

By the mid-1960s, Hewlett-Packard was an established high-technology firm. In addition to its analytical instruments, it began producing engineering calculators, which proved to be its entree into the new world of computers, printers, plotters, and disk drives. In the early 1980s, CEO Young decided to take the company in a new direction that would transform it into a full-service computer company. H-P computers had always been considered highly reliable and advanced in design. Equipped with their unique H-P operating system and software, the company's computers and work stations enjoyed a good market in engineering companies, where their capabilities were most appreciated, and in banks, where reliability was essential. By the late 1980s, H-P's share of the work-station business rose to number two, just behind Sun Microsystems. H-P completely dominated the market for graphics devices, such as pen plotters: Products like Sweet LIPS (low impact plotter system) and Hot LIPS provided higher quality graphics outputs than those of competitors and could maintain a lion's share of the business market while still permitting a premium price. From the viewpoint of design, engineering, reliability, and service, H-P products were considered top-drawer. By 1990, the company had 90,000 employees in 42 operating units around the globe and was producing $13 billion in revenues.

As successful as the company had become, it was clear that development teams were not learning lessons from other projects. The many repeat failures in new product development were just once piece of evidence that the corporation as a whole was not learning from its missteps. If a product team in Division A was far off the mark on bringing a project in on schedule, the reasons were not being communicated to development teams in Division B. The same was true of successful learning experiences.

Young, who had assumed the mantle of leadership directly from H-P's legendary founders, William Hewlett and David Packard, needed to find a new set of challenges for the firm. He wanted to provide it with "stretch goals" that were demanding, important, and clearly stated. For example, in 1979, he had his staff begin tracking warranty failure rates on H-P products. These were found to be in the range of 2 percent per year—an admirable measure of product quality for an American manufacturer at the time, but not good enough for the new CEO. In January 1980, Young told the firm that he wanted to see a tenfold decrease in the failure rate of H-P hardware products by the end of the decade (the "Ten X Program").[4] In true Youngean style, he did not proclaim any method for achieving that goal; his managers were left to figure out how to do it. Particular corporate staffs took ownership of certain of these Young-inspired initiatives.

With the rest of corporate America going bananas over the popular "excellence" and "quality" initiatives of the time, throwing down the gauntlet of time-based competition to H-P personnel seemed appropriate for both the business and the competitive climate. H-P was, after all, a producer of high-tech products and a commercial adversary of dozens of skillful Japanese producers, many of whom had already adopted the gospel of time-based competition. Frustrated with the time it was taking H-P to develop and produce new products, improving time-to-market became a new stretch goal, expressed in 1986 by Young as follows:

> Create best practices across functions to translate new ideas into successful products. Make these efforts pay off in half the time it currently takes.

Cutting development times in half was to be achieved by 1994. As usual, Young did not say how it was to be done; he left that to his managers. Corporate Engineering, then led by Chuck House, became the principal "owner" of the effort to improve time-to-market.

THE SEARCH FOR BEST SCHEDULING PRACTICE

Chuck House was a natural champion for Young's new time-to-market goal. He had a long-standing interest in the general problems of engineering productivity, the business side of R&D management, and best practices for getting H-P products off the drawing boards and into the market. In 1986, he initiated an annual conference on productivity improvement for engineers, drawing up to 600 attendees. He also created an engineering productivity prize for R&D teams (now call the Chuck House Award).

House's response to Young's proclamation on time-to-market was to conduct a study within the firm, looking for practices that contributed to success in terms of break-even time—the firm's own shorthand for time-to-market. In 1987, Hewlett-Packard maintained 56 R&D and product development centers among its corporate and operating divisions. Each of these centers managed a portfolio of a handful to dozens of development projects. This was a large and diverse universe from which to ferret out what Young was looking for.

H-P could have gone elsewhere to discover these processes. Like Xerox, it could have gone outside of its own industry, to firms facing the same *generic* problem with product development; like Ford, it might have tried *competitive* benchmarking of its rivals in the same industry. However, with hundreds of examples inside its own operations—many of them great success stories—the decision was made to conduct the study within Hewlett-Packard. In 1987, the idea of "benchmarking" had not yet entered the business lexicon, even though many firms did it.

Self-evaluation had always been an accepted practice within H-P. The "next bench" philosophy of Bill Hewlett and David Packard—the practice of always looking at what other engineers were developing and then offering review and suggestions—was part of the corporate culture. This practice was very effective, especially when the customer base was other engineers. It was an internal form of customer input, as long as the engineer at the next bench was a reasonable proxy for the final customer.

Corporate Engineering was the right locus for control of the Best Scheduling Practice (BSP) Study—"BSP," as it came to be called. House was an "engineer's engineer" and something of a hero to other managers within the corporation. If he backed something, others took it seriously. Independent and sometimes irreverent, House enjoyed the reputation of being a successful maverick. Once told by the company's venerable founders, Hewlett and Packard, to kill a project he had lots of faith in, House quietly ignored the order and proceeded to make the project a success—and was rewarded for his perseverance.

House made his backing for BSP clear to everyone—an important element in securing companywide support for it—and put one of his top people, Marv Patterson, in charge. Patterson had been a section R&D manager at the San Diego Division, and had joined Corporate Engineering in the same capacity. Patterson and Corporate Engineering proceeded (a) to create a companywide productivity network in which each of the firm's 56 R&D centers had a productivity manager assigned to assess its capabilities, and (b) to conduct best-practice analyses on a handful of projects that had recently run their course. The postmortems sought the factors that had contributed to those projects' success or failure in meeting their scheduling objectives.[5]

H-P was a firm in which R&D project managers enjoyed a great deal of autonomy, so it was not surprising that many R&D centers were not sent a set of specifications on what to measure, how to measure it, and how to write up their reports—the normal and useful procedure when measuring ongoing operations. Instead, House and Patterson were asking people to evaluate historical events, and they left it to their judgment as to how to write them up. The result was a set of project analyses that were far from uniform.

THE SAN DIEGO DIVISION

Hewlett-Packard's San Diego Division was one of its most successful units. It was a reliable cash cow that provided approximately $600 million in sales (almost 10 percent of total corporate revenue) at very high pretax margins; it dominated the markets for its products, and was recognized as being the best H-P division in terms of getting products out quickly, with many of them coming from "clean sheet"

designs. A series of remarkably successful computer-driven ink plotters, thermal ink-jet technology, and product-specific software were
at the heart of San Diego's good fortunes, and the Division enjoyed a
well-deserved reputation for product innovation.

The San Diego Division's R&D Manager, Al Johnson, assigned
Dave Tribolet responsibility for the BSP study at the Division. Tribolet created a task force of 28 other engineers who would zero in on a
dozen lab projects that had completed their cycle of inception-to-
development-to-introduction. These engineers would analyze those
projects in terms of adherence to initial schedule, ferret out causes for
scheduling delays, and look for practical lessons that would lead to
improved scheduling accuracy.

The San Diego Division task force completed its work over a period
of ten months. Each project group provided data on schedule slippage
rates and on the nature of the problems that cropped up during development; each gave its own reflections on how those problems could
be either avoided or mitigated in the future. The individual reports
were compiled by Tribolet into a "Best Scheduling Practices" manual
that covered the critical development activities at San Diego. Figure
5–1 is an abridgment of the contents of Tribolet's final document.

The San Diego study made it clear that, despite the division's development prowess, slippage rates on project schedules were far from
the ideal hoped for by John Young. As Figure 5–2 indicates, slippage
rates (indicated in number of months) were high.

With the exception of one project that came in ahead of its originally scheduled introduction, and one that was on time (but delayed
by shipping), all of the projects in the San Diego study slipped—
some, dramatically. If the McKinsey findings were applicable to these
projects, Hewlett-Packard would have foregone a large part of the potential revenues these new products should have generated during
their first five years in the marketplace. As one would guess, there
was a strong correlation between the duration of the project and the
number of months the original schedule slipped (see Figure 5–3).

The R&D sources within the San Diego Division submitted a number of important lessons about scheduling, and the factors that led to
scheduling failures were reported and compiled. Because the reporting parties had their own areas in mind when they submitted these
lessons, the expressed lessons were more particular than general. Still,
it was clear that, with a bit of study and editing, these lessons about

1. History. An overview of schedule history of San Diego Division projects.
2. Best Lab Practices. Includes a list of best practice, costing best practice, costing history by project, and checkpoints for managing R&D projects.
3. Best Practice for Tooling. In-depth review of two plotter projects, and review of tooling and project schedules.
4. Best Practice for Vendors. With review of procurement issues that impact scheduling.
5. Best Practices for Manufacturing. Lessons from Project Elmo and review of production ramp and bench failure rates on three projects.
6. Best Practices for Marketing. Product introduction time and marketing activities. Time-line guide.
7. Best Practices for Customer Assurance. Product test history. Inspection history.
8. PPMs for Schedule Accuracy. Form for tracking accuracy.
9. Appendix:

   Scheduling pitfalls

   The "Risk Index" method of estimating project duration, with example Historical baseline for project schedules.

Source: Hewlett-Packard, San Diego Division, "Best Scheduling Practices."

Figure 5–1.   "Best Scheduling Practices"—Contents

good scheduling practices could be presented in a way that could generate learning across divisions. Figure 5–4 presents a small sample of the "lessons" of the study within the San Diego Division.

OUTCOMES OF THE STUDY

As they came into Corporate Engineering from the many research centers, the scheduling studies were analyzed in terms of (a) common causes of schedule slippages, and (b) what was needed to move H-P products to market more quickly. The single most frequent cause of scheduling delays came down to this: "Stop changing your mind"

Project	Original Projected Introduction	Actual Projected Introduction	Project Duration (months)	Slippage (months)
A	5/80	3/81	28	10
B	12/81	3/82	20	3
C	11/82	7/82	11	(4)
D	6/83	9/83	14	3
E	12/83	2/84	16	3
F	10/83	4/84	23	6
G	4/84	4/84	23	0/4*
H	3/85	11/85	24	8
I	9/85	8/87	42	23
J	9/85	8/87	42	23
K	2/86	8/86	27	6
L	12/85	3/87	35	15

*First shipment slipped 4 months

Source: Hewlett-Packard, San Diego Division, "Best Scheduling Practices."

Figure 5–2. Project Schedule History

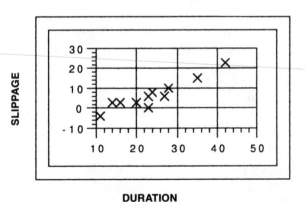

DURATION

Source: Hewlett-Packard, San Diego Division, "Best Scheduling Practices."

Figure 5–3. Project Duration and Project Slippage (in months)

Lesson	Comment
More people in the approval loop means more changes.	Having one person authorized to approve changes late in the project is effective in minimizing changes.
A part that is significantly more complex than average will increase development time.	Develop a measure of part complexity; eliminate outliers. Make part complexity as uniform as possible.
The risk level of a project increases the probability of schedule slippage.	Define and minimize risk levels.
Staffing, in terms of numbers, experience, and training, must be appropriate to the project.	
Schedule in sufficient detail (e.g., include assembly tooling, inspection, etc.).	Make one person responsible for managing the schedule.
When dealing with vendors, avoid new vendors and new processes.	Especially avoid new vendors with new processes. There must be a clear competitive reason to take this risk.
Plan for vendor-purchased parts coming in not to spec.	Have a back-up plan.
Set project and product performance goals (e.g., product cost, build time, number of suppliers, code bugs found, number of parts, etc.).	These give managers a tool to track progress and improve the process.
Assign development engineers to manufacturing at intro, to ensure continuity.	
In the lab phase, go through the entire environmental test cycle plus strife, to minimize future surprises.	Be quality-driven throughout the project, not just at the end.
Assume that all new molds will need rework.	Don't expect mold try-out parts to be used to build machines.

Source: Hewlett-Packard, San Diego Division, "Best Scheduling Practices."

Figure 5–4.   Lessons from "Best Scheduling Practices" (San Diego Division)

[about the product specifications]. With respect to moving to market more quickly, the conclusions were that H-P had two important needs: a common measure of time-based performance, and a better focus on customer requirements (which related directly back to changing specs).

THE PERFORMANCE METRIC

As if following the philosophy of Joseph Juran—"If you want to manage it, you have to measure it"—H-P realized that it needed some common yardstick against which to assess the performance of the many and diverse projects of its R&D centers. The company was, by tradition, a great believer in performance measures. It had created and applied them to operations that are typically immune to measurement: administration, support functions, and marketing. Young was perhaps the leading advocate for metrics: "If you don't have metrics, don't bother getting started [on quality or other business improvement programs]. . . . It won't make any difference."[6]

Candidates for a time-to-market performance metric were not in short supply. "Concept to marketplace" would have made sense, but would have failed to consider cost inputs against revenue outputs; likewise, a simple "payback" analysis would have failed to recognize the time value of money, the mother tongue of finance. Net present value analysis and internal rate of return, by themselves valued tools in modern business, fully recognized the time value of money but did not fully weight the importance of getting to market quickly. The McKinsey study had made it clear that getting to market on time was more important than being on budget, but a project that was both on time *and* on budget was the best of all possibilities.

Based on the results of the BSP, Corporate Engineering led the cross-divisional network of R&D productivity managers in adopting the concept of "break-even time" (BET). A project's break-even time, as defined by Hewlett-Packard, was "the length of time from the beginning of a project until the cumulative net profit resulting from the sales of new and affected products equals the cumulative net project investment." BET was thus equal to the payback time for the net present value of R&D and production investments.[7] BET had three underlying components:

1. The amount of time the project spent in development[8] (where it was a source of cost and not revenue);
2. The rapidity with which newly introduced product generated sales revenues;
3. The after-tax cost of capital to the firm.

Because it related time to money, this new metric was a more robust measure of performance than the simple "concept to market" measure, which could not discriminate between a project that was late but hugely successful and one that was on schedule but a total market dud. Better still, it linked together the important elements and activities of the business—the cost sinks of R&D and production tooling on the one hand, and the revenue-generating activities of manufacturing and sales on the other. Even finance was included: the metric was expressed in its chosen language.

The new performance metric was discussed and developed internally in 1987 and integrated into H-P's new-product development process over the next four years. It was the most tangible outcome of the BSP. In the spring of 1989, a piece of software that simplified and standardized the new metric was released to development and engineering centers companywide. Financial analysts of the firm could then use the same program to monitor ongoing projects, do postmortems, and determine actual results.

Managers could then indulge in cash-flow forecasts—positive and negative, from the time their projects were slated to begin—and get an estimate of their break-even times under a variety of scenarios. At the project level, BET could be used to select among alternative design options and to focus the attention of project managers on the business consequences of their choices. Once the project was actually underway, it could, like any other forecasting tool, be used to monitor progress against forecast at any important project checkpoint. With frequent financial "snapshots" at successive checkpoints in a project's evolution, trends that connote serious problems could be identified and addressed. Experience with a number of projects so forecasted and monitored through BET analysis could help managers develop a better sense for the timing and financial dynamics of similar projects, which could be usefully applied to future projects.

At the level of the research lab, BET could be used to think tactically about the lab's menu of possible projects, and to help managers to determine whether to continue funding existing projects. For corporate and divisional managers, BET information could be a tool for monitoring product development process performance in the aggregate.

Today, Hewlett-Packard Corporate Engineering, which developed the BET metric, provides ongoing assistance to personnel who use it in selecting and analyzing projects. Besides a software package to make the actual calculation, it publishes and distributes a 14-page pamphlet describing BET and how it can be used at the project level. Staff specialists in BET issues are also available for consultation.

Everyone understands that tossing some hypothetical numbers into an equation will do nothing to improve actual performance, but after three years of implementation, there is general agreement that BET has been effective in concentrating attention on speed to market and maintaining it as a goal of the firm.

FOCUS ON CUSTOMER REQUIREMENTS

Engineering-based companies are notorious for producing what can be made. Whether the goods produced meet customer needs is not always thought out. Engineers, after all, are trained to design and make things, not sell them. This is quite the reverse of the market-oriented philosophy of "Find a need and fill it." Hewlett-Packard had been blessed with enough talent and good management to avoid making products for which there was no market. The BSP study revealed, however, that many of its problems with timely product development were associated with having an insufficient grasp on customer requirements early in the development cycle. Among the key elements of schedule slippage were lack of agreement on specifications, and changes made toward the end of the development cycle (two problems that are often associated).

Academic research from several sources supported the notion that understanding customer requirements is an important determinant of business success. Project SAPPHO, a study of innovation in two science-based sectors of industry, conducted at the University of

Sussex from 1970 to 1972, reached a number of conclusions. The first was:

> Successful innovators were seen to have a much better understanding of user needs. They may acquire this superiority in a variety of different ways. Some may collaborate intimately with potential customers to acquire the necessary knowledge of user requirements. Others may use thorough market studies.[9]

Echoing this sentiment, Eric von Hippel of the Massachusetts Institute of Technology has written extensively on the benefits of staying close to product users, not merely to better understand their requirements, but because they are often sources of incremental product innovation.[10]

The connection between time-to-market and understanding customer requirements found its expression in Hewlett-Packard's adoption of Quality Function Deployment (QFD), a Japanese management method that, among other things, demands a systematic approach to understanding customer requirements. This project was championed by H-P's Corporate Quality staff under Craig Walter. By using two staff organizations to drive complementary changes, H-P focused the design teams on the two key elements of schedule improvement. There is no need to change a design specification if it is responsive to the customers' needs.

HEWLETT-PACKARD TIME-TO-MARKET TODAY

The implementation of BET and greater attention to customer requirements through QFD have begun to pay observable dividends at Hewlett-Packard years before Young's 1994 goal for cutting time-to-market in half. For example, under past practices, the hot-selling DeskWriter jet printer would have taken 4.5 years to develop for market; it took just 22 months under the new product development approach. The Draftmaster CAD system, whose first generation took 6.5 years to bring to market, required just 30 months in a subsequent generation.

The disciplines that have been applied to product research and development have carried over to other functional areas of the firm. In response time, H-P has been able to reduce its manufacturing cycle time from 4 weeks to just 2 days on one production line; order turnaround has dropped from 6 weeks to 3 days in another operation.

The methodology underlying these dramatic improvements is not unfamiliar to anyone involved in process control on the factory floor. The necessary steps are:

1. Document the process.
2. Measure the process.
3. Reduce the variability within the process.
4. Think of ways to continually improve the process.

It is easy to lose sight of the fact that product research and development is, like manufacturing or order fulfillment, a process—not as routine, perhaps, but a process nevertheless. Like any other process, its steps can be identified and measured, and causes of variability can be found and reduced. The final improvement step is the creative one: thinking of ways to eliminate unproductive effort, either incrementally or through an entirely new process architecture.

The Best Scheduling Practices Study documented the R&D process for Hewlett-Packard; break-even time allowed it to measure the process; improved understanding of customer requirements helped to reduce both variability and time in process.

6

Conducting a Competitive Benchmarking Study

COMPETITIVE BENCHMARKING

The second type of information-gathering approach for benchmarking focuses on competitors. Competitive benchmarking studies target specific product designs, process capabilities, or administrative methods used by a company's direct business competitors. Studies of this type differ from process benchmarking studies in terms of their depth and the fact that their goal tends to end with measurement rather than with implementing process enablers. Competitive benchmarking studies may be conducted directly with competitors on benchmark processes that are noncontroversial, such as facilities management, internal auditing practices, human resource practices, employee safety and health, compensation and benefits, employee training and development, quality programs and methods, purchasing and supplier management, and industrial policy issues. Often, these studies are conducted by a third party to sanitize competitive information, nominalize sensitive performance information to an agreed-on base measure, and report case study information that has been approved by the contributing company. In these types of studies, several companies from the same industry may participate. It is much more difficult to share competitive information during one-on-one exchanges with competitors because of concerns over antitrust violation and unfair trading practice considerations. Most competitive benchmarking studies are conducted at arm's length from the competitor, and make heavy use of secondary research and consulting firms that mask the interest of the inquiring firm. The fact that a company is interested in a particular process of a competitor is, by itself, of competitive interest: it tends to indicate that the particular process is in need of managerial oversight.

As an example of how a competitive benchmarking study is conducted, this chapter examines how Ford conducted its competitive product analysis and design process benchmarking on the Taurus.

TEAM TAURUS: A CASE OF COMPETITIVE BENCHMARKING

Business was bleak for U.S. automakers in 1980, and Ford Motor Company was the hardest hit. During that fiscal year, Ford recorded losses of $1.5 billion, the second largest single-year loss for one company in American business history. Ford's disappointing sales were a reflection of driver sentiment about its products, which were generally viewed as stodgy; unremarkable in design, innovation, and performance; and of poor quality. National surveys rated Ford cars in the cellar among U.S. autos, and far below the quality ratings being given to the German and Japanese models, which were taking a larger and larger share of the market. Indeed, FORD as an acronym for "Fix Or Repair Daily" had become more than just a joke among car owners. In 1978, the company had recalled more U.S. models than it had produced.

This state of affairs was not lost on Donald Petersen, then president of Ford Motor Company. As a careerist with Ford, he had been with the company since 1949, and had experienced both its days of glory and its days of defeat and disappointment. He could remember the years when the Ford Mustang was all the rage with style- and performance-minded buyers; the success of the Econoline van, in which he played a major role; and the great failure of the ill-fated Edsel. The company whose founder had dominated the infancy of the industry was now out of favor with the buying public. In his book, *A Better Idea,* Petersen records his experience with a focus group brought together in Marin County, California, by Ford's market research department: "In one session, not one owned a Ford or ever had owned a Ford. They scratched their heads, wondering if they'd ever been in a Ford. They thought Ford made a good truck but a mediocre car."[1]

"Why Can't We?"

Petersen, Chairman Phil Caldwell, others at Ford headquarters, and many Ford dealers came face-to-face with the realization that something had to change if the firm was to survive and prosper. In 1980, NBC aired a documentary entitled "If Japan Can, Why Can't We?," in which the contributions of W. Edwards Deming to the success of Japanese industry were notably addressed.

Deming was hailed in the documentary as the man who had taught the Japanese about quality manufacturing. Indeed, the venerable statistician/management consultant had been among the group of American industrial experts brought to Japan by General Douglas MacArthur's occupation administration in the late 1940s and early 1950s. Deming dealt directly with the top leaders of Japan's shattered industries; he taught them the scientific principles of statistical process control and his own humanistic brand of industrial management—both of which had been overwhelmingly ignored in his own country.

Eager to learn and to succeed rapidly, the Japanese leaders embraced Deming's ideas and incorporated them—in top-down fashion—into their operating principles. By 1980, the results were manifested in Toyotas, Hondas, and other Japanese products of elegant design and superior quality.

Petersen was impressed by what he learned in the documentary; he later recalled:

> That NBC documentary triggered me to invite Dr. Deming to visit Ford. He said he would come, but he insisted on meeting with me personally. That's standard procedure for Dr. Deming, because he believes that any serious effort to improve quality has to be supported by top officials.[2]

Petersen became one of Deming's disciples. He began working at infusing the Ford organization with one aspect of Deming's philosophy at a time: first, statistical process control; then, elimination of fear from the workplace, continuous improvement, employee involvement, and customer focus.[3] Petersen, and subsequently the rest of Ford management, came to the realization that if quality could be significantly improved, all other corporate objectives would follow.

An indication of what these methods could accomplish had already been made vividly evident to Petersen. Ford, at the time, had a part-interest in Mazda. The Mazda Hiroshima plant supplied transmissions for the Ford Escort, as did a Ford plant in the United States. Petersen had his engineers break down and compare transmissions from these two sources. The quality differences were painfully obvious. "The Mazda parts," Petersen wrote, "were beautifully manufactured and finished, and every measurement fell within very close tolerances. The Ford transmission met the specifications, but there was a much wider variance in dimensions from one transmission to another."[4]

The relationship between the Ford chief and the tribal elder of quality would be satisfying for both men. Petersen and Ford would learn Deming's powerful lessons about quality management, and Deming now had an opportunity that had been denied to him for decades: to nurture his ideas within one of his home nation's largest industrial corporations.[5]

While Deming served as the oracle to top management, another eminent quality expert, Genichi Taguchi, was enlisted to operational-ize his own brand of quality improvement. Taguchi's method comple-mented the classic Deming/Shewhart model of statistical process control, in which manufacturing processes were monitored to infer the conformance of output variability within upper and lower dimen-sional ranges. Taguchi wanted always to close in on the target specifi-cations, gradually narrowing the range of acceptable output. He justified the investment in this effort with his "loss function," which stated that the cost of deviating from the target specification in-creases quadratically (by squares). Thus, the further the dimensions of a cam shaft or other part varied from the design specs, the greater the cost to the company. This formula allowed design engineers to determine the cost of quality—or, more correctly, the cost of poor quality—and design to optimal standards. Taguchi provided a scien-tific foundation to the idea that cost cutting and quality improvement were not conflicting goals.[6]

At about the same time that Petersen was meeting with Deming, hundreds of Ford executives and supervisors, from all functions, were being sent to Japan to visit Mazda, Toyota, and other auto manufac-turers. The tour, a humbling experience for all concerned, cleared away any lingering belief that Ford's current problems were either short-term or linked to short-term problems in the marketplace.

Those who went to Japan returned with a grudging respect for the operational superiority they had witnessed. Robert Adams, then manager of Ford's Cleveland engine plant, spent two weeks studying engine manufacturing processes in Japan. "I was under the impression that we were doing a good job in this country," he recalled later. "Then, in 1982 on my first visit to Japan, I toured a few engine plants and witnessed their work effort and efficiency. I found out that they were doing things we didn't think were possible."[7]

Ford even invited the venerable Kaoru Ishikawa, Japan's leading quality consultant and senior consultant with the Union of Japanese Scientists and Engineers, to deliver a series of lectures on quality management to its senior staff. Management seemed to want to cover every base in the effort to improve quality.

The insights gained from the visits to Japan and the exchanges with external consultants provided a significant learning for Ford: competitors were outperforming the company on a number of fronts. Not only was overall product quality much better, but the assembly lines were much more efficient. Worse still, firms like Toyota were able to move a new model from concept to showroom in half the time needed by their U.S. rivals.

The Ford people who returned from Japan were clearly ready for a change.

Forming Team Taurus

The gradual adoption of Deming's methods roughly coincided with the decision to develop a new car model, dubbed the "Taurus" (Sable, in its Mercury form). The company had not had a really hot car for years—not since the Mustang—and it needed one now more than ever, if it was to stem its financial and market share losses. Market research indicated that the great "middle market" of American families was abandoning Ford and other U.S.-produced cars in favor of foreign-made models. Ford's mainstay in the market segment had been the LTD, then priced at around $14,000. The new model was planned as a replacement for the LTD, at a price of $15,000 or less.[8]

So important to the firm was the Taurus project that Lew Veraldi, a senior, respected chief engineer, was put in charge. In their book, *Product Development Performance,* which researched product development in 20 auto firms around the globe, Kim Clark and Takahiro

Fujimoto refer to the "heavy-weight project manager"[9]—the senior-level leader who does not have to run around for approvals or await the decision of dozens of committees before things can get done. Veraldi was that type of manager. He was known to be both a personable manager and someone whom others liked to work for, and he had a reputation for making things happen.

Lew Veraldi, a Ford lifer, had started his career as a Henry Ford Trade School student. He had risen through the ranks and had spent a tour of duty with Ford in Europe, where he had been in charge of development of the Fiesta model, a $870-million clean-sheet project. Fiesta had been a great success for the company, so Veraldi was a natural choice for the job. Taurus was a quantum leap in size and risk for Ford. When the company board of directors approved it in the spring of 1980, they estimated its budget at $3.25 billion and expected to see a car come off the line in four years.

As a senior manager, Veraldi was given broad discretion in selecting a multidepartmental team to be members of a Car Product Development Group that would spearhead the project, working jointly on the design, marketing, engineering, and manufacturing aspects of the new model. This inner circle included Veraldi, John Risk (car product planning director), chief engineer A. L. Guthrie, chief designer Jack Telnack, and Philip Benton. Other individuals from various functional groups within the firm were recruited to contribute their special expertise, some as full-time and others as part-time members of the team.

This was not a classic, functional auto development team, with parties representing engine development, body and frame development, safety engineering, and so forth. Team members were selected on the basis of a mapping of all requisite areas of expertise: each would bring in the resources and skills of his or her department. As a result, between 400 and 500 people were working on the development of the new model at any given time. On the surface, this arrangement was not particularly unique, but, in a break with the Ford tradition of new-model development, Team Taurus would not pass the project "over the wall" from design to engineering to manufacturing to marketing. Veraldi's team—which represented each of these areas—was to stay with the project from start to finish, integrating functions ordinarily addressed sequentially. Figure 6–1 represents the unusual organizational structure of Team Taurus.

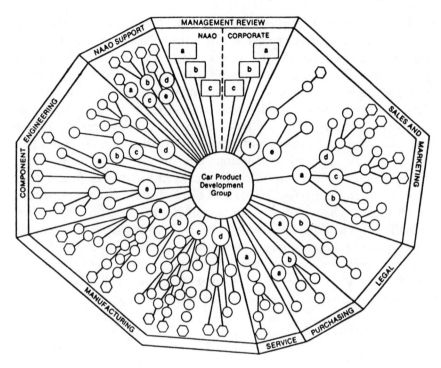

The Car Product Development Group is responsible for overall direction, design, development, control and final approval.

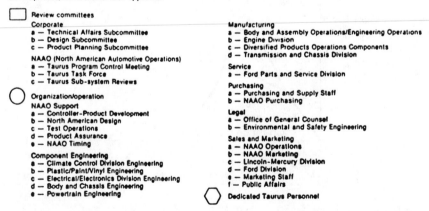

☐ Review committees

Corporate
a — Technical Affairs Subcommittee
b — Design Subcommittee
c — Product Planning Subcommittee

NAAO (North American Automotive Operations)
a — Taurus Program Control Meeting
b — Taurus Task Force
c — Taurus Sub-system Reviews

○ Organization/operation

NAAO Support
a — Controller-Product Development
b — North American Design
c — Test Operations
d — Product Assurance
e — NAAO Timing

Component Engineering
a — Climate Control Division Engineering
b — Plastic/Paint/Vinyl Engineering
c — Electrical/Electronics Division Engineering
d — Body and Chassis Engineering
e — Powertrain Engineering

Manufacturing
a — Body and Assembly Operations/Engineering Operations
b — Engine Division
c — Diversified Products Operations Components
d — Transmission and Chassis Division

Service
a — Ford Parts and Service Division

Purchasing
a — Purchasing and Supply Staff
b — NAAO Purchasing

Legal
a — Office of General Counsel
b — Environmental and Safety Engineering

Sales and Marketing
a — NAAO Operations
b — NAAO Marketing
c — Lincoln-Mercury Division
d — Ford Division
e — Marketing Staff
f — Public Affairs

⬡ Dedicated Taurus Personnel

Source: "Team Taurus," *Ward's Auto World,* February 1985. Reproduced with permission.

Figure 6–1.   Team Taurus Organizational Chart

Two of the most insidious effects of the "over-the-wall" development approach that is typical in the auto industry are (a) time-to-market delays, and (b) a high incidence of quality problems during the period just after the product enters the market. The root cause of both effects is the number of engineering changes that uncoordinated development efforts typically produce. As Figure 6–2 makes clear, Japanese companies not only had a lower level of engineering design changes but, equally important, they worked them out far in advance of actual ramp-up and production. On average, 90 percent of the changes were worked out 14 to 17 weeks in advance of production. (See Job #1 in Figure 6–2.) This lead time gave the process planners a much greater chance of shaking out all the bugs before production actually commenced. The results were shorter development time and fewer quality problems during the early production stage. The American companies, by contrast, required a much higher level of engineering changes, and they were still making these changes during the early stages of production. In effect, their design cycle extended into the

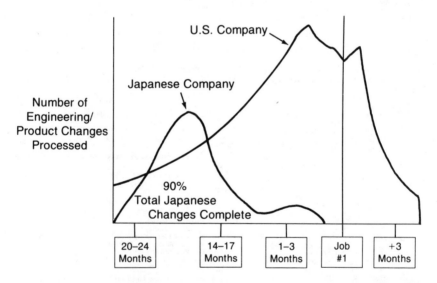

Source: Larry Smith and Hal Schaal, Ford Motor Co. Used with permission.

Figure 6–2. Engineering/Design Changes and the Development Cycle: U.S. and Japanese Companies

first several months of new-model production. This, naturally, played havoc with manufacturing and with the ultimate quality of the vehicle. No wonder savvy car buyers avoided Detroit's new models until they had been in production for six months or so![10]

The Taurus project inadvertently became a first test for the quality-driven, employee-involvement orientation that Petersen and Deming were encouraging. The multidisciplinary team concept, however, can be traced directly to Veraldi's experience in Europe, where he successfully brought management and engineering together on the Fiesta project. When he returned to the United States and took on the Taurus project, Veraldi decided to make his team as eclectic as possible; besides management and engineering, he included marketing, manufacturing, service, and public relations.

This idea was not unanimously embraced in the managerial ranks. Ford, at the time, had its share of fiefdoms and powerful departmental barons. Some department heads, who did not like having their best people pulled away from them for Veraldi's project, at first resisted by putting forth their second- and third-level players. However, top management, which solidly supported Veraldi and his team concept, let it be known that they knew who the top people were in each division, and they wanted them on the Taurus team. The department heads had little choice but to acquiesce.[11]

THE BENCHMARKING EXERCISE

One of the first things Team Taurus did was to develop a list of features that would seem important to the customer, whether largely transparent features (engineering details in the drive train, braking systems, and so on) or customer-perceived features (seat ergometrics, clutch pedal effort, fuel filling ease, and similar details). The list was generated from within the Ford organization and its constituencies: Ford designers, assembly engineers and line workers, marketing personnel, dealers, legal and safety experts, suppliers, auto insurers, auto service mechanics, and a sprinkling of consumers.[12] Anyone who has ever tried to remove a fender to knock out a dent, or has attempted to get a grip onto an inaccessible oil filter, should appreciate the lengths that Veraldi and his team went to in anticipating problems that designers usually overlook and consumers are always stuck with. The team was determined to give the customers not only what they expected, but pleasant discoveries, many of them made months after they made their purchases. "The Service Managers Council was helpful in telling us what steps we could take to make the cars easier to service," Veraldi told researchers from Amos Tuck School of Management. "We also looked very carefully at bodywork repairability by talking to independent repairmen and insurance companies. The repairmen came in and told us where in any body structure it was best to maintain body integrity, ease of repair, etc. . . ."

The list of features was later confirmed by means of Ford customer focus groups. In the past, the design team would have developed the features on its own and passed them on to engineering for elaboration. For this project, Ford workers from many disciplines were given the opportunity to tell Veraldi's team what they would expect in terms of components and features in a world-class car. Ford market researchers also conducted surveys among both Ford owners and drivers of competing vehicles. This outside research, conducted over a period of almost two years, and the input of Ford workers and managers were compiled into a list that was eventually honed down to 400 items within general automaking categories of lighting, power train, brakes, steering, storage, space perceptions, foot comfort, instrument, under-hood accessibility, exterior, windows, comfort, and convenience.

Best in Class

The intended point of this exercise was not simply to be sure that the new model included most, if not all, of these features or components. That, in itself, would not have ensured market success or a quality car. Instead, it was intended that the new Taurus be "best in class" (or at least equal to the best) in each feature. This appears to have been Veraldi's idea. He wanted to build the best car in the world for the middle market. This lofty goal set Team Taurus apart from what might have otherwise been a fairly ordinary auto development project—with ordinary market results. After years of being asked to design and manufacture parts and entire cars within the confines of non-quality-related constraints, Veraldi was challenging Ford people to think beyond the limits of a meat-and-potatoes car company. He was asking them to become the best.[13] Challenge goals are fairly common for development teams throughout industry, but the goals are usually articulated in engineering terms (braking distance; curb weight; trunk volume; and so on). Best in class went beyond mere engineering goals. It was loftier and more customer-oriented, and it unified development specialities.

But what, exactly, was best in class?

Analyzing the Competition

To answer this question, Team Taurus purchased 50 automobiles representing the wide variety of models that catered to the middle-market car buyer. Most were either U.S.-produced cars or foreign cars for sale in the U.S. middle market. Because many of the key Ford managers on Team Taurus had worked for Ford Europe and were familiar with the many top-drawer models available there, a number of automobiles never seen on American roads were included among the 50. Special federal approval to bring these into the country and test them on U.S. roads had to be obtained,[14] because they were not manufactured to meet U.S. safety and pollution standards.

These 50 vehicles were acquired to do competitive product analysis—an early form of benchmarking similar to product tear-down analysis or reverse engineering—on each model, in terms of the list of 400 features. Categories of these features and components were farmed out to team members who had appropriate expertise. For example, determination of best in class in fan noise was given to the environmental control specialists on the team. This same team was responsible for evaluating related climate features like temperature control, air circulation, and air conditioning systems.

The number of different car models broken down and examined was probably excessive, given the purpose of the exercise. The list of purchases include the world-beating cars from Audi, Honda, and Toyota—obvious choices; GM and Chrysler cars were also on the list, as were unlikely cars like the Opel Senator, hardly a main-line competitor. Fifty seems an extreme number, but two things were going on at the time: (a) Ford was sensitive to the fact that the company had erred in not doing sufficient competitive analysis in the past; and (b) Ford was willing to learn from everyone, including companies like Opel.

Competitive Analysis of Manufactured Products

The Ford approach to breaking down a great number of its competitors' products was certainly a good method for determining the design and materials needed for its new Taurus model. This case, however, represents only a limited use of this important methodology.

A "single-point" observation of a competing product can reveal the features, technologies, design rules, and safety standards incorporated into that one product. It fails, however, to reveal the trend of improvement, the mix of new versus old features, the speed with which a competitor is capable of implementing new technologies or adapting to environmental change, or clues as to the underlying process technologies. Doing analysis *over time,* on the other hand, provide insights into these issues.

A robust approach to competitive analysis looks beyond today's product features and production methods to development of a broad profile on a competitor—its core capabilities, its technological velocity and trajectory, its strategic investments. These characteristics cannot be learned from single-point product analysis.

Over a period of months, each of the 50 competing models was evaluated in terms of the 400 features and ranked to determine the best of class for each feature. Final determination of best in class was made by a number of "juries" who had different automotive specialties, under the direction of Ford's chief engineer of test operations, Howard Freer, and William Hahl, manager of the best in class analysis teams.[15] The objectivity of these juries was not questioned; most of the top honors went to non-Ford cars like the Audi 100 (named the 5000 in the United States), the Mazda 626, the Honda Accord, the Opel Senator, the BMW 528E, and the Toyota Cressida. American cars, including Ford's grabbed only a handful of honors. Chrysler products did not score in any of the 400 categories. Figure 6–3 provides a sampling of a few of the 400 features and indicates the winning car models.

With these ratings empirically determined, Team Taurus had effectively established competitive benchmarks on the 400 features that had been deemed important to the overall outcome of the final product. These then became tangible targets for Ford's design and manufacturing units and for its network of parts suppliers.

Feature	Car
Lowest ignition switch effort	Ford
Lowest air register operating	Audi 100
Best accelerator pedal feel	Audi 100
Best accelerator pedal location	Chevrolet Celebrity
Lowest effort to rotate sun visor side-to-side	Honda Accord
Lowest effort to adjust rearview mirror	Toyota Cressida
Best hand control ergonomics	Opel Senator
Best visual ergonomics	Honda Accord
Best night-time illumination of switches	Honda Accord
Best clock readability	Audi 100
Best fuel gauge accuracy	Toyota Supra
Best oil filler accessibility	Nissan Maxima
Best transmission control (travel/feet)	Opel Senator
Least transmission gear noise	Ford Escort, Supra
Best steering wheel feel	Porsche 924
Best outside mirror remote control	Mazda 626
Best oil filter accessibility	Nissan Maxima
Most effective sun visor (travel/feet)	Honda Accord
Best trunk storage capacity	Chevrolet Celebrity

Source: Ford Motor Company, as published in *Automotive Industry,* January, February, and July 1986.

Figure 6–3.   The Best in Class—A Sampling of the 400 Key Features

The Team Taurus approach to the design process is compared to the traditional approach in the profiles shown in Figure 6–4. The important difference between them is in the immediate translations of customer wants into design specifications. These translations become the constraints around which the rest of the process must operate. If the specifications are truly best in class, then there is no problem. The problem with the traditional method was that the constraints were something other than world-class specs. Components and systems had to be jerry-rigged to fit some general car "concept" developed from customer wants; it was never empirically determined what level

Traditional Approach	Team Taurus Approach
1. Customer Want	1. Customer Want
2. Concept Design	2. Specifications
3. Detail Design	3. Concept Design
4. Specifications	4. Detail Design
5. Manufacture	5. Manufacture
6. Delivery	6. Delivery

Source: Larry Wilson and Hal Schaal, Ford Motor Co. Used with permission.

Figure 6–4. The Design Process

of performance should be set for these specifications. In the long run, concepts cannot run the car, provide a quiet fan, allow accessibility to the engine for easy maintenance, or do the hundreds of other things car owners live with over the life of their vehicles.

The whole notion of "best in class" may have been influenced by the Japanese practice of Quality Function Deployment (QFD)—part of the Toyota design system—with which Ford was becoming acquainted at this time. One requirement of QFD is an analysis of customer-perceived features, a task similar to that undertaken by Team Taurus. In the analysis, a firm uses a point system to rate its products against competitors' products along a spectrum of features and performance characteristics. The objectives in the design phase are to eliminate any significant weaknesses relative to competing products, and to gain measurable superiority in those areas that translate into customer satisfaction and sales success.

The Taurus project is, in fact, the earliest known example of a QFD-type analysis in an American product. Since that time, Ford has used QFD as a standard approach for product definition.

THE TAURUS EXPERIENCE

Taurus/Sable was a tremendous success when it hit the market in 1986. *Motor Trend* named it "Car of the Year," comparing it favorably to the fine Japanese models that had taken all the laurels for excellent design, innovative styling, and quality manufacture. *Automotive Industry* named Veraldi "Automotive Man of the Year" in its February 1987 issue. Fully 77 percent of the 400 features benchmarked had been incorporated into the production-line automobile.[16] The dealers could not get enough of the new vehicles. The profits from its new model not only restored Ford to financial health, but put it ahead (in actual earnings) of its long-time rival, General Motors, for the first time in decades. The aerodynamic styling that so radically departed from Ford's clunky tradition was a hit with the public and would soon be imitated by rivals.

Not everything in the new-model development process had gone smoothly. Initial production was a year late, partly because of a rethinking of the overall size of the car. Forecasters at Ford had been predicting $3 per gallon fuel prices by the date of Taurus's introduction. Originally intended as a smaller vehicle with a fuel-stingy four-cylinder engine, sagging fuel prices and market intelligence determined that the Taurus should be a larger car. It was accordingly expanded in almost all dimensions and was given a six-cylinder engine—but at the cost of the original schedule.

Nor was all of Taurus's success attributable to the benchmarking exercise discussed above. The car's radical body styling put Ford far ahead of its U.S. and foreign competitors in one quantum leap. The shape of the Taurus emerged from the minds of the Ford design team—the same group of people who had been doing boxy designs for years—and is evidence of what can happen when rigid management constraints are loosened and people are allowed to do what they do best. Jack Telnack, a 20-year veteran of Ford at the time of the project, and head of the company's design center, called the striking aerodynamic lines of the Taurus the New American Look. (Many at Ford had been deathly afraid that the design was too radical for consumer tastes and would not be accepted by the typical Ford customer. The company's last great design leap had been the Edsel, a disaster of classic proportions. Periodic market research with potential buyers was used to secure feedback on Telnack's design.) "The managers said they wanted something different," Telnack said several years later, "and they were serious this time."[17]

Benchmarking did not create this bold body design; it emerged from the new spirit underlying the management of the company.

Deming had insisted that *fear* be driven from the workplace; Petersen told the designers to create a car they would be proud to have in their driveway; and Veraldi was willing to let his people try things. Telnack, a long-time boating enthusiast who had moonlighted as a boat designer in the 1960s, commented on the satisfying differences between the boating industry and the auto world of that time: "There were no committees. We went directly from a sketch to a full scale model without any intermediate steps."[18] Working with Veraldi, he had finally been given that same opportunity.

Much of the Taurus's success—both in the market and profitwise—came from the adoption of other quality-related programs. Process

Competitive Analysis and Parts Reduction through Redesign at Sunbeam

Spurred by a goal to capture 30 percent of the steam/dry iron markets in which it chose to compete, the Sunbeam Appliance Company in 1982 undertook a detailed study of competing products. Like Team Taurus, Sunbeam researchers obtained and broke down steam irons from all over the world, analyzing each on the basis of number of parts, costs, and labor costs needed for assembly. A two-day conference of the company's engineers from Australia, western Europe, and North America was convened to discuss the analysis.

Sunbeam researchers found wide variations in the parameters under study. Parts counts varied from 147 to 74; fasteners, from 30 to 16; fastener types, from 15 to 9. Sunbeam's own products fell in the middle to lower end of these ranges.

Because a generally linear relationship was found to exist between the number of parts and material and labor costs, Sunbeam determined that a redesign of its line of steam/dry irons, with careful attention to both the number of parts and the labor cost of assembly, would give it a substantial competitive advantage. The resulting product line, launched in 1986, was based on a design with only 51 parts and 3 fasteners in just 2 configurations. Production costs to Sunbeam were substantially below those of its former steam/dry irons and those of its competitors.

Source: Alvin P. Lehnerd, "Revitalizing the Manufacture and Design of Mature Global Products," in Bruce R. Guiles and Harvey Brooks (Eds.), *Technology and Global Industries* (Washington, DC: National Academy Press, 1987).

improvements had much to do with reduced costs and improved quality. The Ford assembly plant in Atlanta had been selected as early as 1981 to manufacture the Taurus. The employee involvement program produced a number of important suggestions from line workers in the Atlanta plant that paid off for the company. For example:

- Side panels were reduced from six to two.
- The number of screws needed to attach the interior molding was reduced.
- Line workers identified potential assembly problems during the design stage that would have created squeaks when the car was in operation.[19]

The design team reduced the number of parts and subassemblies in the vehicle to the point where Taurus labor costs (assembly time) were an estimated 40 percent below those of competing U.S. models. The parts in a newly assembled Taurus were 28 percent fewer than those in the LTD, which it was built to replace.

The combinations of benchmarking, quality initiatives, employee participation, and many important internal changes made Taurus/Sable a tremendous success for Ford. Figure 6–5 indicates, in terms

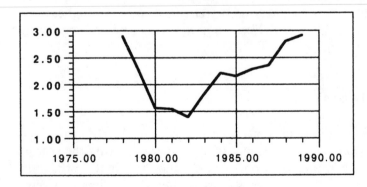

Source: Annual Report, Ford Motor Company.

Figure 6–5. Ford U.S. and Canadian Car Sales (units, in millions), 1978 to 1990

	Taurus Buyer	LTD Buyer
Average age	47	59
Average income	$38,000	$28,000
College graduate	43%	29%
Traded-in foreign make	15%	5%

Source: From *Marketing and Media Decision,* March 1987, as cited in J. B. Quinn and P. C. Paquette, "Ford: Team Taurus," p. 15.

Figure 6–6. Demographics of Taurus vs. LTD Buyers

of U.S. and Canadian unit auto sales, the reviving fortunes of the company.

Equally important, these unit sales translated into big profits for Ford. After years of stripping away the overhead in its plant and work force, sales revenues did not have far to travel to reach the bottom line; margins on the new model were very high—perhaps $1,200 to $1,500 *higher* per unit than on the old LTD.[20] Veraldi's concurrent engineering approach to managing the project may have saved the company between $300 million to $400 million on development costs alone.

Better still, the demographics were just what the stodgy old car company needed to create a clientele for the future: The average Taurus buyer was younger and better educated, had a higher income, and was three times more likely to have been a former import owner. (See Figure 6–6.)

THE TAURUS LESSONS

The success of the Ford Taurus was immediately recognized in the auto world and in U.S. industry in general. During the year following its market introduction, Veraldi and his public affairs manager, Charles Gumushian, criss-crossed the United States in response to dozens of invitations from companies like Hewlett-Packard, Boeing, and others that hoped to learn the lesson of Ford's great new success.

Team Taurus had successfully embodied the "guiding principles" that its company had first articulated just two years before in its Annual Report and public statements:

- *Quality comes first.* To achieve customer satisfaction, the quality of our products and services must be our number-one priority.
- *Customers are the focus of everything we do.* Our work must be done with our customers in mind, providing better products and services than our competition.
- *Continuous improvement is essential to our success.* We must strive for excellence in everything we do: in our products, in their safety and value—and in our services, our human relations, our competitiveness, and our profitability.
- *Employee involvement is our way of life.* We are a team. We must treat each other with trust and respect.
- *Dealers and suppliers are our partners.* The company must maintain mutually beneficial relationships with dealers, suppliers, and our other business associates.
- *Integrity is never compromised.* The conduct of our company worldwide must be pursued in a manner that is socially responsible and commands respect for its integrity and for its positive contribution to society. Our doors are open to men and women alike without discrimination and without regard to ethnic origin or personal beliefs.[21]

Ford learned two important lessons from the Taurus experience:

1. Competitive product analysis can provide perspective and guidance on critical design and development issues.
2. The process is as important as the product.

The efforts of Petersen and Veraldi integrated into the company many new processes for developing and manufacturing, at the same time that the product was being created. Employee involvement, empowered individuals and teams, Taguchi methods, and other new approaches to manufacturing were important legacies of the Taurus experience.

At Ford, the best in class approach to benchmarking the competition and Veraldi's cross-functional team model were both carried forward to other car development projects, most notably the redesigned Continental and the new Explorer,[22] both of which have been market successes. The extent to which the firm is able to institutionalize both the best in class method and Veraldi's team model throughout the company will be the measure of success for the Ford Design Institute, an educational center established to improve the effectiveness and efficiency of the design process for Ford cars.

7

Performing a Functional
Benchmarking Study

FUNCTIONAL BENCHMARKING

Functional benchmarking investigates the performance of a particular function within an industrywide application. This comparison is sometimes extended to a broader definition of industry than a stock analyst would define as a competitive industry. This type of study offers a good opportunity to develop breakthrough results in terms of identifying and understanding process enablers. Because of the need for logistical coordination and the potential need to produce "blinded" results, this type of study is usually facilitated by an external consultant; however, the study criteria are developed by the host company. One variant to this approach is to target specific companies that fit the study criteria and work with them, using a nondisclosure agreement as a means to establish the sharing conditions. General Motors Corporation (GM) conducted such a study in the early 1980s and it provides an interesting insight into how benchmarking studies progress.

THE GENERAL MOTORS CROSS-INDUSTRY STUDY

In September 1984, GM circulated the findings of a two-year study of quality practices within a number of prominent American companies which, by all accounts, were "excellent" firms. GM's documentation of its methodology in the study provides us with a richly detailed picture of how a multidivisional organization went about a large-scale benchmarking exercise at a time when there were few precedents or explicit guidelines for this type of study.

The major quality themes unearthed by the study were:

1. The companies studied embraced a quality culture in which employees committed themselves to quality output and quality improvement;

2. Management converts quality attitudes into action through a number of strategies:
   - Processes, goals, accountability, standards, and policies;
   - Organization mechanisms;
   - Enlisting the support of employees;
   - A constant flow of communication that reinforces the quality commitment;
   - Training programs;

3. Quality starts in "upstream" activities: product design and development;

4. Inputs and outputs are thoroughly tested as products move toward production; suppliers are made part of the team;

5. Measurement and testing are thorough; nothing is left to chance;

6. Custom satisfaction is a top operating priority.

From the perspective of the 1990s, GM's findings seem unremarkable, but in 1984 they merited a great deal of attention, particularly within America's largest auto company, where managers felt the tide of commercial power running against them and saw their public reputation slipping. J. D. Power Associates had published its customer satisfaction and quality surveys at about this time. In the first of these surveys, Japanese cars swept all the top ratings; GM cars were visibly absent from the winners' circle of top-ranked automobiles. *Motor Trend* magazine seemed to pick one or another Japanese model as its Car of the Year with disturbing regularity. Feedback on quality and customer satisfaction from many other sources was consistent in reinforcing these disappointing ratings. The giant automaker's only satisfaction was that its domestic rivals, Ford and Chrysler, ranked even lower.

The origins of the GM cross-industry study can be traced back to a 1982 internal report to top management on the causes of disasters that had accompanied development of the firm's "X" and "J" cars. The X-cars, first released in 1979, had been GM's response to the oil crisis of the 1970s; they were new designs intended to meet the growing market demand for the smaller, more fuel-efficient cars that Japanese automakers were quickly monopolizing. But the X-cars—the Chevrolet Citation model, for example—had been plagued by engine and assembly problems. The J-cars—among them, the Chevrolet Cavalier and Pontiac Sunbird, introduced in 1981 after five years of development—were deeply flawed during their first two years of production. They missed design targets for curb weight, fuel consumption, manufacturing cost, power-to-weight ratio, and tailpipe emissions, and they resisted starting in cold weather. Body parts for the new J-cars, originally drilled with round holes, could rarely be made to match up in the assembly plant, so "oval" holes—a GM tradition of that era—were required.

To determine what had gone wrong in the development of these two troubled series of vehicles, a cross-functional group of 75 GM managers and engineers had been recruited by GM's Corporate Quality and Reliability (Q&R) Department, in late 1981, to brainstorm the issues surrounding the X- and J-car projects and to appraise GM product development practices in general. J-car veterans purged themselves in these sessions, describing how the pressure to keep to schedules and avoid reporting bad news to top management had led them to take shortcuts, compromise on quality, and even fudge test results on the J-car. It was revealed that when then-President and CEO James McDonald arrived with his entourage at the Arizona test track to try out the preproduction J-car, he unknowingly got behind the wheel of a vehicle whose engine had been secretly souped up and filled with special fuel to conceal its anemic performance. The test track itself had been redesigned during the previous few days to eliminate grades the car could not master.

These and other findings were incorporated into a report presented to McDonald, who professed disbelief and remained solid in his conviction that GM was the largest and finest manufacturing company in the world, the corporation against which others measured their own manufacturing and quality competencies.

If GM was to change, the people in command—at the corporate and division levels—had to change their thinking about quality. Getting them to change would become the goal of a number of dedicated GM employees, notably those in Corporate Q&R.

LAUNCHING THE CROSS-INDUSTRY STUDY

In the summer of 1982, several months after McDonald's chilly reception of its X- and J-car report, Corporate Q&R took a first major step in changing conventional thinking on quality within General Motors. Working closely with consultants from the Sandy Company, a Troy, Michigan, firm, it brought together 150 managers from many levels of the organization to formally study the firm's larger quality issues and to pinpoint matters of product quality, dependability, reliability, and performance that failed to match the expectations of customers.

General Motors had traditionally maintained Q&R functions and conducted the daily details of standards, inspections, and quality assurance within its operating divisions. The recent formation of a corporate-level department had not been a popular idea within the divisions, where it was viewed with a mixture of suspicion and annoyance as yet another bureaucratic level to pass down requirements or otherwise impinge on the freedom of the operating divisions. Robert Decker, who had broad manufacturing experience, had been placed in charge of the new corporate entity. He enlisted Cardy Davis as its director, responsible for staffing the new department and developing its mission and policies. Davis had an engineering background and had had four years of quality and reliability experience at Buick and Cadillac.

Davis understood the territorial concerns of the operating divisions. He knew that Corporate Q&R would have to find a role for itself that provided the leadership that top management hoped for, without becoming the meddlesome bureaucracy that the divisions feared. In discussions with the divisions, it became clear that Corporate Q&R would have to be "process-oriented": It would have to deal with quality issues from a strategic standpoint, leaving the details to the divisions. In that capacity, it would be fulfilling top management's intentions without duplicating other ongoing Q&R activities. To avoid starting from scratch, Davis hoped that GM could learn how other companies were dealing with strategic quality issues and the related subject of customer satisfaction. The firm had already been getting advice from W. Edwards Deming, Joseph M. Juran, and Philip B. Crosby—the leading quality experts of the time—but, according to Davis, "what we really needed to do was go out and see what other companies were doing with this quality job, particularly those that were doing it successfully." He suggested a formal study of important companies that had already demonstrated success in quality and customer satisfaction.

There was little enthusiasm for Davis's proposed study outside the offices of Corporate Q&R. Looking back from the perspective of a decade, he recalled: "There was lots of initial resistance to damn near anything from the corporate level, as it was perceived as interference with the operating level." But he persevered, urging GM top management to approve the initiative, and seeking support for it within his own department and GM operating divisions.

Davis's urgings came at a time when the giant automaker's idea of quality was still hidebound in the traditional methods of assurance and inspection ("the little q"), before quality-as-business-ethic had really caught on in North America. Quality directors like Davis existed all over American industry, but the larger sense of quality they were beginning to see in the early 1980s ("the Big Q"—Total Quality Management) was still not part of the corporate consciousness. They would be its missionaries.[1]

Davis eventually won the support he needed to conduct the study. The firm would look beyond its own fences—indeed, outside its own industry—to the experience of firms that had demonstrated success on the quality front. It would attempt to determine how and why other companies had attained high standards of quality and customer satisfaction, and whether those experiences were transferable to GM. There was also a possibility that GM could save time and money if it simply learned from the experience and successes of other firms. Finally, Corporate Q&R saw a value in establishing network relationships between peer groups at GM and quality-oriented companies.[2]

SELECTING THE BENCHMARKING TARGETS

Every benchmarking exercise begins by answering two questions: Whom should we benchmark? and What should we benchmark? In answering the first question, and working closely with Sandy Company consultants Stephen Wells and Bruce Pince, the GM study group came up with a list of 92 companies for possible investigation. That list was reduced through a number of qualifying screens, such as number of employees, productivity ratios, profitability and other measures of return, performance rankings among peer groups of companies, technological comparability to GM, and quality stature. These selection criteria filtered out firms whose characteristics would make them too dissimilar to GM, although it was understood that the "product" of these companies mattered less than the "process." A good quality and reliability process was thought of as transferable, no matter what the product. None of the other U.S. carmakers was put on the list; it was felt that they were farther behind than GM on quality issues. GM had no access to the most obvious models: the Japanese auto firms.

In the end, a group of 20 companies was selected for study. Of these, Wells and Pince were able to win the cooperation of 11: Boeing, Cincinnati Milacron, John Deere & Co., GE Medical Systems, Hewlett-Packard, IBM, Maytag, Rockwell International Automotive, Texas Instruments, 3M, and AT&T Technologies. It was probably no coincidence that most of these had been prominently featured in Tom Peters and R. H. Waterman's book, *In Search of Excellence,* which had recently been published and was becoming something of a sensation among business managers all over North America. Many of the 150 managers in the study group had been among its enthusiastic readers.

There was a great deal of enthusiasm for the general goals of the study among the 11 companies. "Quality," as we have seen in previous cases, was on the minds of most thoughtful American managers. The dramatic invasion of their domestic markets by foreign competitors gave managers in different industries—and even among traditional competitors—a sense of fraternity and shared danger. This atmosphere created a mood of cooperation and facilitated the decision of the target companies to join the study as "hosts." Every one of these firms was keenly aware that GM was "in trouble" (more aware than GM top management at the time) with respect to its market share and the quality of its products, and they wanted to help the auto giant improve its quality practices. All would prove generous with their time and resources. John Deere went so far as to bump its own board of directors from use of the corporate jet, to make it available to the visiting GM team.

Virtually all of the host firms were farther along the quality curve than was GM, but their understanding of Big Q ideas was still far from complete. Hewlett-Packard, for example, was a leader in the American quality movement, and its quality director, Craig Walter, was among the most respected in the business. Yet, in 1983, HP was only halfway toward becoming a total quality management organization. Like everyone else, HP was learning many quality ideas from the Japanese, but was getting only one piece of the puzzle at a time.

THE GENERAL MOTORS HYPOTHESIS

Unlike most benchmark exercises, the GM study began with a hypothesis that identified ten factors (Figure 7–1) as distinguishing quality-competent companies and contributing to their success. Instead of the normal approach of observing competitors, peers, or other target companies along some focused set of activities, this study chose to state a broadly framed hypothesis and go out to find data to test against it. This hypothesis testing approach was used as a way to focus the data-collection process.

The objective of GM's cross-industry study was to verify this hypothesis empirically. The hypothesis was sufficiently broad to cover many of the objectives that would be addressed in any quality benchmarking study.

CONDUCT OF THE STUDY

Organization and Preparation

Each of the 25 GM divisions participating in the study contributed two or three individuals, all experienced managers, to what would be company "study teams." Collectively, they represented a broad range of functions within the firm—purchasing, engineering, and manufacturing—and roughly half represented divisional Q&R units. The

1. *Core Concepts.* A pervasive philosophy—core concepts—guides and perpetuates [quality firms'] reputation for quality. These core concepts originate and issue from the firm's senior management.

2. *Quality Mechanisms.* Quality companies have mechanisms which convert their core concepts into people-oriented strategies and tactics that employees can act upon.

3. *Standardize Performance.* Encouragement and rewards support quality concepts and lead to standardized performance at all levels.

4. *Transfer Quality Performance.* Quality firms know how to transfer methods and practices within and between their organizations.

5. *Establish a Quality Culture.* [Quality] firms inculcate themselves with cultural patterns in support of quality that transcend technology issues, its products, organization, and management.

6. *Production is Subservient to Quality.* Quality, and not production schedules, techniques, or cost, comes first.

7. *QRDP Disciplines.* These firms employ quality, reliability, durability, and performance disciplines rigorously, consistently, and at all levels.

8. *Unselfish in Seeking Customer Satisfaction.* Their ceaseless quest for ways to please their customers has positive effects on investment returns and long-term corporate value.

9. *Resist the Temptation for Short-Term Financial Success.* All levels of the firm reject short-term financial goals that would lead it away from its core values.

10. *Learn from Failure.* Failure heightens vigilance, and successful companies continually adapt to quality change and challenge.

Source: General Motors Corporation, Cross-Industry Study Report, September 24, 1984.

Figure 7–1.   Ten Elements of the Quality Null Hypothesis

backgrounds and schedules of these individuals were considered in assigning them to particular "host" companies. The study teams were made up of three to four GM managers, one or more staffers from Corporate Q&R, and a consultant from the Sandy Company.

As preparation for site visits to the host companies, team members were invited to an orientation workshop held, in May 1983, by Corporate Q&R at the GM Training Center. Robert Decker, vice president of Corporate Q&R, prefaced the working sessions with an overview of the company's involvement with the quality movement and the current commitment of top management to its principles in all aspects of GM operations. The working sessions of the orientation meeting were devoted to the purposes of the cross-industry study, site visit protocol, team assignments, and review of specific quality activities the teams should look for. The teams were given GM's model of the "Quality Process" (see Figure 7–2) as a framework for seeking sources of quality values and enabling mechanisms that would lead to quality performance.[3]

Just as the stage was set for conduct of the study, its greatest proponent was promoted and reassigned within GM: Cardy Davis was named director for Q&R within the critical Assembly Division. His leadership was lost to the study, but another capable individual, Al Billas, whom Davis had recruited to Corporate Q&R, would see it through to the end.

Site Visits

Visits to the 11 host companies began in June and ended in August of 1983; each visit lasted three to five days. Typically, several divisions of each host company were visited. The visits had the following pattern:

1. The GM team listened to the host company's formal presentation of its quality program and processes. These presentations were described later as "structured, detailed, and candid."

2. The GM team made its own presentation, explaining the nature of its study and the ongoing quality efforts at GM.

3. Senior managers of the host company were interviewed to determine their "core quality concepts" and the mechanisms they used to inculcate the concepts in the organization as performance standards.

4. Middle managers and supervisors were interviewed to determine their quality implementation and measurement methods.

5. GM team members spoke with workers, in an effort to assess their roles, attitudes, authority, and responsibilities for quality outcomes.

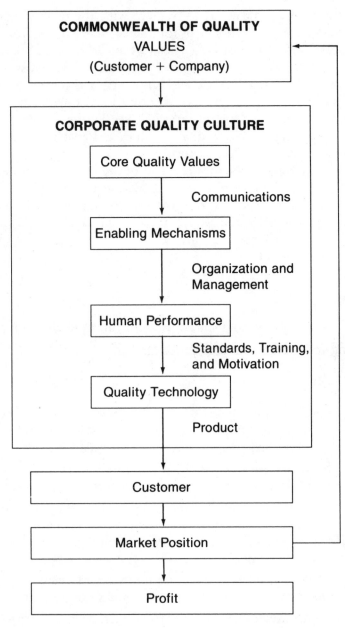

Source: General Motors Corporation.

Figure 7–2. The GM Quality Process Model

6. Processes and procedures were observed in laboratories and offices, and on the production line.

7. Information relevant to the production of quality goods and services was collected.

8. Team members looked for patterns, cultural elements, and strategies that contributed to success and change.[4]

The host companies were described by GM team members as very candid in describing both their successes and failures with quality initiatives, and several managers of host companies expressed an interest in site visits to General Motors.

Site Visit Wrap-ups

Despite the fatigue that followed each three- to five-day site visit, each team held a meeting at the conclusion of the visit, to record and evaluate its collective experience while impressions were still clear. The Corporate Q&R staff and the Sandy Company consultant assigned to each team played leadership roles in these meetings. Each wrap-up meeting followed a four-step procedure in getting all the pertinent facts out into the open:

1. The host company was evaluated in terms of quality, reliability, dependability, and performance. How it stacked up against GM in these terms was also considered.

2. The processes used by the host company to produce quality products and services were identified, and their transferability to GM was evaluated.

3. The degree to which the host company conformed to the ten key factors in the GM quality hypothesis was assessed using a numerical scale (0 to 10).

4. Other impressions or insights of team members were shared.

Information recorded at these wrap-up meetings, along with documents collected during the actual visits, formed the basis of the study team reports. Corporate Q&R and the participating Sandy Company consultants compiled the reports into a standard format that analyzed each of the host companies along several dimensions: the degree to which it fit the ten key hypotheses, overall QRDP rank, common quality practices, and so forth. These company reports were presented to study participants at an all-teams workshop, held in October 1983. Members of the different teams, who had worked independently, had an opportunity to share their experiences, suggest changes and additions to the Q&R reports, and discuss practices that seemed transferable to GM.

REPORTING THE FINDINGS

Some months after the October workshop, a final and official report of the cross-industry study was released within GM and the 11 host companies. The 136-page report was divided into three parts:

1. Results of the hypothesis testing;
2. Summary of the findings in strategic and managerial terms;
3. Separate reports on each of the 11 host firms.

Hypothesis Testing Results

The scores given to each company during the visit wrap-ups were tabulated and summarized in the final report. There was a fair amount of variation (from several 10s to a low of 4.8) from company to company, in terms of individual conformance to the hypothesized ten key quality factors. When averaged out, the mean score for the companies as a group conformed fairly well to the hypotheses.[5] The scores were highest in those categories that related to top management's commitment to the quality ethic (core concepts, quality culture, etc.) and lower in those areas more closely tied to implementation.[6] The report made the comment that, although evidence of other quality precepts was sought, none was identified that "seemed to . . . contradict, displace or amplify on [the] ten hypotheses." Either the designers of the study had a very complete sense of the universal drivers of quality, or the site teams saw the world through only the particular set of lenses they were given.[7]

Summary of Findings

An early section of this chapter presented the study's findings in abbreviated form, and they will not be repeated here. They dealt with issues of core concepts and attitudes, managerial strategies, product design and development, manufacturing, measurement and testing, and customer focus. Each of these issues was examined generally in the report, often using examples drawn from the host companies. In approaching these issues in a general way, the similarities that bridge companies, industries, and regions were drawn into sharper focus. The study's discussion of these findings was universally positive.

The reporting of these findings was undoubtedly useful to just about all of the participants in the study, both at GM and at the host companies, because it integrated the many parts of the puzzle, allowing those who had seen just a few pieces to get a sense of the whole.

Individual Host Company Reports

Perhaps more useful from the standpoint of practice transfer were the detailed reports done on each of the host companies. Each of these reports very systematically presented a brief overview of a host company's quality improvement efforts, and followed with very detailed information on that firm's quality and reliability mechanisms.[8] The latter laid out the Q&R mechanisms used by the firm, how those mechanisms worked, and the results that followed. Figure 7–3 provides an example, from the study, of just a few of the mechanisms used by one of the host companies.

Reporting the Test Results to the Host Firms

GM's Corporate Q&R was systematic in disseminating the results of its study to the host companies. Staffers were sent out to each of these firms, and copies of the study results were distributed at management presentations. The host firms were offered the opportunity to visit GM to conduct their own benchmarking studies; by most accounts, this offer was generally accepted, and groups of managers from the

Name of Mechanism	How Mechanism Works	Results
Reliability Testing "to Failure"	• Establish realistic factors and test 'til fails • Product must meet customer environment requirements and not just specifications. • Data fed back to product development teams continuously. • STRIFE (stress test to life of product) at every stage of product development.	• Products which satisfy customer expectations of reliability.
Consequence Systems	• All know that their job and its benefits are tied to total quality performance. • Failure to conform to teamwork practice or to goal of customer satisfaction can result in "exclusion" from Company X.	• Work force motivated to perform positively because of clear understanding of the results of their behaviors.
Product Development Teams at Core of Quality Effort	• After market need is identified, interdisciplinary team is set up to design solution; team includes Quality Assurance. • Team is autonomous and responsible for product to General Manager.	• More product ideas than they can produce. • Clear-cut responsibility and accountability for new products.

- Designs are carefully reviewed and follow development, testing and process review procedures rigorously.
- Original design teams follow product into and after SOP and even physically moves to manufacturing to help product reach full maturity.

- Close-working relationship and communications laterally, especially between R&D and Marketing and between R&D and Manufacturing.

Vendor Development Process

- Careful development of good relations training and support assures quality from suppliers.
- 90 percent of the total number of parts for Company X products are purchased from suppliers.
- Materials Engineering is responsible for technical quality of suppliers.
- Company X purchasing agents are becoming "professionalized" by placing engineers or MBAs in these roles.

- Very satisfactory and colleagial relationship with vendors, solving Quality and Reliability problems together.
- Vendors as "partners in quality."

Source: General Motors.

Figure 7-3. Quality and Reliability Mechanisms, Company X

host companies trooped through GM facilities both during and after the period of the study.

THE LONG-TERM RESULT OF GM'S CROSS-INDUSTRY STUDY

The presentation of the study to GM's executive committee in September 1984 did not go over well. President McDonald, as in the case of the X- and J-car report, refused to take the study seriously; he questioned the validity of the J. D. Power quality data on GM that had prefaced the study's presentation, stating that "We're not that bad"—an opinion he would eventually change.[9] The patient did not like the taste of the medicine the study was serving up, and Decker, Billas, and others knew that their job of integrating their findings with GM practices would not be easy. In January 1985, they followed up their report with a three-day conference in which Corporate Q&R brought together 110 managers, in an attempt to convert the benchmark findings into some form of tangible company quality strategy and policy statement.[10] This task was accomplished, but the timing could not have been more inopportune. By then, GM's top management and McKinsey Company consultants were launching plans for a major reorganizing of the corporation; two of its largest divisions, Assembly and Fisher Body, were to be eliminated. Managerial personnel were so involved in job changes, new reporting responsibilities, and so forth, that there was little interest or reaction to the study report or the policy recommendations. By all appearances, the cross-industry study had fallen into an organizational abyss.

GM has made a number of important advances in quality and customer satisfaction, the twin objects of the study, since the events just described: development of a very credible supplier quality program (Targets For Excellence); the Cadillac Division's winning of the Malcolm Baldrige National Quality Award; recognition in the early 1990s for the Oldsmobile Ciera as the highest-quality car built in North America; and J. D. Power & Associates' naming of GM's Oklahoma City assembly plant as the best in North America (and second in the world). During the past decade, GM has moved away from its early "conformance to specifications" mentality to the model of continuous improvement. The UAW/GM Quality Network (1989), the firm's current mechanism for integrating quality efforts, incorporates many of the recommendations of the 1984 cross-industry study.

Direct linkages between these successes and the study cannot be firmly established. Nevertheless, almost all of its lessons have been learned and adopted by GM. According to Davis, who views the impact of the study as having had subliminal effects on the company rather than creating a legacy of specific programs, "It clearly got the quality and reliability leadership in the company to start thinking in the right way, so that over time they were able to make many important things happen. Also, there were lots of people involved in the cross-industry study who, later on, were put in positions where they could really make important changes." Counting himself as one of those people, Davis, who is now platform manager for GM's A and W cars, is responsible for just about everything but marketing, for a number of the best-rated cars sold in North America. Al Billas, who managed the cross-industry study following Davis's departure, has moved to a key post within the Inland Fisher Guide Division. Scores of other individuals who served on the study teams became converts to the quality disciplines they found outside GM, and they have served as a "fifth column" within the giant automaker, creating change through their daily activities—outside the boundaries of official corporate programs.

QUALITY AND RELIABILITY MECHANISMS

General Motors Corporation's cross-industry study listed 151 quality and reliability mechanisms that appeared tied to positive outcomes in the 11 host companies. Many of these, like "supplier quality policy" and "quality training" repeat themselves across the firms. Even after eliminating these repetitions, at least 100 different mechanisms are mentioned. Today, most quality managers refer to these mechanisms as "enablers"—factors that enable behavioral change.

Figure 7–4 lists a number of the mechanisms, with the comments they drew. Mechanisms deemed company-specific were eliminated for this listing.

Q&R Mechanism	Comments
No defects in Unit 1	For major job shop projects, forcing defects out of Unit 1 sets the processes to drive defects out of subsequent units.
Have a system to collect, analyze, distribute, and require quality data	
Budget responsibility to lowest unit	
Cost of quality	Dollarize quality performance to emphasize profit potential; emphasize the cost of doing things wrong.
System for delegating consequences for quality success and failure	Desirable quality behavior is rewarded; undesirable behavior has consequences.
Review of exceptions by management	All events falling outside limits are reviewed.
Standardized quality policies, procedures, and practices	Corporatewide.
Quality assurance system and policy	Corporatewide.
Quality-oriented product development	
Prime division has product responsibility	This division has authority to enforce quality standards in other divisions.
Change control system	Multifunctional committee must approve design changes.
Program manager selects own team	Recruitment from throughout the firm.
Quality supplier policy	Suppliers have quality assurance programs; monitor suppliers; eliminate the worst, support the best.

Source: General Motors Corporation.

Figure 7–4. Sample of Q&R Mechanisms (Enablers) and Comments, GM Cross-Industry Study

Q&R Mechanism	Comments
State-of-the-art information management system	Make production control and quality monitoring possible.
No work advances with quality problems	
Absolute honesty required on quality issues	Encourage workers to speak up about quality problems; no punishment of whistle-blowers.
Customer satisfaction as Job 1	Supported by feedback and problem resolution system.
Employee satisfaction as Job 2	Keep work units small as possible; promote from within; share pain and rewards proportionately; few privileges for executives.
Guarantee product performance over time	All quality efforts are directed toward meeting those guarantees.
Education and training	
Management contact with customers	
Quality starts "upstream"	Periodic checkpoints in product design and development catch future problems.
Liaison between product engineers and manufacturing	
Product engineer stays with the product from conception to market release	Establishes accountability for quality.
Management by walking around	Encourages communication and team spirit.
Reliability testing "to failure"	
Top management commitment to action	Not talk.
New products must be of better quality than products being replaced	Even in the first model year.

Figure 7–4. *(Continued)*

Q&R Mechanism	Comments
Quality measure part of personnel evaluations	
Union/management cooperation	Partners for quality.
Q&R, JIT, etc., as strategies for profits	Higher quality equals greater margins.
Quality improvement teams	Formed at all levels.
Common language of quality	Through training process.
Statistical process control used at many stages	
Product-by-product quality audit system	
Plant manager accountable for product quality	
Any employee can stop movement of the product because of defects	Applies within the firm and to the customer.

Figure 7–4. *(Continued)*

8

Developing a Generic Benchmarking Study

GENERIC BENCHMARKING

Generic benchmarking represents the broadest application of data collection to company partners. In conducting a generic benchmarking study, a company is not confined to a competitive or industry border; it is confined only by its ability to develop an analogous process and understand how to translate across industries, using its partner's selection criteria. This most innovative approach to benchmarking can result in changed paradigms and reengineering of business operations. Perhaps the best known benchmarking study is the generic study conducted by Xerox Corporation of L. L. Bean, to understand Bean's shipment processes.

XEROX FINDS BEST PRACTICE "DOWN EAST"

In 1979, Charles Christ, then vice president of Xerox copier manufacturing, sought out a variety of productivity measures of the firm's rising Japanese competitors. He was looking in particular for factors such as the ratio of staff personnel to direct labor, product quality, and levels of parts inventory. The measures he found were compared to those of Xerox and drawn up in a report in early 1981.[1] The data for the report were generated through what may have been the first benchmarking exercise within Xerox Corporation. Christ's manager,

149

Frank Pipp, vice president of development and manufacturing for the entire copier business, had become aware of substantial cost differences between Xerox's U.S. copier production and the costs experienced by the firm's Japanese joint venture, Fuji Xerox Company Ltd. Pipp learned that Fuji Xerox, through its competitive intelligence unit in Japan, had access to cost information about the competitive Japanese products. Pipp asked the unit's president, Yutaro "Tony" Kobayashi, to study copier producers in Japan, determine their cost structures, and report on these to Christ's staff, which was assigned to develop the report.

Christ's study confirmed the growing body of evidence that Japanese competitors in the plain paper copier business—Minolta, Ricoh, Canon, Toshiba, and others—were profitably selling their high-quality products in the United States at prices below those of Xerox's own cost of production. This evidence, and Pipp's championing of its significance to the firm, convinced Xerox management that new ways of operating would be required if the once "Cinderella company," the pioneer of xerography, were to avoid a slow slide into obscurity.

In 1980, the plain paper copier industry was a $26 billion worldwide business. Xerox had developed the industry and, so far, had remained its leading producer. Its first copier, the 914, introduced in 1960, had revolutionized the white-collar workplace and had been described as "the most successful product ever marketed in America." Xerox quickly broke into the ranks of the Fortune 500, and its stock went onto the "nifty fifty" list of blue-chip growth companies that virtually every institutional investor had to own. The company's ascent between 1960 and 1980 had been nothing less than dramatic: employment skyrocketed from 3,000 to over 100,000, and revenues hit the $8 billion mark.

By the late 1970s, however, the bloom was off the rose. From the perspective of 1987, William Glavin, then executive vice president of Xerox, wrote: "Our manufacturing facilities were highly labor-intensive. We built up a huge overhead structure of indirect white-collar workers. Our organization was bogged down with far too many checks and balances."[2]

By the late 1970s, a growing number of competitors had entered the field: Kodak, IBM, 3M, and the Japanese firms previously mentioned. Xerox's 1976 estimated market share of 82 percent slid substantially over the next five years. By 1981, Xerox still accounted for about 60 percent of all the revenues in the copier industry, but the income was derived mostly from its placement of machines in the high and middle segments of the market. After their usual fashion, the upstart Japanese were coming to dominate the low end of the market.

Typical of American producers in the 1970s, Xerox managers had expected the greatest competition to come from other American firms—IBM and Kodak, in particular. Meanwhile, the Japanese were busily developing the new products and process technologies that would soon become the real threat. Minolta, for example, had been studying Honda and learning Toyota's just-in-time approach to quality and manufacturing. And Minolta was not unique. Japanese firms in a variety of industries had been quick to ferret out whatever industrial practices worked well, and had adapted them to their particular situations. Canon, Minolta, and Ricoh had applied typical Japanese ingenuity and method to the copier problem: They had increased reliability and reduced cost by designing the product to operate using the fewest possible number of parts. When combined with stringent levels of quality control and the Toyota-inspired system of manufacturing, these firms developed significant cost and time advantages over their American rivals.

David Jorgensen, chairman of Dataquest, is quoted in Jacobson and Hillkirk's study of Xerox as saying:

> I remember going and visiting the factories at Canon and Minolta in the latter seventies. Compared to the way Xerox made machines, it was night and day. The Japanese were putting machines out every fifty seconds. At Xerox, there was a huge area at the end of the assembly lines where they did quality assurance and quality control. In Japan, they were put in a box and shipped. It was obvious . . . Xerox was far behind.[3]

The growing strength of the Japanese in the market, and the new evidence about their manufacturing cost advantage—determined to be 50 percent lower than that of Xerox—stirred then-CEO David Kearns to launch a broad-based counterattack in August 1981. Dubbed "Business Effectiveness," the new program was designed to turn back the Japanese offensive. It contained a new philosophy for quality and organizational effectiveness, and had as its goal the renewal of Xerox's original innovative spirit and market power. The principal tools of Business Effectiveness would be employee involvement and benchmarking.[4] Top management directed all units and cost centers to adopt benchmarking techniques.[5]

During the 1980s, Xerox successfully reformed its operating practices to the point where it closed the manufacturing-unit cost gap with Japan, cut its product development cycle time, eliminated mountains of burdensome overhead, and came to be recognized as one of the most quality-conscious corporations in the world. It may well have been the first major U.S. manufacturer to have successfully recaptured its markets from Japanese competitors, a point made apparent in Jacobson and Hillkirk's *Xerox: American Samurai*.

A remarkable point about the Xerox story is the extent to which the new operating philosophy permeated that huge organization. The battle for the copier market was not won in corporate headquarters, nor in the R&D labs alone, or even on the factory floor; success was the result of firmwide operational improvements, even down to the most unglamorous functions. One of these many points of improvement was the Xerox warehouse and distribution system—not an area that most business strategists would normally get excited about, but an important interface with customers and a key part of the firmwide productivity and quality improvement puzzle.

The Logistics Problem

Within the Xerox Logistics and Distribution (L&D) unit, annual productivity had been increasing at roughly 3 to 5 percent until 1981, but that was not seen as sufficient to meet the challenges of the business environment then or in the future. A number of improvements were already in progress. The inventory control system had done benchmarking of best practice, and was applying the lessons learned to its own operations. The Christ study presented in 1981 had revealed that Japanese producers kept roughly a one-month inventory of parts on hand, compared to Xerox's 3.2 months' parts inventory, which cost roughly $33 million per month.[6] Figuring that the Japanese would drive their already low number still lower in the years ahead, Xerox got busy with an ambitious program to reduce the need for its costly inventory.

In the field of transportation, the Reagan Administration had carried over many of the Carter Administration's deregulation initiatives. The results were greater flexibility and more opportunities to reduce transportation costs within the United States. For an operation on the scale of Xerox, these would translate into better service and cost savings.

Within L&D, warehousing was the next likely place to seek out sources of operational improvements. Warehousing entails receiving raw materials and components from suppliers, maintaining accurate records of quantities and locations, providing timely service to the manufacturing function, and fulfilling finished goods orders (receiving, picking, packing, and shipping)—for both new machines and follow-on replacement parts and supplies. Distribution manager Robert C. Camp[7] decided to focus first on order fulfillment, and, within that general area, on the smaller but important issue of "picking," which was viewed internally as an important bottleneck in the company's receiving/shipping cycle. The flow of materials through the warehouse had to be streamlined somehow, to increase productivity and minimize the time and effort taken to pick, pack, and ship a customer order. Camp, a PhD in logistics/operations research from Penn State, had been a distribution manager for the company for ten years. It would be his job to provide the ideas that would help Xerox break through its current bottleneck.

The "science" of improving warehouse productivity was already well-developed by the early 1980s. Automated storage and retrieval systems (ASRS), an optimizing approach to the design of warehouse layout, were readily available. The company already had one ASRS warehouse in Webster, New York, to support its manufacturing operations, and there were plenty of warehouses around the country where these systems could be observed and benchmarked. However, the logistics groups had already decided that the high initial cost of these systems was not justified for the order picking and fulfillment activities faced by Xerox. Xerox's picking operations were not characterized by the truckload and pallet-size orders that these elaborate systems so ably served. When these kinds of orders occurred at Xerox, they were the exception. Instead, orders of two screws, a replacement photoreceptor, cartons of copying paper, a box of transparencies, or five toner cartridges were more typical. Picking and shipping items on this scale was seen as a generic function that might be benchmarked in any number of related or unrelated industries. The idea of benchmarking against competitors was already accepted in Xerox at the time, and there was a growing body of experience within the operating and staff units on how to conduct a benchmarking study against competing firms. The idea of looking outside Xerox's industry had not yet been accepted. Camp's feeling was that, if one looked only at competitors, the best one could hope for was learning enough to gain parity with them. His group was looking for practices that would put Xerox out ahead, and it seemed that these might be found by expanding the universe of benchmark candidates to include companies that were first-rate in *a particular function.*[8]

Identifying the Benchmarking Target

Formal benchmarking procedures were begun as soon as the general warehouse problem had been identified and agreed on by the logistics group. The first order of business was to determine a benchmarking "target" company: one (or more) organizations that defined best practice in materials handling in general, and picking operations in particular.

In January 1981, it was determined by the logistics group that one person would be assigned, part-time over an extended period,[9] the task of filtering through all public sources of information that might provide clues to the current definition of best practice in picking operations. Camp took on this responsibility and began filtering any and all information on this subject. His twin goals were to determine which activities were leading-edge, and to find companies that were within the definition of "best practice." Three primary sources of information were investigated:

1. Trade journals in materials handling and logistics, going back three years, were screened for articles on the subject;

2. Professional associations were contacted, to determine which individuals or firms were providing practical leadership in this area;

3. Management consultants specializing in materials handling were contacted informally to obtain their insights.

From this initial screening, which lasted for ten months, a report was developed that listed companies, distributors, and dealers that had developed reputations for good practice in the generic area under investigation. The specific companies included Bergen, Sears Roebuck, Tandy, American Hospital Supply, and Westinghouse. The unique characteristics of their systems were arrayed in tabular form.

Like most benchmarking investigations, this initial effort served to highlight the broad differences between what Xerox was doing in its warehouse and what the literature and personal contacts had described as best practice. It also whetted the logistics group's appetite for more and specific knowledge about companies and practices. There was an obvious opportunity to learn a great deal that would lead to improved warehouse productivity and service within Xerox— enough so that a full-time benchmarking position was created for Camp within the logistics group.

An article entitled "A Truly Outstanding System for Manual Order Picking" had appeared in *Modern Materials Handling,* the trade periodical of the Council of Logistics Management, less than a year before.[10] The article described L. L. Bean's operation as manual, but efficiently directed by a computer system that minimized the amount of labor and time involved in locating and picking the millions of items ordered by customers during the year. During its peak season (fall), 60 Bean stock pickers could pick up to 33,000 orders per day—a level of productivity that far exceeded the Xerox rate. Business circumstances at Bean had made this productivity level a necessity. Sales had grown at a 10 percent compounded rate over the previous ten years, and the distribution operation would have been swamped had it not been able to reach greater levels of efficiency. Bean had made a quantum leap of 45 percent in picking productivity within just two months of its installation of the computer-assisted system. Best of all, this improvement had been accomplished without a mountain of capital costs. Tom Day, then director of distribution, quality control, and engineering at Bean, was quoted as saying: "With our order profile, that is, an average of 1.9 small items per order, our system compares favorably with any automated storage and retrieval system. We have a relatively low capital investment featuring standard racks and push carts. Most of the investment is in software and controls."

The Xerox team was excited by what they read. The Bean warehouse was picking and packing a small package of trout flies here, an 18-foot canoe there, and thousands of other items of varying shapes, sizes, colors, and weights. Best of all, outgoing accuracy, an important performance measure, was touted in the article as 99.85 percent. This was the type of quality figure that Xerox top management wanted to see associated with its own products and services.

On the surface, Bean and Xerox had much different forms of warehousing operations. To the logistics professional, form mattered less than function, and the functions performed at the Bean warehouse were strikingly analogous to those required by the copier firm. Camp later made these comments about the analogies between L. L. Bean and Xerox:

> I was particularly struck with the L. L. Bean warehouse system design. Although extremely manual in nature, the design minimized the labor content, among other benefits. The operation also did not lend itself to automation. The design therefore relied on very basic handling techniques, but it was carefully thought out and implemented. In addition, the design was selected with the full participation of the hourly work force. It was the first warehouse operation designed by quality circles.[11]

THE HUMMING WAREHOUSE IN FREEPORT

It is a long way from the concrete-and-glass canyons of downtown Rochester, New York—company town for Eastman Kodak and Xerox Corporation—to the seacoast community of Freeport, Maine. It would seem unlikely that a global manufacturing giant would find much to emulate among the clapboard colonial homes and factory outlet stores that line the main thoroughfare of Bean's hometown.

Freeport is undoubtedly the most visited single location north of Boston—doubly so during the fall foliage season, when both "leaf peepers" and shoppers converge on the town. They crowd the outlet stores of Patagonia, Dansk, Nike, Liz Claiborne, Timberline, and dozens more that are the town's chief industry. The centerpiece and magnet of Freeport is the cavernous L. L. Bean store—right on Main Street—in which all the catalog items so familiar to Beanophiles from

Toledo to Tokyo can be seen, handled, and discussed with knowledgeable employees. For long-time mail-order customers from outside of New England, a visit to Bean's is an unforgettable experience. The store is open 24 hours a day, every day, and 4 million people pass through its doors each year.

About a mile down the street, on the south edge of town, is the 310,000-square-foot L. L. Bean warehouse and distribution center, where some 13,000 regular items are stocked and sold through hundreds of thousands of annual direct mail orders. Like the store, the direct mail center is humming 24 hours a day, seven days a week. As if to demonstrate that practice makes perfect, Bean and systems vendor Kurt Salmon Associates have used those many transactions to develop a stock picking and order fulfillment process that is highly praised by customers for its accuracy and speed.

Like Xerox, L. L. Bean is not in the truckload or pallet-size distribution business. Its stock pickers are filling orders for "one of these and two of those," shipped together in a small box via UPS for rapid delivery. An expensive and automated materials handling system, although useful to bulk order distributors, would not be cost-effective. To the logistics group in Rochester, Freeport seemed like an excellent place to see firsthand how to improve its own picking operations.

PREPARATION AND EXECUTION OF THE SITE VISIT

Camp had already made the acquaintance of L. L. Bean's distribution director, Tom Day, at a recent conference of distribution managers. Camp reestablished contact with Day in early 1982, explained his interest in the Freeport distribution operation, and asked whether a site visit would be feasible. Day was agreeable, and all the arrangements were made.

The Xerox team made its visit to the Freeport facility in February 1982. Team members came armed with a questionnaire and a list of points to discuss, both of which had been developed in Rochester during the preceding month. The questionnaire had been prepared in cooperation with the line managers at Xerox who would be involved with both the execution of the site visit and implementation of any changes that the benchmarking study might lead to. (In the end, this proved to be an important element in gaining acceptance for future changes within the Xerox distribution system.) The team was prepared to spend a productive day with the head of distribution and supervisory personnel, seeking answers to the questionnaire, observing operations, and comparing these to their own practices. Figure 8–1 identifies the participants on both sides of the site visit.

The morning was spent with Day and his operations supervisors. Each of the items on the Xerox questionnaire was discussed, and the visitors received an overview of order handling practice at Bean. After lunch, Day provided his guests with a complete tour of Bean's sprawling warehouse, which employed between 200 and 480 people, depending on the season.

Some distribution people swear that they can spot a well-run warehouse/distribution operation as soon as they walk through its door. A first-rate warehouse/distribution center is well-lighted and neat as a pin. No bulky items are piled up in corners; aisles and rows are clear and well-marked; no empty soda cans or lunch bags inhabit the storage bins. This is the type of operation the Xerox team found; Camp later remarked on the "efficient and excellent housekeeping" of the Freeport facility. The order picking area, which was the primary focus of the visitors' attention, accounted for about one-sixth of the total square footage. This area was organized into zones from which pickers fanned out into adjacent aisles. Each picker had a cart with shelves that could be segmented by partitions to accommodate each order.

Xerox:

Benchmarking manager

Headquarters planning manager for products of interest in
   the study

Field distribution center manager

L. L. Bean:

Director of distribution, quality control, and engineering

Distribution operations supervisors

Warehouse personnel

Figure 8–1.   Personnel Involved in the Xerox/L. L. Bean Benchmark[12]

To the untrained eye, the movement of order pickers and their carts through the many stock zones might have seemed unremarkable, but to the Xerox team, which was prepared to compare the finer points to other systems, including their own, Bean's ingenuity and efficiency were delightful to observe.

Order pickers received a computer-generated pick list. This graphically demonstrated how the shelves on the picker's cart were to be partitioned into compartments to hold all the items on the list. Each item would occupy a specific partition on the cart. The computer even determined the size of each compartment, according to the size of the assigned item.

The computerized pick list determined a route that minimized the picker's travel distance. Because there were no permanent storage locations within the zones, the fastest moving items for a particular season were stored by a logic that further minimized the distance traveled.

After the picker made his or her assigned rounds, the cart went to a packing station. Here again, the Xerox team found that the computer had minimized effort: individual items on the cart were arranged in correct packing order. Even the size of the appropriate shipping boxes was determined in advance.

After observing the process, the team from Xerox concentrated on the individual parts of the operation, interviewing managers and order pickers about their work.

ANALYZING THE DATA

The site visit had been activity-packed, and the Xerox team came away with a great deal of valuable information, all of which needed to be organized, analyzed, and disseminated to the appropriate parties within the company. The first step in this process took place at the Freeport airport: A debriefing was held as the team awaited the flight that would return them to Rochester, New York. Team members conducted a verbal reconstruction of the L. L. Bean operation, each adding a piece to the larger puzzle and contributing what others might not have seen or remembered. Notes were made of all narrations.

When team members were back in their Rochester offices, the analysis was pursued more methodically. The first task was the development of a "trip report" that recorded the particulars of the site visit and the team's collective observations. Follow-up calls between the Xerox team and L. L. Bean yielded added particulars. Specific practices of the Bean distribution center were compared to those currently used by Xerox. (See Figure 8–2.)

Put Away. At Bean, computer-selected storage locations for incoming materials were based on availability of specific rack locations, volume requirements of the incoming materials, and minimization of the travel distance to the rack locations.

Compared to traditional methods, which either assigned incoming inventory to specified locations or required visual searching for open storage areas, this approach proved to be a time-saver and a better utilizer of limited rack space.

Picking Order. The put-away logic of the computer-located inventory matched the daily order activity: Fast-moving items were stocked closest to the beginning of the picking route. Infrequently ordered items (and some bulky items) were located farthest away. The travel route of the stock picker was thereby minimized.

The computer accumulated orders for short periods (usually hourly) throughout the day, and then consolidated like items. Described as "short interval scheduling," this methodology further minimized the travel route of the stock picker. It also accumulated all orders of a single stock item so that only one visit would have to be made to that stock location during a given period.

Shipping. Bean documented the shipping weight and dimensions of each stock item. Supportable computer records of items shipped in any given period allowed Bean to pay UPS charges based on these records. Transactional labor time and money were substantially reduced.

Activity Analysis. Bean's computerized systems made it possible to track both the level of activity and the error rates of both individual order-fulfillment personnel and teams. Thus, productivity measures and standards could be established, managed, and rewarded.

Figure 8–2.   Observations of L. L. Bean Distribution Activities[13]

	L. L. Bean	**Xerox**
Picking activities		
Orders/man-day	550	117
Lines/man-day*	1,440	497
Pieces/man-day	1,440	2,640
Total warehouse activity		
Orders/man-day	69	27
Lines/man-day	132	129
Pieces/man-day	132	616

*Lines/man-day, representing the number of trips made by a picker to bin locations, is an indicator of travel in the warehouse. (The equivalent term in current usage, lines/person/day, has been used in the text discussion.)

Source: Benchmarking, p. 159. Used with permission.

Figure 8–3. Comparative Performance Data (February 1982)

The observations of L. L. Bean's distribution activities suggested a number of ways in which Xerox could improve its own operations. To compare them carefully, a number of performance criteria were established as significant, and these were generated for both firms (using Xerox's most efficient warehouse). These criteria, shown in Figure 8–3, were related to stock picking and to overall warehouse output.

This comparison highlighted the striking performance superiority of the Bean distribution operation in specific—and significant—activities: order picking, line picking, and overall orders/person/day. For these activities, Bean's level of productivity was roughly three times that of Xerox. Xerox's superiority in pieces picked/person/day, and in the overall level of pieces/person/day shipped out the door, was attributed to differences in the relative pieces per order. The distribution in pieces per order at Xerox had a higher bias toward pallet-sized orders of dozens of pieces; at Bean, the bias was toward small orders.

TRANSFERRING THE DATA AND FINDINGS

Seeds scattered on unprepared fields usually do not result in a good crop, and the benchmarking team seemed to understand this from the very beginning of the project. Robert Camp knew that if the study produced a set of transferable ideas, those ideas would have a better chance of taking hold if the people responsible for adopting them were somehow involved with the study. Among the measures taken to secure their involvement with the benchmarking exercise were: wide circulation of the *Modern Materials Handling* article, which had been instrumental in stimulating the benchmarking project, and circulation of the trip report and analysis within Logistics and Distribution. These deliveries generated interest, commentary, and debate.

Some of the companies designated earlier as possible benchmarking targets were visited, as a means of validating the Bean study.

OUTCOME OF THE STUDY

In their study of the Xerox revival, authors Jacobson and Hillkirk note that "Xerox had done thousands of little things to improve the company," but they view the turnaround as having hinged on a list of ten key success factors, and leading the list is a step involving competitive benchmarking. (See Figure 8–4, in a later section, for the complete list.)

The L. L. Bean experience was one of the many activities that helped revive the fortunes of Xerox Corporation. As a result of the benchmarking exercise, a number of acquired practices were incorporated into Xerox's warehouse operations, including the computer-assisted stock picking logic observed in Freeport. Looking back on the experience, Camp commented:

> Benchmarking has become an ongoing practice at Xerox Logistics and Distribution. The requirement to carry on the procedure has been pushed down the organization to individual operations, which now do their own benchmarking rather than have a specialist perform it. Because the process is well understood and because the people who undertake it are the ones who implement the findings, benchmarking is so much easier to carry out than before.[14]

The L&D Group's order picking study very quickly became a classic story within the Xerox Corporation and entered into its corporate

Planning

1. Identify Benchmark Outputs
2. Identify Best Competitor
3. Determine Data Collection Method

Analysis

4. Determine Current Competitive "Gap"
5. Project Future Performance Levels

Integration

6. Establish Functional Goals: Communication of Data/Acceptance of Analysis
7. Develop Functional Action Plans

Action

8. Implement Specific Actions
9. Monitor Results/Report Progress
10. Recalibrate Benchmarks

Maturity

11. Leadership position obtained
12. Process fully integrated in our practices

Source: Competitive Benchmarking: The Path to a Leadership Position, Xerox Corporation, 1988, p. 11. Used with permission.

Figure 8–4.   Xerox's Ten Benchmarking Steps

lore. Everyone in-the-know in Rochester, all the way up to Kearns, heard about it and talked about it. The fact that L. L. Bean had been the target company no doubt played an important part in the notoriety the study gained within the firm. Bean was, after all, a household name and had a reputation for excellent products and outstanding service. Many Xerox managers were undoubtedly Bean customers or were on its catalog mailing list. If Camp and his group had chosen an obscure farm equipment supplier as their target company, the study would not have had as much impact on the firm. The fact that it was L. L. Bean made it special.

L. L. Bean was not untouched by the experience. The Xerox visitors learned something they did not already know about distribution, and their company learned the value of looking beyond its own industry;

L. L. Bean learned about benchmarking. Although Bean employees never took up Camp's open invitation to visit the copier manufacturer, various teams from L. L. Bean did in fact conduct studies at other companies in the months and years that followed.

XEROX BENCHMARKING TODAY

From its beginnings in the Christ study and early efforts like the L. L. Bean venture, Xerox has institutionalized benchmarking as an operational technique. In the manufacturing division alone, some 200 benchmarking studies were conducted in the period from 1989 to 1992. Perhaps one of the important outcomes of the L. L. Bean study was its confirmation of the benefits of looking beyond competitors and products to generic functions. Top management's support of benchmarking has been so frequently articulated that it has become core doctrine, just as continuous improvement, employee participation, six-sigma quality, and best in class have been adopted by other firms.

Corporate Level Support

About the time of the Bean project, Xerox's Printing Systems Division, on the west coast, developed a pilot training program on benchmarking techniques. Put together by Bob Edwards and Jules Cochoit, the materials for this program evolved into a standard set of training documents that could be used by anyone in the firm. Another document, known in the firm as the "Little Red Book" (officially, *Competitive Benchmarking: What It Is and What It Can Do for You*, Xerox Corp., 1987) was being assembled by Richard Barchi, a Government Accounting Office executive on leave to study business practices. Barchi traveled throughout the Xerox system, interviewing managers and staff on their methods of conducting studies of outside firms. The Little Red Book described the philosophy and benefits of benchmarking and offered some rudimentary approaches to doing it; most of these are now common knowledge among employees. This publication was succeeded by the "Little Tan Book" (*Competitive Benchmarking: The Path to a Leadership Position*, Xerox Corp., 1988), which was distributed free to all Xerox employees.[15] This booklet contains the firm's ten key steps to conducting benchmarking studies. The steps themselves, which many attribute to Bob Camp, are subsumed within a number of process phases, as presented in Figure 8–4.

In awarding the Baldrige National Quality Award to Xerox in 1989, the judges cited the exceptional excellence of the firm's benchmarking programs as key in their decision, noting that 400 or so studies had been undertaken by Xerox up to that date.

Robert Camp, who spearheaded the L. L. Bean project for Logistics and Distribution, was given responsibility for several large-scale benchmarking investigations of product delivery and business process. In 1990, he was made manager of benchmarking competency, and began pursuing that mission from within the Quality Office for the corporation's U.S. Customer Operations (USCO). Camp was then responsible for expanding and intensifying benchmarking in all USCO units. Operating without a special staff, Camp is neither a "benchmarking czar" nor a bureaucrat; he describes his job as "coordinator" for benchmarking efforts by corporate and division-level teams, and for a growing network of employees within the vast Xerox population who now conduct their own studies. He also responds to the requests of outside firms to benchmark particular Xerox operations.

Unit-Level Operations

The fact that Camp is at the center of Xerox's U.S. corporate benchmarking, but does not have an army of assistants, analysts, and internal consultants, indicates how deeply benchmarking philosophy and methods have embedded themselves into the fabric of the company. By the late 1980s, all of the larger Xerox units—technical services, manufacturing, and so on—had full-time staff persons assigned to benchmarking programs. In smaller functions such as finance and human resources, one individual had part-time responsibility for benchmarking studies. Typically, if a unit manager wants to do a benchmarking study, the staff person will act in an advisory capacity, sharing his or her expertise with respect to carrying out the study, analyzing the results, and turning the results into action. Studies of non-U.S. firms are conducted through Xerox's foreign divisions. Studies of Japanese companies, for example, are conducted by employees of Fuji Xerox, who are familiar with the business terrain and have their own network of benchmarking contacts around Japan.

One of these specialists is Warren Jeffries, a full-time benchmarking manager in the Technical Services Division, a unit of some 15,000 headquarters- and field-based employees who are the foot soldiers of Xerox's customer services. Jeffries sees himself as "a facilitator and focal point for benchmarking" within his division. Like his peers in other operating units, his job is to provide coaching and resources to the teams that arise spontaneously to conduct studies on technical service-related practices. Part of Jeffries's value to these teams lies in his knowledge of developments taking place in the customer service field. To develop and refresh that knowledge, Jeffries, like other benchmarking specialists, subscribes to service industry publications, maintains memberships in professional associations, and attends conferences at which new practices in customer service are discussed. If a manager within Technical Services wants to study best practice in some function, Jeffries can provide him or her with a list of potential benchmarking target firms—many of which might be totally outside the manager's circle of experience—and a matching list of individuals to contact in getting the study moving. For example, if a manager wants to evaluate self-managed work teams, Jeffries can provide a name at a major Chicago bank, where just such a study has been conducted. (See Chapter Nine for a discussion of the benchmarking experience of First Chicago Bank.)

The BEST Network

Being a huge enterprise, Xerox recognized early that some system of cooperation would be useful in sharing information and avoiding duplicated efforts among the firm's many foreign and domestic units. The result was BEST, the Benchmarking Effectiveness Strategy Team. BEST is an informal network of benchmarkers within the sales, service, and administrative functions of the corporation; it has been instrumental in helping otherwise isolated teams to answer one of the two important questions: Whom should we benchmark? The collective experience within the network represents a proprietary data base of firms known for superior practices, and the names of individuals to contact.

Another benefit of the BEST network is its ability to handle incoming benchmarking requests, which may enter the firm through Camp or through one of the divisional specialists. Xerox's success in reforming its own business has not gone unnoticed: The corporation receives dozens of requests each month from firms that are eager to study particular Xerox operations. The network has proven valuable in channeling those requests to the units in the best position to respond to them. Because all such requests raise issues of proprietary and competitive information, the Xerox doctrine has been to let the operating units—those closest to the situation—determine whether the company's competitive assets would be threatened by any particular study.

The BEST network is held together through informal contacts, periodic meetings, and a regular newsletter.

9

Expanding Benchmarking for Broader Applications

BENCHMARKING IN SERVICE ENVIRONMENTS

In preceding chapters, we have considered benchmarking initiatives by a number of organizations, each a major manufacturer—Hewlett-Packard, Ford, General Motors, and Xerox. It would be a mistake, however, to conclude that benchmarking techniques are suitable only for industrial firms. Xerox was, after all, studying the distribution function of a direct mail retailer; Hewlett-Packard's study was of the scheduling problems of product development teams, and manufacturers are not the only businesses that develop products or experience scheduling problems. General Motors was testing a hypothesis about quality practices and their management, and these practices and management requirements could be applied equally to service quality and to the quality of assembled goods.

Benchmarking, as defined in Camp's book, is the search for best practices that will lead to superior performance,[1] and those practices exist in virtually every industry. Why has Federal Express been so successful in its goal of providing next-day package delivery? How has Wal-Mart outpaced rivals like Sears and K mart on almost all important measures of business success? What does Marriott do to earn such high marks from its hotel clients? Each of these service firms follows practices that result in superior performance, and these practices can be observed, measured, and often transferred through the benchmarking process.

This chapter looks at benchmarking initiatives by three nonmanufacturing organizations in which the primary emphasis is on service. The first is the International Facilities Management Association, a professional trade group. Its goal was to use the rich data available within its membership to determine and circulate measures that were associated with superior practice.

The second organization described is First National Bank of Chicago, which conducted a benchmarking study of employee empowerment and self-directed teams.

The third study is of Healthcare Forum; its interest was in a common administrative procedure that it hoped to improve through a benchmarking study: the admission of patients.

BENCHMARKING BEST PRACTICES IN FACILITIES MANAGEMENT

The International Facilities Management Association (IFMA) is a trade group dedicated to improving facilities management and the professionalism of its members. Often overlooked as a business function, managing large private and public facilities is a major endeavor and has a tremendous impact on the operating profits of corporations and on the budgets of public institutions.

The magnitude of facilities management requirements can be deduced from the statistics on just one of the IFMA's large and active members, United Services Automobile Association (USAA), an insurance/financial services firm. At its 286-acre headquarters facility in San Antonio, Texas, USAA:

- Garages 6,700 automobiles in a typical day;
- Runs six employee dining facilities with 190 personnel who make 12,000 customer transactions each working day;
- Owns a fleet of 750 vehicles;
- Services office spaces of 3.2 million square feet (just slightly smaller than the Pentagon);
- Maintains fire protection and security.

On top of all of these tasks, USAA facilities management has responsibility for courier and shuttle services, safety, special events, pest control, trash removal, energy conservation, and recycling programs. Thus, facilities management at a large corporation like USAA is a major business in its own right, and IFMA sees one of its roles as providing information that will assist its members in that important function.

Establishing a Baseline of Performance

As early as 1984, IFMA had begun providing research reports to help define the functions of facilities management, and collecting data on trends and demographics that were of interest to its members. In 1987, it provided data on occupancy expenses that served as an early form of benchmark information, allowing members to compare their own expenses to those of a sampling of their peers.

In August 1990, IFMA's newly formed Research Committee proposed a formal benchmarking project; it took six months to form a "focus group" to plan and execute the project. This group, which was limited to 40 participants with common interests in benchmarking, quality programs, and best practices, met in Houston in February 1991. Agreement was reached on a project aimed at determining the key indicators of facilities management performance by means of benchmark research within its member organizations. These indicators were to be determined through a questionnaire sent to individual members.

Over the next several months, the questionnaire was developed and pretested. Typical questions focused on quantifiable issues:

- The cost of various forms of janitorial services, measured in cents per square footage; the number of crew per foreman; and so on;
- The frequency of commonly performed operations (vacuuming common areas, stripping and waxing floors, washing windows, and similar activities);
- Wage rates paid to various categories of maintenance employees, and related benefits.

Some questions were not quantifiable. For example, respondents were asked to report whether they recycled office paper, and by what measure customer satisfaction with facilities management was reported.

Results of the pretest were circulated to the focus group and suggestions were accepted on improving the questionnaire as an instrument to ferret out the true indicators of performance. A new questionnaire was developed and sent to focus group members in May 1991. By August, analysis of the responses had begun. Later that same month, the preliminary results of the benchmarking study were reviewed by the focus group at a meeting in Seattle. Six months later, the complete results and analysis were mailed to all IFMA members, and this information became the centerpiece of the focus group's February 1992 meeting in Houston.

Study Results

The study provided a useful baseline of information to practitioners about how their organizations stood on each of many operating parameters. However, from the implementation point of view, the study lacked two important elements: the identities of the questionnaire respondents and the enablers of good performance. The IFMA study was done in a blind; thus, organizations could not identify the top performers and go directly to them for more in-depth study. Because the questionnaire was not designed to probe the enablers that led to good performance, the ways in which any firm could improve its performance were not indicated. The anonymity of respondent companies was deliberate on the part of the IFMA researchers. A broad data baseline was the primary objective, and it was felt that wider participation would be ensured if the identity of companies was not revealed in the study.

No sooner had the first IFMA benchmark study been completed and sent to members than plans were being made for other studies to explore specific aspects of facilities management performance: customer satisfaction, quality, and "right-sizing."

The Focus Group Approach

Member firms found that the focus group approach provided a useful opportunity to meet and network with a manageable set of peers that had similar interests. Focus group meetings provided a setting within which partnerships for future benchmarking projects, arrangements for site visits, and sharing of other information could take place. This helped to eliminate the barrier to more effective follow-up activities that some of the study participants had found in the first study.

At the February 1992 meeting, attending members of the focus group expressed their opinion that the group's primary purposes should be:

- To explore the newest issues and trends of importance to facilities management;
- To provide examples of best practice in the industry;
- To help IFMA's Research Committee to identify and develop research projects that are of critical concern to facilities managers;
- To serve as a pretest group for those future research projects.
- The focus group saw the dissemination of research results as its greatest challenge.

Associations as Facilitators of Benchmarking

Professional and trade associations are well-positioned to conduct benchmark research and circulate results to where they will do the most good. Many associations cut across industry lines, including member firms from both related and unrelated industries. IFMA, for example, includes companies such as Ford Motor Company, Warren Petroleum, the U.S. Government Service Administration (GSA), U.S. West, Bell Canada, Hewlett-Packard, State Farm Insurance, Digital Equipment, Shawmut Bank, and Kodak among its members. In most instances, the sharing of data on facilities management issues is not perceived as revealing competitive information. Thus, associations like IFMA are natural repositories and potential clearinghouses of information on generic business functions as defined by the focus of their association.

The IFMA Information Clearinghouse

The information function of associations is important to both the dissemination of benchmark findings and the development of further studies. As central and neutral clearinghouses for information, professional and industry associations are natural matchmakers for member firms. As early as 1991, the IFMA focus group had suggested the establishment of an information clearinghouse to support benchmarking, and an informal one was established soon thereafter. Frank Yockey, a member from Hewlett-Packard, took responsibility for soliciting best practices studies from members of the focus group; a number of firms, including IBM, Northrop, USAA, and Hewlett-Packard, made contributions of their own internal studies. The intent of IFMA is to continue building a body of knowledge and experience on which the entire membership can draw. The future success of the clearinghouse, according to Yockey, will depend on the active participation of the IFMA Research Committee and member firms.

THE BENCHMARKING BANKERS

One of the greatest benefits of the Malcolm Baldrige National Quality Award to American business has been the extent to which thousands of organizations have scrutinized their own practices, either as part of the examination preparation itself, or out of a more detached curiosity about the criteria of the Award. Both levels of involvement with the Baldrige Award have provoked abundant constructive self-evaluation.

The First National Bank of Chicago (First Chicago), the largest bank in the Midwest, with assets of $47 billion, applied for the Baldrige in 1991. In the processes of self-assessment, First Chicago decided to conduct a study of employee empowerment—a practice central to the concept of continuous improvement, as contained in the Award.

The subject of continuous improvement has been widely reported with respect to the American industrial sector. High-quality, low-priced manufactured goods from new competitors in Europe and Asia have battered U.S. auto, steel, and electronics firms, forcing them to either adopt the modern practice of industrial management or disappear. Much less is heard about continuous improvement or its enablers in service-sector companies, some of which have been as deeply troubled as manufacturing.

Banking is one of the service industries that has experienced tremendous challenges over the past 15 years. During that period, large commercial banks have seen much of their most lucrative business disappear. Financial innovations like commercial paper and the Euromarkets have made it possible for the banks' largest and most creditworthy customers to obtain financing on better terms elsewhere—a process known as *disintermediation*. Deregulation of interest rates forced banks to compete on price (i.e., rates), and the ensuing competition has cut margins to the bone. Meanwhile, the explosive growth of money market mutual funds has sucked billions of low-cost deposits—the "raw material" of the lending industry—out of passbook accounts, forcing bankers to replace them with funds acquired at much higher costs. Brokerage firms, insurance companies, and nonbank institutions like GE Capital have invaded the turf of retail banking with a full menu of competing financial services.

Given this intensely competitive environment, forward-thinking American bankers have had to reexamine their operating practices and improve their levels of transactional productivity and customer service.

Within First Chicago, the Service Products Group began a major initiative with regard to the Baldrige Award. As part of the effort, senior management identified ten areas as important to the forward progress of the bank, two of which were employee empowerment and self-directed work teams. Support for these concepts was particularly strong in the commercial loans operations area, where the quality of loan servicing was viewed as an important competitive factor that demanded greater flexibility on the part of employees than did more routine, transactional jobs found elsewhere in the bank. First Chicago's Operating Services Department (OSD), headed by senior vice president Joe Spadaford, was asked to study these concepts more fully.

The OSD had already done some of the foundation work that was intrinsic to progress toward employee empowerment. As early as 1988, it had converted many of the departments' clerical positions from what had been perceived as "fragmented" jobs to "whole" jobs. This had been accomplished through job redesign and follow-on training. OSD managers perceived this change as merely one step along a continuing path that led, by stages, to employee empowerment, and further on, to self-directed teams. The path to more advanced stages was murky and demanded investigation.

In early 1992, Spadaford and his OSD management team began the first phases of a study that addressed the question: Can we improve productivity and service quality through empowerment and self-directed work teams? They began with a survey of the literature on these two topics, which was determined to be anemic compared to coverage of other areas in the human resources field. Still, enough was learned to begin developing a list of critical questions about empowerment and self-directed teams.

It was quickly determined that very little was to be learned from within First Chicago's own operations, or within the banking industry, and that other organizations might provide greater insights. This was confirmed through a very successful meeting arranged by a commercial loan officer with one of the bank's own clients, a firm that had had some experience in the issues under investigation. This initial meeting kindled great enthusiasm among OSD managers, and led to an equally successful site visit with this company and with yet another.

Line Involvement in Benchmarking Network

The fact that a loan officer provided the First Chicago study team with its first outside contact underscores the importance of networking as a facilitator of benchmark studies. Corporate loan officers continued to play a useful role in First Chicago's study as it extended out to other firms.

In the banking industry, loan officers are the eyes and ears of their institutions; they have intimate knowledge of particular outside companies, their managements, and the business challenges they face. In other industries, sales engineers, purchasing managers, officers who serve on other companies' boards, and others who have frequent extracorporate contacts can be the conduits of information on potential benchmarking targets.

At this point, OSD, encouraged and aided by one of the bank's quality coordinators, Obie LeFlore, decided to conduct a full benchmarking study of firms with experience in empowerment and self-directed teams. A project team was assembled, headed by Spadaford; six other OSD managers and a human resources executive completed the team.

Conducting the Benchmark Study

A kickoff meeting was arranged by LeFlore, who brought in Sy Zivan, a retired Xerox benchmarking specialist, to instruct the team in benchmarking techniques. Team members came prepared with "homework" completed: Each had been assigned to read and report to the group on some portion of the literature first surveyed. These reports became the basis of further generation of questions about empowerment and self-directed teams, for which answers would be sought in the field. Figure 9–1 contains just a few of the many questions generated at the kickoff meeting. The actual list contained 29 questions about empowerment and 23 on self-directed teams, a few of which repeated themselves.

Selecting Benchmark Targets

As in the Xerox/L. L. Bean study reported earlier, a list of companies chosen as benchmark targets was generated through a literature search and the personal knowledge of team members. In all, 14 companies were selected, representing an interesting mix of industries: 70 percent were in manufacturing—consumer products, photocopiers, publishing, pharmaceuticals, and wood/paper. Several financial service companies were on the list; these included one bank (not a direct competitor in the regional market) and two insurance companies. The experience of these firms with employee empowerment and self-directed teams varied greatly: one firm had begun implementing these concepts as early as 1983; others were just getting started. The cooperation of the individual firms was enlisted through the personal acquaintanceship of team members, by Obie LeFlore, or by other bank officers. A banking relationship was instrumental in enlisting a few firms for the study, but, in the end, the network of quality managers at First Chicago and the other firms led to the cooperation that made the study possible.

Executing the Study and Reporting Its Conclusions

The degree to which members of the study team were able to penetrate the host companies varied greatly, from a telephone interview on the low end to sitting in on a meeting of one company's self-directed

Empowerment	Self-Directed Teams
• How did empowerment start?	• How did the decision to implement self-directed teams (SDTs) come about?
• Why did you decide to use empowerment?	• How long ago did you start to use SDTs?
• What is the executive commitment? How is it demonstrated?	• What were the major hurdles in terms of production, people, and systems?
• Which employees or groups are empowered and why?	• How did your systems and work processes fit with SDTs?
• What are the measures or success?	• What kinds of training have team members received over the past 12 months?
• What training resources were used?	• How do jobs grow and change as a team continues to function?
• Are empowered employees compensated differently? If so, how?	• What measures are used to assess team efforts?
• How much time was allotted for individuals to adapt to the changes?	• How well have managers/ supervisors adjusted to SDTs and their new roles?
• What are the most positive and negative outcomes of empowerment?	• What (if any) have been the dollar savings?
• What would you do differently?	• Would you recommend using SDTs?

Source: "Empowerment and Self-Directed Work Teams," First National Bank of Chicago, August 1992, p. 7.

Figure 9-1. Sampling of First Chicago's Benchmarking Questions

team on the high end. In the course of these contacts, a one- or two-person OSD team obtained answers to its list of questions (later determined to be too long), and observed a spectrum of practices with respect to employee empowerment and self-directed teams. Their observations and conclusions were reported to management in a formal document in August 1992, and the details of their findings were organized under the following general categories:

- Origin of empowerment and self-directed work teams;
- Senior management support;
- Role of middle management;
- Training and support;
- Implementation of empowerment;
- Implementation of self-directed work teams;
- Rewards and recognition;
- Results;
- Risks.

Each of these categories was richly detailed with observations and examples, "lessons learned," and what the team described as "noteworthy practices." OSD team members found similarity in the conceptual approach to empowerment and many of the implementation techniques among the companies studied. The stage of empowerment, however, varied dramatically between firms—primarily, the team concluded, because of different business objectives. What was an "ideal" degree of empowerment for one firm was less than ideal for another. Thus, there was no best in class insofar as empowerment and self-directed teams were concerned. The need to match the degree of empowerment to business objectives was seen to be an important conclusion and a significant discovery of the benchmarking study. The study concluded:

> [E]mpowerment is a viable business strategy in many environments, including financial service organizations. Focusing on empowering the organization provides solutions to the multiple challenges of improving productivity, service quality, job fulfillment, staff commitment and flexibility. Most of the companies we interviewed were able to cite tangible monetary benefits as a result of their efforts.[2]

"Lessons Learned" for Other Benchmarkers

The First Chicago study underscores many of the important benefits of benchmarking to managers contemplating changes in operations or strategy. Pushing forward into areas that are uncharted by the organization is always risky. It is always possible to "think ahead" to some of the problems or opportunities of a new situation, using experience with current practices as a guide—as did the study group in its generation of questions to be answered. However, lack of experience limits the range of this forward probing, casting no light onto shoals that experience would not reveal. The findings of the First Chicago team revealed instances of surprise and discovery, risks, impediments, and opportunities not expected.

It is too early at this writing to speculate on the impact of First Chicago's benchmarking study on internal operations, but its thoroughness with respect to the issues involved in launching empowerment initiatives and self-directed teams has certainly given the bank's managers the information they will need to reach an informed decision.

This first benchmarking experience, according to Spadaford, raised the comfort level of OSD and the bank management team with the methodology of dealing cooperatively with outside firms. Thus, when the bank began serious consideration of a new product area—servicing corporate and commercial real estate mortgages—it benchmarked some of the larger companies in that business, and was able to learn a lot about how these companies conducted their operations.

PHYSICIAN, HEAL THYSELF

As anyone who follows the news surely knows, healthcare costs in the United States have been on a skyrocketing trajectory for years, greatly outpacing growth in gross national product and the public's ability to pay. Many believe that healthcare costs now put American corporations—the sponsors of the major medical insurance plans—at a competitive disadvantage in international competition. According to American Hospital Association statistics, expenses per patient-day among U.S. community hospitals increased a whopping 175.6 percent during the 1980s. Faced with upward internal cost pressures, and external pressures from government, health insurers, and the public to cap payments, hospital managers throughout the United States have been seeking cost-effective solutions. That search has led them to examine their own internal operations. As in other industries, health-care providers have begun to adopt the concept of quality improvement. Organizations such as SunHealth Alliance (Charlotte, NC) and The Healthcare Forum have been leaders in this movement.

The Healthcare Forum (THF) is a San Francisco-based not-for-profit association of healthcare individuals and organizations in all 50 states and in many countries around the world. Its broadly stated vision is "to create healthier communities by engaging leaders in building new visions and models of care." To accomplish that mission, THF provides educational and research resources. Among its initiatives are the four Quality Improvement Networks (QINs) that THF has established among its member organizations. The purpose of these networks is to enhance quality efforts among leading U.S. healthcare organizations through collaborative learning. Each QIN is composed of approximately 15 organizations committed to total quality improvement. The QINs meet three times each year to share information on innovative programs and to provide mutual support. Within the QINs, successful models of practice can be studied and transferred, thus accelerating healthcare quality progress on a wide front.

Healthcare Forum's national base has placed it in an ideal position to spearhead the QINs; it serves as convener, resource center/clearinghouse, and professionally staffed research arm. It has furthered the aims of the networks by sponsoring the The Healthcare Forum/Witt/Kieffer, Ford, Hadelman & Lloyd: Commitment to Quality Award, an annual recognition of healthcare institutions committed to total quality improvement (and modeled after the Malcolm Baldrige National Quality Award).

Impatient Admitting

One problematic function shared by all hospital members of the QINs, and one they wanted to investigate, was the business of admitting patients. As anyone who has been a hospital patient knows, this is the customer's first point of contact with the hospital, and that contact can be difficult and sometimes unpleasant.

From the hospital's viewpoint the admissions process is often difficult and requires many steps. Some patients have already been scheduled into the hospital by their physicians; others have not—

they require emergency treatment. The various tests that need to be performed, may have been done by the outside physician, but sometimes they are not. The means of payment must be verified, considering the literally hundreds of possible exceptions to standard health insurance arrangements. Scheduling treatment and dealing with the issue of space availability are additional steps in the hospital admissions process.

The THF staff and QIN members knew that a great deal could probably be learned about admissions procedures from within the healthcare community. They also understood that other industries dealt with similar operations. Hotels, for example, had to register guests and verify payment methods—and do it efficiently, to meet their bottom-line requirements; airlines had to book space, "admit" travelers, and verify payments—and accomplish all this in a way that was fast and customer-pleasing.

The ideas of benchmarking thus seemed to be the best methodology for obtaining and transferring the information needed by the QIN members.

In May 1991, THF President/CEO Kathryn E. Johnson opened communications with the International Benchmarking Clearinghouse (IBC), a unit of the Houston-based American Productivity and Quality Center (APQC). As noted earlier, the APQC is an association of firms from many industries; its membership numbers several hundred, ranging from small and medium-sized firms to multinational Fortune 50 companies that are interested in developing and sharing knowledge on management approaches to improving practices. For a variety of reasons, APQC members desiring to establish special interest groups to undertake studies on productivity advancement, quality improvement, or benchmarking, will contract with consultants within APQC to manage a benchmarking study, much as Sandy Corporation did for General Motors. (See Chapter 7.) The APQC IBC retains a small staff of specialists, under the leadership of Carla O'Dell, who conduct studies and lend support to a network of benchmarkers within IBC's broad membership.

In January 1992, THF's staff, under director of quality Keith L. McCandless, and a group of 28 hospitals began development of a plan to study the admitting process. For nearly all of the hospitals, this would be their first experience with benchmarking.

Planning Phase

It quickly became evident that "the admitting process" was too broad to study effectively because it involved a variety of patient classes (inpatient, outpatient, emergency room patient, and so on). After considerable debate, the group limited its study to the admitting process for elective acute care (EAC) patients.

By March 1992, the IBC and an advisory group of hospital members had developed a plan for the study and had mailed a survey questionnaire, designed to collect necessary data, to 28 participating hospitals. The plan was to have three objectives:

1. Identification of best practice candidates. Best practice would be defined in terms of a hospital's development of quantifiable measures, its recognition among peers as an innovator, and its dedication to continuous improvement of processes based on both internal and external customer information.

2. Measurements of the admitting process. The plan involved collection and categorization of EAC impatient admitting processes among the benchmarked hospitals in terms of efficiency, economy, and effectiveness.

3. Identification of the process enablers, inhibitors, and improvements. These would represent the guides to future action.

Analysis and Results

THF staff, QIN members, and IBC consultants spent five months in gathering and analyzing information prior to issuing a study report in August 1992. The report made clear that five or six of the 28 hospitals were candidates for the classification of "best practice." These institutions reported patient waiting times (one of the criteria) of less than five minutes, and accuracy of patient information greater than 95 percent.

Twenty-five flow charts of the admitting process were submitted by the surveyed hospitals. The study team determined that only six of the charts provided sufficient detail; from those six, a baseline macro flow chart of the EAC admitting process was developed (Figure 9–2). Each part of the process, in turn, was exploded out into its own details

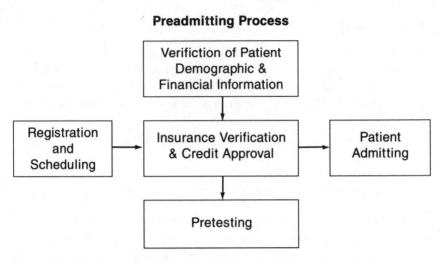

Preadmitting Process

Source: "Benchmarking the Inpatient Admitting Process: Phase I," The Healthcare Forum/ APQC, 1992, p. 7.

Figure 9.2   EAC Inpatient Admitting Process: Macro Flow Chart

in order to establish its subset of processes and customer-triggered events.

After gaining insight into the subprocess components, the next step was to differentiate among the 28 hospitals in terms of key criteria determined by the study group to be highly relevant to the EAC inpatient admitting process:[3]

- Understanding the admitting process;
- Process innovation;
- Measurement;
- Customer satisfaction and focus;
- Information technology;
- Quality improvement initiative;
- External search for improvement.

Each of the hospitals was then rated by the study group in terms of its "opportunity for improvement" (Figure 9–3).

Hospital	Understanding of Process	Process Innovation	Measurement	Customer Satisfaction & Focus
A	3	4	1	3
B	3	1	1	2
C	2	2	3	2
D	3	1	3	2
E	2	1	2	3
F	3	2	3	2
G	3	3	4	3
•	•	•	•	•
•	•	•	•	•
•	•	•	•	•
Y	2	2	2	3
Z	4	4	2	2
AA	3	1	2	2
BB	3	2	1	2
Criterion Average	2.9	2.6	2.1	2.5

Hospital	Information Technology	Quality Improvement Initiative	External Search for Improvement	Hospital Average
A	3	3	3	2.9
B	2	1	1	1.6
C	2	1	1	1.9
D	2	1	3	2.1
E	2	3	1	1.9
F	1	2	1	2.0
G	1	4	4	3.1
•	•	•	•	•
•	•	•	•	•
•	•	•	•	•
Y	3	1	1	2.0
Z	4	2	4	3.1
AA	2	2	2	2.0
BB	2	3	1	1.9
Criterion Average	2.5	2.2	2.4	

Improvement Opportunity

1 = Excellent   2 = Great   3 = Good   4 = Some

Adapted from "Benchmarking the Inpatient Admitting Process: Phase I," The Healthcare Forum/APQC, 1992, p. 15.

Figure 9–3. Improvement Opportunity Ratings

The study identified a number of key enablers that would help organizations to improve their admitting practices: adequacy of training and staffing, centralization, and information technology. It found that cross-training of admitting employees, flexible staffing patterns, centralization of in- and outpatient admitting, the use of a direct admitting process, and a reduction in the number of required admitting forms would help hospitals to improve.

The study was Phase I of a planned two-phase study by The Healthcare Forum and QIN members. Phase II (in progress at this writing) was to go outside the healthcare industry to analogous processes. Among the target companies for Phase II would be airlines, hotels, rental car agencies, and insurance companies. Each of these performs operations similar to those experienced at the hospital admitting desk: taking down personal information about the customer, credit verification and payment determination, and scheduling of service.

The Healthcare Forum study, like that of the International Facilities Management Association cited above, indicates how the richness of different experiences within a professional association or an affiliation of institutions can be tapped to improve the learning of its individual members. These types of organizations are natural networks—one of the key elements of the benchmarking process. Successful beginnings, as those of the EAC inpatient admitting study appear to be, lead to further cooperation and study of other common problems. As of late 1992, THF member organizations had indicated their interest in doing benchmark studies of other common healthcare processes.

10

Creating a
Benchmarking Capability

BENCHMARKING THE BENCHMARKING PROCESS

Most of the Malcolm Baldrige National Quality Award winners cite benchmarking as a key enabler for their quality improvement efforts. Richard W. Allen, director of quality at Solectron Corporation, the San Jose, California, company that was a 1991 winner, commented: "Benchmarking fostered leapfrog improvements in our quality efforts by providing key learnings from leadership companies."[1] Benchmarking is a process and, like any other process, may be studied for improvement. For instance, in 1989, when Hewlett-Packard wanted to initiate benchmarking as a business process, it first studied the Xerox approach. Because Xerox was the best early example of how to implement this methodology, many other companies benchmarked the Xerox benchmarking method and, in turn, became benchmarking models or sources of benchmarking lessons. This chapter provides advice from people who have started benchmarking in their organizations and describes, from their perspective, what to avoid and what to pursue in implementing benchmarking. The chapter closes with a description of how to implement benchmarking as a management initiative to improve business processes.

WHAT TO AVOID

Although benchmarkers often focus on learning from successes, they can also learn from implementation failures and problems observed at

187

other companies. A variety of pitfalls await companies that are beginning a benchmarking effort. Perhaps the most important lesson to be learned is how to overcome resistance to change, in order to implement benchmarking. Executive-level excuses for not benchmarking reduce down to a single basic theme: We don't believe that we have anything to learn from other companies. An observation made of the American automotive industry by George Romney, then president of American Motors, was recalled by David Halberstam, *New York Times* journalist and author: "Success breeds arrogance."[2] Successful companies do not feel that they need to learn from companies that have not achieved an equivalent leadership position. Other excuses include: Our company [or industry] is different; we can't learn from others. This phrase indicates a failure to build an adequate analogy for truly understanding the process similarities between organizations. The fundamental reason for benchmarking is to learn from organizations that have experienced similar situations and dealt with them. If they have been successful, then the benchmarkers gain positive lessons from their success; if they have not succeeded, then insights are gained on the pitfalls to avoid. As Otto von Bismarck, the Prussian military strategist, observed: "Fools you are . . . to say you learn by your own experiences . . . I prefer to profit by others' mistakes and avoid the price of my own." Companies that do not overcome this attitude will not gain from a benchmarking effort.

Another mistake to avoid in beginning benchmarking is not factoring customer expectations into benchmark studies. The reasons for improving a company may be to provide better customer service, more adequately meet customer expectations, achieve a higher return on assets, improve the shareholders' value, and so on. It is important to remember the customer when conducting a benchmarking study; otherwise, it is possible to suboptimize the study and produce results that reflect only internal improvements that are not carried forward to the bottom line. The Ford Taurus competitive benchmarking project took this into account. Ford sought not only to achieve customer satisfaction with the design effort, but also to achieve a market success that would improve the company's financial performance. The company succeeded on both counts!

Another factor to avoid is process owners not participating in the benchmarking process. In almost every major successful company change effort, an enabling factor has been the participation of those who are charged with implementation of the change. In short, the process owner should buy into the need for the change and the proposed improvements before executing the recommendations of the study team. The best way to achieve this is through active involvement in the study effort. One reason for the success of Hewlett-Packard's best scheduling practices study, which effected change in the company's approach to new product development, was the active involvement and participation of the engineering community. Had this study been driven from a staff function, acceptance of the division level undoubtedly would have been different.

These words of advice came from Al Mierisch, manager of the quality service department of Florida Power & Light, winner of the Deming Prize in 1989: "Don't penalize middle management or employees for the current gap in performance observed during benchmarking."[3] Mierisch also recommended not delegating responsibility to consultants for the conduct of the study; it does not help in building internal benchmarking capability. Charles O. Lybeer, vice president of manufacturing for Stone Construction Company, a small business in Honeoye, New York, recommends that beginning benchmarkers avoid benchmarking with companies that are a poor cultural fit in any dimension: too large/small, too centralized/decentralized, too formal/informal, or too authoritarian/participative. He also underscores the need to understand one's own process and to avoid too much informality in the method of benchmarking.[4]

WHAT TO PURSUE

Perhaps the best advice to encourage beginners in benchmarking was given by Samuel W. Bookhart, Jr., manager of benchmarking for DuPont Fibers and one of the authors of the Benchmarking Code of Conduct: "Follow the Code of Conduct."[5] Using the Code as a starting place, beginners can understand the conventions and expectations that have developed among professional benchmarkers since the early 1980s. Other experienced benchmarkers will have their own recommendations for how to begin benchmarking.

Ken Karch, manager of total quality at Weyerhauser Company, offers the following reminders for organizations beginning benchmarking efforts:[6]

- Top management commitment and participation are necessary;
- Team members often have biases that need to be dealt with;

- Team approaches are absolutely critical;
- The benchmarking process cannot be rushed;
- Education and training for the team are needed;
- Benchmarking is resource-intensive: people, travel, research, consultants, and other factors are involved;
- Process rigor is necessary for a successful study;
- Securing quantitative data is often difficult.

Florida Power & Light's Al Mierisch believes that benchmarking should be a key corporate strategy and that it should focus on corporate goals: "Make benchmarking an ongoing process within normal business operations, e.g., business planning or strategic planning. Benchmarking should be a key to achieving your company's vision and strategies."[7] Mierisch's advice is to get middle management to sponsor the studies and drive them from the business unit. Driving them from the staff level is ineffective because the staff does not own the process. He also believes it is important to select knowledgeable team members (people with a balance of functional, technical, analytical, and benchmarking process expertise) and empower them to implement the results. Mierisch says that benchmarkers must be sure to allow adequate time for the study and must provide sufficient resources for the team in terms of both funding and adequate training.[8]

From a small-business perspective, Charles O. Lybeer provides some sound pointers: ensure team commitment through visible management support, focus on the process being studied and on how to achieve improvement, and follow up with action. He believes that much of the benefit of benchmarking comes during the preparation process, as a team discovers the weaknesses of its own process through self-analysis.[9]

THE BENEFITS OF BENCHMARKING

What can a management team expect to get out of benchmarking? Some significant behavioral shifts occur as a company begins to recognize that "gaps" exist between its performance and the performance of other organizations. First, competitive benchmarking provides a better understanding of the needs of the customer and the dynamics of the particular industry. Competitive benchmarking can help to build sensitivity to changing customer needs. An example can be drawn from the Ford Taurus. Many of the comparisons that Team Taurus made for its business process improvements were against the Toyota production system; Toyota had been using a similar design methodology for years. In a recent article in *USA Today,* Chrysler's 1993 LH car series is described as the product of benchmarking studies and assessment of customer requirements. When Glenn Gardner, the chief engineer for the LH series (Dodge Intrepid, Eagle Vision, and Chrysler Concorde), came to his present job from Diamond-Star, the Chrysler joint venture with Mitsubishi, he was given free reign to build a world-class car. To ensure that it would meet this goal, Gardner's team used a combination of competitive benchmarking and customer responsiveness, making the car more amenable to the way people drive.[10]

Another advantage of benchmarking is its acknowledgment of the fact that another organization has been able to perform the same process at a higher performance level. The organization's example—especially the observation of its specific set of enabling actions—provides a vision of the potential end state for similar process improvements within one's own organization. It also helps to establish realistic, actionable objectives for the implementation of process improvements. Charles Lybeer observed a lesson learned from his experience: Benchmarking provides "positive team member reinforcement and a feeder effect for realistic goal setting and long-range planning."[11] The goals that represent the end state desired by an organization can be based on performance relative to observed benchmarks. This approach helps to develop realistic stretch goals as performance targets; they can be both challenging and attainable because a concrete example of this level of performance has been observed by the process owners during their benchmarking study. This experience encourages their emotional buy-in to achieving similar performance for their team. Chrysler engineers cited their observation of the 1985 Ford Taurus/Sable project as a factor in their own approach to the problem of clean-sheet automobile design.

Longer range advantages come from changing the way that an organization thinks about the need for improvement. Benchmarking provides a sense of urgency for improvement, by indicating performance levels that have been previously achieved in a study partner's process. A sense of competitiveness arises as a team recognizes improvement opportunities beyond its direct observations, and team members become motivated to strive for excellence, innovation, and the application of breakthrough thinking to achieve their own process improvement. The advice for a manager who discovers that a benchmarking team has become so motivated has a familiar ring: Lead, follow, or get out of the way!

THE ROLE OF SENIOR MANAGEMENT

Where does a company start, when it is interested in applying benchmarking? Many executives, like Frank Pipp, former vice president of development and manufacturing at Xerox and a champion of Xerox's first benchmarking study in 1979, want to begin with a competitive cost analysis, comparing the organization's current cost performance status against the competition. Other common starting points for management-sponsored benchmarking studies include: manufacturing cost overhead analysis, new product development cycle time, and customer service improvement. These topics are chosen according to the strategic imperatives a company is facing and its identification of the areas where the greatest need exists for performance improvement.

Once a company decides to start a benchmarking project, it should follow a time-tested, generic approach for implementation. This approach begins at the top level of the company with a presentation of an executive overview of benchmarking to the management team, to obtain its support for the pilot project. This presentation, which sets corporate expectations and establishes top-level awareness of the pilot study, will help the management team to understand the significance of the results when the completed project is reported and recommendations for change are made. One outcome of this presentation will be the identification of the pilot study's subject by the management team. Given this responsibility, the team will buy-in to the value of the methodology. In addition, the management team should review the project outline and approve the potential partners for the study. Nothing will deflate a study more quickly than a senior manager who "doesn't respect" the benchmarking partner and is therefore unwilling to learn from the partner's example.

Experience facilitates success. It is important to select an experienced benchmarker to facilitate the first project—either an internally developed benchmarker who has practiced on some less visible projects, or an outside consultant. However, if an outside consultant is used, his or her role must allow the team to learn how to conduct the study so that a knowledge transfer takes place. Without it, the organization may become reliant on the consultant for future benchmarking studies. It is also important to get the process owner involved in the study, to ease the team's ability to implement the findings of the project.

It is especially essential that a first project follow a rigorous benchmarking process. Xerox uses a learning experience model called LUTI (Learn—Use—Train—Inspect) for its implementation of change. This PDCA-like model helps to underline the need for experiential learning to establish true understanding of process improvements. Using the LUTI approach, management would be trained, develop experience by participating in its own benchmarking project, participate in the training or mentoring of others in the benchmarking method, and, finally, inspect the use of benchmarking as part of its review of process improvements and business operations. The Xerox LUTI approach to change implementation underscores the need for continuing involvement of senior management in the process. After receiving both interim and final reports of the study progress and results, senior management should take action based on the study results and provide resources to implement the recommended change. Once the team has completed its work, management should ensure that the recommended change is facilitated and should monitor its progress to verify that the projected results are obtained. The final role of senior management, when success is observed in the pilot study, is to establish follow-on benchmarking project requirements for addressing other "strategic issues" where improvements are needed. This will help to make benchmarking a natural part of the company's planning process.

BENCHMARKING AS AN INTERVENTION

Specialists in the field of organizational development speak of making an *intervention* in their clients' organizations. The term intervention means a change that is imposed externally from the organization, originating either from a consultant or from management. Benchmarking is such a change to the management process of most organizations. It must be treated as a significant change and handled carefully, or, like many other systemic transformations, it may suffer rejection, much like a heart transplant that doesn't take. If benchmarking is mandated by the senior management team, it can suffer the fate of many other enforced interventions. Carla O'Dell, senior vice president at the American Productivity & Quality Center and director of the International Benchmarking Clearinghouse, proposed a tongue-in-cheek list of ways for a change agent to ensure the maximum degree of management resistance to systemic change:

- Mandate the change from the ivory tower of "corporate" headquarters;
- Disregard the opinions of the management team;
- Make ambiguous expectations of the management team for implementing the change;
- Avoid training management in the new roles;
- Give management irrelevant training;
- Allow the management team no involvement in design;
- Provide the management team with no involvement in change;
- By-pass managers in communicating to their teams;
- Reduce or threaten to reduce the number of managers.

Resistance to change and change-blocking behavior by the management team are **NOT** desired behaviors. The key is to build support for the change throughout the entire management team. O'Dell also offered a prescription for obtaining support and consensus for major change:

- Invest time to prepare and plan the change;
- Involve as many of the affected parties in the change definition as possible;
- Ensure that the purpose and direction of the change are clear;
- Specify new expectations and functions for all involved;

- Clarify advantages for managers and their teams;
- Provide timely training required to perform the new activities;
- Start at the top of the organization and cascade down to the individual contributors;
- Respond to skepticism and questions with open, honest responses.

This list of change implementation behaviors should be kept in mind as a new process or methodology is being implemented in an organization.[12]

THE WEYERHAUSER EXAMPLE

The experience of Ken Karch, who led Weyerhauser's benchmarking implementation, can provide a practical lesson in what works for starting a long-term benchmarking effort. Karch recommends the following ten-point approach:[13]

1. Provide leadership from the senior management team, to communicate its support and provide resources to the pilot study; then get managers involved in a benchmarking project of their own, requiring them to actively study the strategic planning or behavioral approach of a senior manager whom they admire. The surest way to get long-term management support is to have managers involved in benchmarking. Larry Osterwise, currently director of market-driven quality for IBM and formerly general manager of IBM's Rochester, Minnesota facility (a 1990 recipient of the Malcolm Baldrige National Quality Award), tells a story about when David Kearns, former CEO of Xerox, visited his facility. Osterwise asked him if he would like to see the plant, to which Kearns replied: "Of course, I need to keep current on my benchmarking." Kearns's attitude, developed over years of exposure to the value of benchmarking, represents an acute awareness of each individual's responsibility to capture every learning experience as a potential stimulus for organizational change.[14]

2. "Adopt a new philosophy." This point, modeled after Deming, means to adopt the philosophy of continuous learning and improvement. Organizations need to eliminate any not-invented-here (NIH) syndrome that may exist and get rid of the following attitudes (excuses):
   - "We can't learn anything from others."
   - "We're as good as you can get."
   - "There's no one outstanding in this area."
   - "Our work is different—it can't be measured against others'."

One senior executive of a Fortune 500 company, discussing why his company had not entered into a benchmarking study for time-to-market of new-products developments, summed up all of the above excuses in one succinct phrase: "We don't want to taint our performance by learning how mediocre companies develop products." The truth is: Every company has something to learn, and few companies have provided their shareholders with the long-term return on investment that they would like to see.

3. Create an executive steering committee that is charged with creating and monitoring a plan for implementing benchmarking. The role of the steering committee is to encourage the integration of benchmarking data into strategic planning and facilitate the establishment of common performance measures. Committee members should be trained in benchmarking and need to get excited about their involvement; they will be promoting the value of benchmarking to the entire organization.

4. Create a support structure. A long-term benchmarking program includes training for benchmarking teams; vehicles for communicating on studies underway and for reporting study results; access to library and information services; and in-house capability to facilitate benchmarking teams. These support services may be purchased by contract for a pilot study; however, a long-term benchmarking effort will require dedicated resources.

5. Find one or more pioneers who are willing to attempt a study, and support them from the quality office. They should be

encouraged from the top of the organization to pursue the study, and their results should be communicated to encourage others who have a need for benchmarking. The activities of the pioneering benchmarkers should be envisioned as a paradigm shift toward a learning organization.

6. Educate people in the practice of benchmarking; incorporate it into the core quality training.

7. Communicate, through internal newsletters and company publications, the concept and applications of benchmarking.

8. Find and use success stories from both inside and outside the company.

9. Make benchmarking a part of the planning process. Build it into strategic business plans as a means for goal-setting. To do this, a company must have a reliable benchmarking process— one that gets both accurate measures of performance and good definition of performance enablers.

10. Recognize and reward successful benchmarking efforts; use an internal conference or "benchmarking days" to spotlight individual team practices. Public acknowledgement by senior management is an important factor in reinforcing benchmarking as a desired activity. Recognition can also take the form of sending teams to conferences or entering them in a benchmarking competition such as the APQC contest for a benchmarking prize.

Karch's approach may appear to be a cookbook to some, but it provides a sound set of elements that can be tailored to an organization's culture. The goal is to have a capability to produce benchmarking studies that change the behavior of the company and increase its effectiveness and efficiency.

WHAT TO DO WITH A USED STUDY

Benchmarking studies are, by nature, perishable and time-sensitive. What was a standard of excellence today may be expected performance tomorrow. Thus, competitive excellence is an ever-increasing standard, and benchmarks are only observations of excellence at a particular point in time. Because the techniques and enablers that companies use to "ratchet-up" their performance may not apply in the future, benchmarks, like any other measurement instrument, need to be recalibrated over time. Benchmarking is an evergreen process that requires revisiting studies to ensure their lasting significance. It is not an end in itself; it is a means to the end of business process excellence in a competitive environment where technology is always increasing the potential for improvement. In the electronics industry, employees once manually inserted electrical components into printed circuit boards. The next generation of improvement came when machines could perform the same function. Another level of improvement came when the machines did not have to insert the components into holes through the boards, but could place them directly on the board, thereby increasing reliability and process quality. At any point in this "electrical component insertion process," a different answer as to the performance benchmark for process quality, cycle time, and cost-effectiveness would have been obtained and would then have been made obsolete by the next generation of technology. Some of the earlier lessons for materials handling and component reliability would still apply and would have been carried over to the next generation. Benchmarking, therefore, must be a continuous practice for those key business processes that affect the competitiveness of the organization.

WHERE TO GET SUPPORT

As benchmarking becomes recognized as an important business practice, more and more information will become available. It will also become increasingly difficult to sort out the resources of value from those that are purely commercial in nature. Many organizations will undoubtedly attempt to imply that their capability (financial analysis or a consulting practice approach) is the true approach to benchmarking. History is the most reliable guide. The appendices of this book have been developed to provide a starting place for companies interested in benchmarking. The Benchmarking Code of Conduct is presented in Appendix A. Appendix B provides a listing of secondary research tools that can be helpful in a search for information about potential benchmarking partners. Appendix C provides the Benchmarking Recognition Award Criteria, issued by the APQC International Benchmarking Clearinghouse. These criteria can be used to assess an organization's progress in developing its benchmarking capability. Appendix D, a sample procedure for benchmarking, is intended to provide general guidance to teams on how to conduct their studies. This procedure may be appropriate for adaptation by organizations that record their processes in a formal manner, or it may be used as a guide for organizations that do not have a high degree of formality. Appendix E is a bibliography of benchmarking books, reports, and articles, compiled in cooperation with the APQC. These materials can be studied to help develop the breadth and depth of knowledge of a company's internal benchmarking experts. Appendix F provides a glossary of benchmarking terms, to aid communication with benchmarking partners by providing a common meaning of terms.

WHERE IS BENCHMARKING GOING?

What is the future of benchmarking? Fred Bowers, corporate benchmarking program manager at Digital Equipment Corporation, predicts that benchmarking, as we know it today, will be greatly changed by the year 2000. Bowers envisions companies performing most studies by the use of information networks that connect clearinghouses and trade associations. He sees companies using benchmarking as a way to engineer competitive uniqueness. He also believes the day of the benchmarking department will pass as benchmarking becomes as natural a part of work as answering a telephone.[15]

BENCHMARKING AS AN AGENT FOR CHANGE

This book has noted how benchmarking is a vehicle for stimulating change in an organization. Another perspective on this application of benchmarking is provided by William Lehman, managing director of the Price Waterhouse Manufacturing Management Consulting Practice. As the keynote speaker at the APQC's first benchmarking conference, Lehman commented about the root cause for some organizations' lack of success in implementing benchmarking:

I maintain that the failure of benchmarking to generate the kind of impact that it should in most organizations is tied up with a misunderstanding of the magnitude of organizational change required to achieve that impact. The real effectiveness of a benchmarking program lies in its ability to generate large, structural shifts in business processes, and hard benefits to the bottom line of the organization. Defining "World Class" practices that enable the delivery of these benefits requires a benchmarking process that is specifically linked to the change planning and integration processes of the organization, its environment for change, and management's vision of the future.[16]

The challenge lies ahead. If you are in the management of a company that is not using benchmarking, you should ask yourself some hard questions:

Am I interested in driving my organization to the leadership position within our industry?

Do I believe that benchmarking can provide my company with the opportunity needed to learn about how and where to improve the organization's performance?

The recipe for successful benchmarking requires three basic ingredients: a supportive management team that has a real problem to be solved; access to prospective benchmarking partners who have previously resolved this problem; and a knowledgeable benchmarking team with the ability to use basic quality tools and research practices to investigate process problems to their root cause. To these three basic ingredients must be added a dash of research perseverance and a whole bunch of patience. If your company is beginning its benchmarking journey, I wish you the unique and abundant success that comes from both the discovery and the application of profound process knowledge!

Chapter Notes

Preface

1. Robert C. Camp, *Benchmarking: The Search for Industry Best Practices That Lead to Superior Performance* (Milwaukee: WI: Quality Press/American Society for Quality Control, 1989).

2. Michael J. Spendolini, *The Benchmarking Book* (New York: AMACOM/The American Management Association, 1992).

3. Gregory H. Watson, *The Benchmarking Workbook: Adapting Best Practices for Performance Improvement* (Cambridge, MA: Productivity Press, 1992).

4. Gerald J. Balm, *Benchmarking: A Practitioner's Guide for Becoming and Staying Best of the Best* (Schaumberg, IL: Quality and Productivity Management Association, 1992).

5. Kathleen H. J. Leibfried and C. J. McNair, *Benchmarking: A Tool for Continuous Improvement* (New York: HarperCollins, 1992).

6. American Productivity & Quality Center, *Planning, Organizing, and Managing Benchmarking Activities: A User's Guide* (Houston, TX: APQC, 1992). This guidebook was published by the International Benchmarking Clearinghouse (IBC), a service of the American Productivity & Quality Center (APQC). The results of the IBC's survey of 87 member companies are presented along with an analytical model for cost comparison of benchmarking projects. This book is being published in 1993 by Productivity Press as *The Benchmarking Management Guide*.

7. *Ibid.*, p. 15 of the first appendix.

Chapter 1

1. Roger Milliken, CEO of Milliken Company, in his address at the National Quality Forum, following his company's receipt of the Malcolm Baldrige National Quality Award.

2. Lois Therrein, "The Rival Japan Respects," *Business Week,* November 13, 1989, p. 67.

3. Quotation from a 1986 tape-recorded lecture by W. Edwards Deming at Hewlett-Packard.

4. As quoted by Paul R. Adam, senior consultant, Westinghouse Productivity and Quality Center, *Proceedings of Benchmarking Week '92* (Houston, TX: APQC, 1992), presentation notes.

5. Id.

6. Fred Bowers, *Proceedings of Benchmarking Week '92* (Houston, TX: APQC, 1992), presentation notes.

7. *Planning Organizing, and Managing Benchmarking: A User's Guide* (Houston, TX: APQC, 1992), p. 4.

8. Robert C. Camp, *Benchmarking: The Search for Industry Best Practices that Lead to Superior Performance* (Milwaukee, WI: Quality Press/American Society for Quality Control, 1989), p. 196. Enablers are activities that facilitate the performance improvement observed at a best-in-class benchmark company. For example, in a distribution process capable of picking and packing orders faster than any other, an enabler could be the stocking locations of frequently ordered items.

9. Deming lecture, note 3.

10. PDCA—the Plan–Do–Check–Act cycle—is the fundamental management method taught by W. Edwards Deming. This model of thinking about process was derived from Walter Shewhart's earlier work and is sometimes called the Shewhart Cycle or the Deming Cycle. Shewhart was influenced by the scientific method of Frederick Taylor, who proposed an approach of plan–do–see, and the educational methods of John Dewey, whose four-step model for learning was: discover new insights, invent new possibilities, produce action, and observe the consequences. In more recent times, Xerox took the model and adapted it as a model for change management to describe the role of the manager–change integrator: Learn–Use–Train–Inspect (LUTI). However the pedigree of this model is identified, it is a universal model for considering management actions when attacking a problem.

11. Taiichi Ohno, *Toyota Production System: Beyond Large-Scale Production* (Cambridge, MA: Productivity Press, 1990), p. 25.

12. *Ibid.*, p. 26.

13. Paul Howell, *Houston Chronicle*, December 16, 1991, as quoted by C. Jackson Grayson at the APQC Benchmarking Week '92 Conference: May 4–8, 1992.

14. An unpublished study by research librarian Joy K. Holland of the American Productivity & Quality Center, Houston, TX, 1992.

15. Alexandra Biesada, "Strategic Benchmarking," *Financial World*, September 29, 1992, p. 31.

16. *Ibid.*, p. 30.

17. Robert D. Buzzell and Bradley T. Gale, *The PIMS Principles: Linking Strategy to Performance* (New York: Free Press, 1987). This relationship of perceived quality to profitability is clearly demonstrated in Chapter 6, "Quality is King."

18. *Ibid.*, p. 109.

19. Noriaki Kano has displayed his model at numerous presentations on quality; I have witnessed them twice at GOAL/QPC Quality Conferences. His model is slightly modified for a Western Audience in this presentation.

20. John Doyle, speech to a class of group quality managers in training as assessors for Hewlett-Packard's Quality Maturity System, February 1989.

21. The idea of a "re-creative" cycle is taken from William Miller, author of *The Creative Edge*. Miller's concept came about as we discussed applications of Kano's model to Miller's work in the field of creativity and innovation.

22. Paul M. Smith, benchmarking program manager—order fulfillment, at Hewlett-Packard, first pointed out the model of the competitive dimensions of a company as related to its ability to protect against the inadvertent release of intellectual property.

23. George Stalk, Jr., and Thomas M. Hout, *Competing Against Time* (New York: Free Press, 1990), pp. 58–60.

24. Theodore Levitt, *Levitt on Marketing* (Cambridge, MA: Harvard Business School Press, 1991). This book is a collection of Levitt's 14 articles from *Harvard Business Review* which describe his concepts that lead to marketing excellence.

25. Alexandra Biesada, "Strategic Benchmarking," p. 34.

26. As an example, see Brian Dumaine, "Corporate Spies Snoop to Conquer," *Fortune*, November 1988, p. 88.

27. Gregory H. Watson, Samuel Bookhart, et al., "Applying Moral and Legal Considerations to Benchmarking Protocol," *Planning, Organizing, and Managing Benchmarking: A User's Guide* (Houston, TX: APQC, 1992), appendix 2.

28. Richard Foster, *Innovation: The Attacker's Advantage* (New York: Summit Books, 1986), pp. 139–142.

29. Danny Miller, *The Icarus Paradox: How Exceptional Companies Bring About Their Own Downfall* (New York: HarperBusiness, 1991), pp. 19–20.

30. Foster, *Innovation*, p. 29.

Chapter 2

1. Bruce D. Henderson, "The Origins of Strategy," *Harvard Business Review*, November–December 1989, p. 5.

2. Sun Tzu, *The Art of War*, ed. by James Clavell (New York: Delacorte Press, 1983), p. 29.

3. The sayings of Miyamoto Musashi appear in *The Book of Five Rings*, ed. by Victor Harris (Woodstock, NY: Overlook Press, 1974).

4. As quoted in Yoji Akao, ed., *Hoshin Kanri* (Cambridge, MA: Productivity Press, 1991), p. xxi.

5. Gregory H. Watson, "Understanding Hoshin Kanri," in Yoji Akao, ed. *Hoshin Kanri* (Cambridge, MA: Productivity Press, 1991), p. xxv.

6. Yoji Akao, *Hoshin Kanri*, appendixes 1, 2, and 3.

7. Gary Hamel and C. K. Prahalad, "Strategic Intent," *Harvard Business Review*, May–June 1989, pp. 63–76.

8. C. K. Prahalad and Gary Hamel, "The Core Competence of the Corporation," *Harvard Business Review*, May–June 1990, pp. 79–91.

9. George Stalk, Philip Evans, and Lawrence E. Shulman, "Competing on Capabilities: The New Rules of Corporate Strategy," *Harvard Business Review*, March–April 1992.

10. Hamel and Prahalad, "Strategic Intent," p. 64.

11. *Ibid.*

12. Sun Tzu, *The Art of War*, p. 28.

13. The story of Canon's attack on Xerox is partially told in a book compiled by the Japan Management Association, *Canon Production System: Creative Involvement of the Total Workforce* (Cambridge, MA: Productivity Press, 1987).

14. Prahalad and Hamel, "The Core Competence of the Corporation," p. 82.

15. *Ibid.*, pp. 83–84.

16. *Id.* Prahalad and Hamel use Canon as a key case study throughout their article on core competence.

17. Stalk, Evans, and Shulman, "Competing on Capabilities," p. 62.

18. Gary Hamel and C. K. Prahalad, "Letter to the Editor," *Harvard Business Review*, May–June 1992, p. 164.

19. Bill Lehman, *Proceedings of Benchmarking Week '92* (Houston, TX: APQC, 1992), presentation notes.

20. This operational definition of world class comes from an unpublished General Electric benchmarking study that evaluated strategic change implementation among nine strategic partners.

21. Robert S. Kaplan and David P. Norton, "The Balanced Scorecard— Measures that Drive Performance," *Harvard Business Review,* January– February 1992, p. 74.

22. John A. Young, CEO of Hewlett-Packard Company, in an address to senior executives of Chevron, June 1990.

23. Roger Milliken, CEO of Milliken Company, in his address at the National Quality Forum, following his company's receipt of the Malcolm Baldrige National Quality Award.

Chapter 3

1. The *International Quality Study: Best Practices,* conducted jointly by the American Quality Foundation and Ernst & Young, is available through the American Society for Quality Control.

2. Philip B. Crosby, *Quality Is Free: The Art of Making Quality Certain* (New York: McGraw-Hill, 1979), pp. 25–40.

3. Joseph M. Juran and Frank M. Gryna, eds., *Juran's Quality Control Handbook,* 4th ed. (New York: McGraw-Hill, 1988), p. 9.2.

4. Internal customers are those individuals, teams, or organizations to whom an internal product is delivered. For development of this concept, see Richard J. Schonberger, *Building a Chain of Customers: Linking Business Functions to Create the World Class Company* (New York: The Free Press, 1990), and John Guaspari, *The Customer Connection: Quality for the Rest of Us* (New York: AMACOM/The American Management Association, 1988).

5. The ISO 9000 standard is actually a set of three company models for quality assurance systems. ISO 9001 applies to companies that ensure quality during the design of custom products for individual orders. ISO 9002 applies to companies that ensure quality during the manufacture of products for a standard price list. ISO 9003 applies to companies that ensure quality in distribution and in the final testing of products or services. ISO 9004, a general guideline for interpretation of the quality models, provides a more detailed description of a quality system.

6. Robert C. Camp, *Proceedings of Benchmarking Week '92* (Houston, TX: APQC, 1992), presentation notes.

7. *Ibid.*

8. *Ibid.*

9. Comments by Noriaki Kano at the 1989 GOAL/QPC Conference.

10. Some readers of the Benchmarking Code of Conduct have remarked that it merely represents the fundamentals of business ethics and is not required. The Code was judged to be necessary by some of the "old-timers" of benchmarking, who continue to observe a lack of professionalism among some companies that begin benchmarking and do not understand the protocols and conventions that govern intercompany relationships. For further background readings on business ethics and related problems, see the collection of *HBR* articles brought together in: Kenneth R. Andrews, ed., *Ethics in Practice: Managing the Moral Corporation* (Boston, MA: Harvard Business Review Press, 1988).

11. The Benchmarking Code of Conduct is reprinted in Appendix A of this book. Both APQC and SPI encourage wide distribution of the Code.

12. Xerox Corporation, *A Guide to Benchmarking in Xerox* (Rochester, NY: Multinational Customer and Service Education, 1990), p. 8. (Pub. no. 700P91713.)

13. Todd Lambertus, *Surveying Industry's Benchmarking Practices* (Houston, TX: APQC, 1992). The full results of this survey are unpublished, but this executive overview is available from APQC.

14. H. James Harrington, *Business Process Improvement: The Breakthrough Strategy for Total Quality, Productivity, and Competitiveness* (New York: McGraw-Hill, 1991).

15. John A. Young, CEO of Hewlett-Packard Company, in an address to senior executives of Chevron, June 1990.

16. Gregory H. Watson, *The Benchmarking Workbook: Adapting Best Practices for Performance Improvement* (Cambridge, MA: Productivity Press, 1992), pp. 18–21.

17. Xerox Corporation, *A Guide to Benchmarking in Xerox,* p. 24.

18. Watson, *The Benchmarking Workbook,* pp. 15–41.

19. *Ibid.,* p. 41.

20. *Id.*

21. *Id.,* p. 40.

22. This methodology for demonstrating process interactions is from Geary Rummler and Alan P. Brache, *Improving Performance: How to Manage the White Space on the Organization Chart* (San Francisco: Jossey-Bass, 1991).

23. Gregory H. Watson, "Comparing Process Models for Benchmarking," *Planning, Organizing, and Managing Benchmarking: A User's Guide* (Houston, TX: APQC, 1992).

24. *Ibid.*

25. The organization of my previous book follows a six-step process that differs from the process used in this book in its emphasis on secondary research and adapting enablers. Otherwise, the processes map identically. *The Benchmarking Workbook* also includes forms to help facilitate teams' progress through the benchmarking steps.

26. John A. Young, address to senior executives of Chevron, June 1990.

27. *Webster's Ninth Collegiate Dictionary* (Springfield, MA: Merriam-Webster, 1987), p. 257.

Chapter 4

1. Shoshanna Zuboff, *In the Age of the Smart Machine: The Future of Work and Power* (New York: Basic Books, 1988). Zuboff goes on to explain how learning the focus of an organization requires a new vocabulary, "one of colleagues and co-learners, of exploration, experimentation, and innovation" (p. 395). Out of this new workplace evolves a new structure:

   > The informated organization is a learning institution, and one of its principal purposes is the expansion of knowledge—not knowledge for its own sake (as in the academic pursuit), but knowledge that comes to reside at the core of what it means to be productive. Learning is no longer a separate activity that occurs either before one enters the workplace or in remote classroom settings. Nor is it an activity preserved for a managerial group. The behaviors that define learning and the behaviors that define being productive are one and the same. Learning is not something that requires time out from being engaged in productive activity; learning is the heart of productive activity. To put it simply, learning is the new form of labor. (p. 395)

2. David E. Meen and Mark Keough, "Creating the Learning Organization," *The McKinsey Quarterly* (1), 1992, p. 59.

3. *Ibid.*, p. 60.

4. The idea of "re-creation" and the linkage of quality and innovation come from a series of discussions with William Miller, President of Global Creativity, Inc.

5. Tracy Kidder, *The Soul of a New Machine* (New York: Avon Books, 1982), pp. 31–32.

6. Meen and Keough, "Creating the Learning Organization," p. 59.

7. Gary Hamel and C. K. Prahalad, "Strategic Intent," *Harvard Business Review,* May–June 1989, p. 71.

8. C. K. Prahalad and Gary Hamel, "The Core Competence of the Corporation," *Harvard Business Review,* May–June 1990, p. 82. Core competencies are very unlike many of an organization's other resources. They do not deteriorate and depreciate over time; rather, they multiply as they are transferred and they appreciate in terms of the capability of the organization to cope with its future.

9. Arie P. de Geus, "Planning as Learning," *Harvard Business Review,* March–April 1988; republished in *The State of Strategy* (a Harvard Review Paperback, 1991, p. 130).

10. *Ibid.*

11. John A. Young, CEO of Hewlett-Packard Company, in an address to the senior management team of Chevron, June 1990.

12. *Ibid.* Young described how he sought to change H-P and keep it in a leadership position in its industry, a position it had already achieved.

13. De Geus, "Planning as Learning, p. 130.

14. A detailed description of this model is found in Gregory H. Watson, *Benchmarking for Competitive Advantage* (Cambridge, MA: Productivity Press, 1993).

Chapter 5

1. These findings were later published in Preston G. Smith and Donald G. Reinertsen, *Developing Products in Half the Time* (New York: Van Nostrand Reinhold, 1991).

2. George Stalk and Thomas Hout, *Competing Against Time: How Time-Based Competition Is Reshaping Global Markets* (New York, The Free Press, 1990), p. 58.

3. *Ibid.,* p. 156.

4. As to his decision to ask for a tenfold improvement, Young once remarked that he had pulled the number out of the air: "I hadn't any idea if this was the right number, and didn't even know if it could be done." He did know that if he had asked for a twofold improvement, very little would have been accomplished. Giving the company a decade to accomplish this seemingly impossible goal was a signal of his seriousness. Young's use of stretch goals was a Japanese management practice called Hoshin Kanri, a planning system with feedback, a review cycle, reward, recognition, and teamwork built in. (See Yoji Akao, ed., *Hoshin Kanri* (Cambridge, MA: Productivity Press, 1992)). Hoshin Kanri gave Young a way to take his strategic initiatives and drive them into action.

5. Postmortems on completed operations can be extremely useful as a means of fostering continuous improvement. The U.S. Army Infantry School has, for decades, managed a Lessons Learned center where knowledge gained from past engagements is identified and recorded for current and future infantry personnel. At Merck Corporation, each project manager keeps track of what went well and what went badly; for his or her own benefit and for the benefit of other researchers, these lessons are contributed to a companywide "Book of Knowledge."

6. John Young, CEO of Hewlett-Packard Company, to managers at Chevron, 1989.

7. The standard net present value (NPV) calculation is:

$$NPV = \text{cash flow}_1/(1 + i)^1 + \ldots + \text{cash flow}_n/(1 + i)^n$$

where i = the firm's cost of capital; and the initial cash flow periods will be negative. Therefore, the "break-even point" for the NPV is really the number of cash flow periods needed to get to an NPV of zero. In keeping with financial theory, the relative risk of various projects subjected to BET analysis can be factored in through the cost of capital rate (i).

There is a long-standing tradition of using NPV analysis within Hewlett-Packard. Bill Hewlett was a strong advocate of advanced capability hand-held calculators, partly because of his strong belief that engineers should have a handy tool for doing NPV analysis. Not coincidentally, the first of the now-famous line of professional quality H-P calculators had all the important financial formulas programmed into it.

8. Scholars of product development have been quick to note that development cycles as reported by various companies cannot always be accepted at face value. A principal reason is the fact that the official "starting time" for one company's development project may be different from that of another. Per Hewlett-Packard's printed guide to doing BET analysis:

> The BET period should begin with the formation of the investigation team (including project manager or leader). For example, if there is a sparsely staffed, very fundamental technology research project which eventually develops into an investigation, the BET period should not start with the beginning of the fundamental research but should begin with the formation of the project investigation team.

Once the BET period has started, the BET clock should not be suspended even if the project is put on hold or suspended for a period of time. ("Break-Even Time at Hewlett-Packard," Hewlett-Packard Co., 1990.)

9. Science Policy Research Unit, University of Sussex, *Success and Failure in Industrial Innovation* (London: Centre for the Study of Industrial Innovation, 1972), p. 5.

10. See Eric von Hippel, *Sources of Innovation* (New York: Oxford University Press, 1990); also "Get New Products From Customers," *Harvard Business Review*, March–April 1982, pp. 117–122.

Chapter 6

1. Donald E. Petersen and John Hillkirk, *A Better Idea: Redefining the Way Americans Work* (Boston, MA: Houghton Mifflin Co., 1991), p. 18.

2. *Ibid.*, p. 6.

3. *Id.*, pp. 7–10.

4. *Id.*, p. 15.

5. Worth mentioning is the fact that Petersen was on the board of Hewlett-Packard, and H-P's CEO, John Young, was on Ford's board. The two men became good friends. Because HP was among the most advanced U.S. firms on quality issues, one might suspect that the influence of Young was an important element in Ford's increasing interest in quality.

6. "Ford: Team Taurus," case study by James Brian Quinn and Penny C. Paquette, Amos Tuck School of Business, Dartmouth College, Hanover, NH, p. 7.

7. Quoted in Robert L. Shook, *Turnaround: The New Ford Motor Company* (New York: Prentice-Hall Press, 1990), p. 76.

8. Petersen and Hillkirk, *A Better Idea*, p. 69.

9. Kim B. Clark and Takahiro Fujimoto, *Product Development Performance* (Boston: Harvard Business School Press, 1991).

10. Ford learned this lesson through some of the literature that started appearing in the early 1980s. Productivity Press, a small Cambridge, Massachusetts, firm, became the translator and publisher of many works then only obtainable in Japan. Notable among the early authors were Shigeo Shingo and Taichi Ohno, two of the guiding spirits of the Toyota production system. Shingo was the chief industrial engineer for Toyota manufacturing and Ohno was the firm's vice president of manufacturing worldwide. Together, they put together the pace-setting Toyota system of manufacturing.

11. This same phenomenon was observed when Admiral Bobby Inman put together the Microelectronics Computer Consortium (MCC), in Austin, Texas, in the early 1980s. As a research consortium of major electronics

firms, MCC was to be staffed with top scientists and engineers from each member firm, with all results to be shared. Inman quickly noticed that many firms were sending their second-string players. He fired a salvo to tell the CEOs of the member firms: "I'm not running a turkey farm down here!" The firms sent their best people after that.

12. Quinn and Paquette, "Ford: Team Taurus," p. 9.

13. The extent to which Ford developers had been working within constraints, and not toward higher potentials, is best told by Petersen, who described a visit to the Ford design center in 1980 in company with Jack Telnack, its manager, and a number of the design staff. "I was disappointed with what I saw," Petersen relates. "I asked them if they like the new cars they were working on. [These included the 1983 Thunderbird.] . . . they said that they didn't, and we talked about why. It had a lot to do with lists of restrictions—assumptions about what they could or could not do, based on past experience and a general sense of resignation. That's when I asked them if they would design a 1983 Thunderbird that they would be proud to drive and to park in their driveway." Petersen and Hillkirk, *A Better Idea*, p. 70.

14. Eric Taub, *Taurus: The Making of the Car That Saved Ford* (New York: E. P. Dutton, 1991), p. 57.

15. Joseph M. Callahan, "Ford Finds 400 Ways to Say Quality," *Automotive Industry*, 166 (1), January 1986, p. 44.

16. Ford later reported that a full 100 percent achievement was not possible because some best-in-class features block others.

17. Jack Telnack, quoted in *Fortune*, January 5, 1987, p. 78.

18. *Ibid*.

19. Petersen and Hillkirk, *A Better Idea*, p. 75.

20. Quinn and Paquette, "Ford: Team Taurus," p. 14.

21. Ford Motor Company, Annual Report, 1984.

22. The team approach has actually been strengthened. The team members who worked for Veraldi on the Taurus project never really left their own departments. Today, Ford uses a "co-locational" approach, assigning individuals directly to teams for the duration of their projects.

Chapter 7

1. GM was a combination of "little q" companies at the time, and was trying to learn to become a "Big Q" firm. Its tradition—indeed, the tradition of the U.S. auto industry—was to work against standards, looking always for "repeatability." Where those standards were placed,

and when they should be challenged, was not open for discussion. This was in marked contrast to the quality culture of the Japanese auto firms, in which the "standard" was always questioned or challenged. For a good discussion of the global automobile industry, see James P. Womack, Daniel T. Jones, and Daniel Roos, *The Machine That Changed the World* (New York: Rawson Associates, 1990).

2. Quality managers in those early days of the "movement" had to learn, and sometimes draw morale sustenance, from each other, because so few of their regular colleagues shared their commitment to quality principles. There was, in fact, an old-boy network of quality directors, most of whom knew each other through membership in the American Society for Quality Control, conference seminars, and career migrations. Their shared concerns for product quality united them into a kind of fraternity.

   This network of quality managers proved to be an important facilitator of benchmarking studies in the years that followed. Strategic alliances between firms, major vendor–customer relationships, and working relationships between CEOs on each other's boards, also served to cross-pollinate American industry with quality principles.

3. General Motors Corporation, "Cross-Industry Study," September 24, 1994, pp. 8–10.

4. *Ibid.*, pp. 8–9.

5. The actual mean ratings for all 11 companies were as follows:

Core concepts	8.68
Quality culture	8.26
Transfer of quality	8.15
Learn from failure	8.14
Unselfish customer satisfaction	7.95
Resist short-term temptations	7.92
Standardize performance	7.82
Quality mechanisms	7.80
Subordinate production	7.67
QRDP Disciplines	7.12

(Source: General Motors)

6. This should not be surprising. Experience seems to indicate a gap of about 18 months between the proving-out of a new quality management idea and its adoption by operating managers. A time gap of this length exists even in some of the most quality-conscious firms with which I have had experience.

7. With the benefit of hindsight and another 10 years of experience in industrial benchmarking on record, writers pick away at some points of GM's benchmarking methodology. However, General Electric undertook a similar study of much different companies, used another methodology, and came up with many of the same conclusions as did GM.

8. This study uses the term "mechanism" in the same way that many today use the term "enabler." The latter was first used by Bob Camp, and is probably the better term: it is broader, taking in topics like "employee involvement."

9. Corporate Q&R vice president Robert Decker, appalled by McDonald's disbelief in GM's quality problems, quickly called IBM's CEO, John Ackers, and asked him to intercede. IBM had been a participant in the study, and Decker knew that its prowess was respected by GM management. Ackers arranged for McDonald to visit IBM headquarters and spend the day with his quality managers. The visit to IBM appeared to have altered McDonald's thinking, because he later declared himself to be "born again" on quality issues.

10. Robert Decker, who had been unswerving in his attempts to reform GM quality practices, died from a series of heart attacks. His position as vice president of Corporate Q&R was taken over by Don McPherson, who carried on the effort with equal vigor.

Chapter 8

1. Gary Jacobson and John Hillkirk, *Xerox: American Samurai* (New York: Collier Books/Macmillan, 1986), pp. 233–234.

2. William F. Glavin, "Competitive Benchmarking, A Technique Utilized by Xerox Corporation to Revitalize Itself to a Modern Competitive Position," *Review of Business,* 6 (3), Winter 1984, p. 10.

3. Jacobson and Hillkirk, *Xerox,* pp. 105–106.

4. *Ibid.,* pp. 172–173.

5. Frances Gaither Tucker, Seymour M. Zivan, and Robert C. Camp, "How to Measure Yourself Against the Best," *Harvard Business Review,* January–February 1987, p. 8.

6. Jacobson and Hillkirk, *Xerox,* p. 234, Glavin, "Competitive Benchmarking," p. 10.

7. Bob Camp wrote the first definitive book on the subject of benchmarking, and his assistance in the development of this chapter is gratefully acknowledged.

8. Interview with Robert C. Camp.

9. Robert C. Camp, *Benchmarking: The Search for Industry Best Practices That Lead to Superior Performance* (Milwaukee, WI: Quality Press/ American Society for Quality Control, 1989), p. 71.

10. "A Truly Outstanding System for Manual Order Picking," *Modern Materials Handling,* March 1980, pp. 48–53.

11. Camp, *Benchmarking,* p. 286.

12. *Ibid.,* p. 103.

13. *Id.,* pp. 146, 148.

14. Tucker, Zivan, and Camp, "How to Measure Yourself Against the Best," p. 10.

15. In 1989, the firm's Corporate Education and Training department published an even more complete "Reference Guide" for teams involved with benchmark studies.

Chapter 9

1. Robert C. Camp, *Benchmarking: The Search for Industry Best Practices That Lead to Superior Performance* (Milwaukee, WI: Quality Press/ American Society for Quality Control, 1989), p. xi.

2. "Empowerment and Self-Directed Work Teams," First National Bank of Chicago, August 1992, p. 34.

3. "Benchmarking the Inpatient Admitting Process: Phase I" (San Francisco: The Healthcare Forum/APQC, 1992), p. 14.

Chapter 10

1. This quote is from Richard Allen's presentation at the APQC Conference, Benchmarking Week '92, held in Dallas, TX, May 4–8.

2. Halberstam quoted Romney in his keynote address to the GOAL/ QPC Conference in 1989.

3. From Al Mierisch's presentation at the APQC Benchmarking Week '92 Conference.

4. *Ibid.*

5. *Id.*

6. *Id.*

7. *Id.*

8. *Id.*

9. *Id.*

10. As quoted in an article by James Healey, "Firm Taps Rivals' Gains in Big Gamble," *USA Today,* October 21, 1992.

11. APQC Benchmarking Week '92.
12. *Ibid.*
13. *Id.*
14. *Id.*
15. *Id.*
16. *Id.*

Appendix A

Benchmarking Code of Conduct

Benchmarking—the process of identifying and learning from best practices anywhere in the world—is a powerful tool in the quest for continuous improvement.

To guide benchmarking encounters and to advance the professionalism and effectiveness of benchmarking, the International Benchmarking Clearinghouse, a service of the American Productivity and Quality Center, and the Strategic Planning Institute Council on Benchmarking have adopted this common Code of Conduct. We encourage all organizations to abide by this Code of Conduct. Adherence to these principles will contribute to efficient, effective, and ethical benchmarking. This edition of the Code of Conduct has been expanded to provide greater guidance on the protocol of benchmarking for beginners.

BENCHMARKING CODE OF CONDUCT

Individuals agree for themselves and their company to abide by the following principles for benchmarking with other organizations.

1. Principle of *Legality*

- If there is any potential question on the legality of an activity, don't do it.
- Avoid discussions or actions that could lead to or imply an interest in restraint of trade, market, and/or customer allocation schemes, price fixing, dealing arrangements, bid rigging, or bribery. Don't discuss costs with competitors if costs are an element of pricing.

- Refrain from the acquisition of trade secrets from any means that could be interpreted as improper, including the breach or inducement of a breach of any duty to maintain secrecy. Do not disclose or use any trade secret that may have been obtained through improper means or that was disclosed by another in violation of a duty to maintain its secrecy or limit of use.
- Do not, as a consultant or a client, extend one benchmarking study's findings to another company without first obtaining permission from the parties of the first study.

2. Principle of *Exchange*

- Be willing to provide the same type and level of information that you request from your benchmarking partner to your benchmarking partner.
- Communicate fully and early in the relationship to clarify expectations, avoid misunderstandings, and establish mutual interest in the benchmarking exchange.
- Be honest and complete.

3. Principle of *Confidentiality*

- Treat benchmarking interchange as confidential to the individuals and companies involved. Information must not be communicated outside the partnering organizations without the prior consent of the benchmarking partner who shared the information.
- A company's participation in a study is confidential and should not be communicated externally without its prior permission.

4. Principle of *Use*

- Use information obtained through benchmarking only for purposes of formulating improvement of operations or processes within the companies participating in the benchmarking study.
- The use or communication of a benchmarking partner's name with the data obtained or practices observed requires the prior permission of that partner.
- Do not use benchmarking as a means to market or to sell.

5. Principle of *First-Party Contact*

- Initiate benchmarking contacts, whenever possible, through a benchmarking contact designated by the partner company.
- Respect the corporate culture of partner companies and work within mutually agreed upon procedures.
- Obtain mutual agreement with the designated benchmarking contact on any hand-off of communication or responsibility to other parties.

6. Principle of *Third-Party Contact*

- Obtain an individual's permission before providing his or her name in response to a contact request.
- Avoid communicating a contact's name in an open forum without the contact's permission.

7. Principle of *Preparation*

- Demonstrate commitment to the efficiency and effectiveness of benchmarking by completing preparatory work prior to making an initial benchmarking contact and following a benchmarking process.
- Make the most of your benchmarking partner's time by being fully prepared for each exchange.
- Help your benchmarking partners prepare by providing them with an interview guide or questionnaire and agenda prior to benchmarking visits.

8. Principle of *Completion*

- Follow through with each commitment made to your benchmarking partners in a timely manner.
- Complete each benchmarking study to the satisfaction of all benchmarking partners as mutually agreed.

9. Principle of *Understanding and Action*

- Understand how your benchmarking partners would like to be treated.

- Treat your benchmarking partners in the way that each benchmarking partner would like to be treated.
- Understand how each benchmarking partner would like to have the information he or she provides handled and used, and handle and use it in that manner.

Appendix B

Tools of Secondary Research

Finding information is often the most difficult task in benchmarking. Access to a good business library and a research librarian will solve most of the information problems that occur. However, sometimes getting started is the hardest aspect of an information search. To provide a starting place for benchmarking information needs, the following resource materials, which can be ordered for business libraries, are recommended:

- *Moody's Industrial Manual*—Corporate history, capital structure, financial statements, and analysis of management for publicly held businesses. One of eight financial manuals published by Moody Investor Services.

  Moody's Investor Services, Inc.
  99 Church Street
  New York, NY 10007

- *Value Line Investment Survey*—An investment advisory service that provides financial analyses of 1,700 stocks in 95 industries.

  Value Line Inc.
  711 Third Avenue
  New York, NY 10017

- *Wall Street Transcript*—An information service that abstracts information, by company, from the publications of Dow Jones (e.g., *The Wall Street Journal*).

  University Microfilms International
  300 North Zeeb Road
  Ann Arbor, MI 48106

- *Business Periodicals Index*—Provides abstracts of articles about business from leading business journals.

  W. W. Wilson Company
  950 University Avenue
  Bronx, NY 10452

- *U.S. Industrial Outlook*—Published by the Department of Commerce; tracks trends in American business.

  Washington Service Bureau
  1225 Connecticut Avenue, NW
  Washington, DC 20230

- *Directory of On-line Data Bases*—Descriptive listing of on-line data bases and information sources, categorized by subject or specialty area.

  Cuadra/Elsevier
  655 Avenue of the Americas
  New York, NY 10010

- *Principal International Businesses*—An annual listing of the principal public and private companies in 133 countries.

  Dun & Bradstreet
  Three Sylvan Way
  Parsippany, NJ 07054

- *Standard & Poor's Register of Corporations*—A three-volume listing of basic information about corporations and business executives.

  Standard & Poor's Corporation
  25 Broadway
  New York, NY 10004

- *Thomas Register of American Manufacturers*—A 25-volume set; the standard for buyers to use for identifying sources of product.

  Thomas Publishing Company
  One Pennsylvania Plaza
  New York, NY 10119

- *Directories in Print, Encyclopedia of Associations, Subject Directory of Special Libraries and Information Centers*—Sources that provide great assistance in finding additional sources of information.

  Gale Research Company
  835 Penobscot Building
  Detroit, MI 48226

Appendix C

Benchmarking Recognition Award Criteria

1992
Benchmarking Award Criteria

INTERNATIONAL
BENCHMARKING
CLEARINGHOUSE

**A Service of the
American Productivity & Quality Center**

■ TABLE OF CONTENTS

■ INTRODUCTION

APQC is pleased to announce the creation of three awards which recognize achievements in benchmarking.

- ❏ Benchmarking Research Prize

- ❏ Benchmarking Study Prize

- ❏ Award for Excellence in Benchmarking

The purpose of the first two of these awards is to promote benchmarking activities by recognizing the contributions of individuals and teams.

The third award for Excellence in Benchmarking encourages the development and maturity of formalized benchmarking activities at an organization-wide level. It complements the Malcolm Baldrige National Quality Award by focusing on the approach and deployment of the benchmarking process, as well as on the results from benchmarking studies. The guidelines for this third award can also be used by organizations as a self-assessment tool for evaluating and improving their benchmarking process.

These awards will be administered by the Director of the APQC International Benchmarking Clearinghouse and applications will be evaluated by an independent panel of recognized experts and leading practitioners of benchmarking who will serve as examiners.

A panel of judges will be appointed to provide senior management oversight, assure the continuing objectivity of the award process, and improve the definition and applicability of the award criteria. Examiners will be appointed by the award administrator and will serve in a voluntary capacity for terms up to three years.

Notice of intention to apply for an award in a given category must be postmarked by November 16, 1992 to be eligible to submit an application. The deadline for application for these awards will be December 18, 1992. All awards will be presented during May 1993 at the APQC Benchmarking Week awards ceremony.

■ BENCHMARKING RESEARCH PRIZE

Purpose: To extend the body of benchmarking knowledge through the recognition of innovative contributions, developments, and research in techniques, methods, and tools of benchmarking.

Categories: The Benchmarking Research Prize is awarded in two categories: academic research and applied research. Up to two awards per category will be granted.

Criteria: This award encourages the development of the technical aspects of benchmarking by seeking original contributions in the areas of data collection, analysis, and integration of benchmarking techniques. This award is intended to encourage and reinforce the increased usage of statistical techniques and managerial tools for benchmarking. Individuals are encouraged to be innovative and scholarly in the development of their papers. It is expected that all applications will be original research. An applicant is allowed to author or co-author only one entry per year. Papers submitted jointly by both academic and industry authors will be evaluated in the academic category if the industry author was a student of the affiliated academic institution, and in the industry category if the academic was on contract to the business.

Eligibility: Individuals or teams may submit an application for this prize. To be eligible for the academic award, the principal applicant must be associated with a college, university, or not-for-profit educational institution. The applied research category is open to all individual or team applicants, regardless of academic affiliation or size of business. Research Prize recipients are ineligible to apply for another award in the same category for a period of three years.

Fees: There is a $100.00 processing fee which must be submitted with each application.

Examination Process: Applications should be prepared in a manner which facilitates blind reviews. Each application will be examined for its own merits. The examination process is two-tiered. The first is an evaluation of the paper by a panel of examiners. The first panel of examiners will evaluate the paper using rules similar to those applied by editorial boards of refereed journals for evaluating submitted articles. This first level review provides an analysis of each paper submitted and summarizes its contribution to the body of benchmarking knowledge. A sponsor for the paper will be appointed from the examiner panel to argue its merits at the second stage review. The second stage review is conducted during a meeting of the examiners. The purpose of the second review is to recommend the best papers to the judges for selection.

Applicants are required to submit a paper copy of the application, limited to 20 pages in length, and an electronic file in ASCII format, or other convertible format.

Publication Rights: Award winners will be invited to present their papers at the next annual APQC Benchmarking Conference. APQC retains the right to publish, in any format, any or all papers submitted for competition. Individual authors may also submit their papers for independent publication. All papers submitted for evaluation for the Research Prize will remain in the possession of APQC and will be available through the International Benchmarking Clearinghouse.

■ BENCHMARKING STUDY PRIZE

Purpose: To promote, encourage, and recognize excellence in the execution of a benchmarking study.

Categories: This award is provided to individuals or teams. There is no distinction as to award category. Each year up to five awards will be presented.

Criteria: This award reinforces the deployment of the benchmarking process by recognizing excellence in the execution of benchmarking principles. Teams are requested to submit applications which document their process for conducting a benchmarking project. The application should describe thoroughly:

- the rationale for selecting the project
- the process used in benchmarking
- the benchmarking study plan and team responsibilities
- the benchmarking questionnaire and results of secondary research
- the results and conclusions of the study
- the action plan recommended to management
- the results achieved

Use these seven bulleted items to form the outline for your application. Teams are evaluated on their approach to the project, the quality of their analysis and execution of the study, and the results obtained from the study. An endorsement by the project sponsor or management representative is required to testify to the importance of the study.

Eligibility: Any individual or team who has conducted a benchmarking project that has been completed, through recommendation to management and subsequent implementation of those recommendations, within two calendar years before December 1, 1992 is eligible to prepare an award submission package.

Fees: There is a $100.00 processing fee which must be submitted with each application.

Examination Process: Applications should be prepared in a manner which facilitates blind reviews. Each application will be examined for its own merits using the examination criteria found in the application guidelines. The examination process is two-tiered. The first is an evaluation of the benchmarking study report by a panel of examiners working independently. The first panel of examiners will evaluate the report using the examination criteria as stated above. This first review provides a rough screening for the applicants. Applications that continue on for consideration at the second stage review are evaluated by a team of examiners which will review the merits of all finalists.

Applicants are required to submit a paper copy of the application, limited to 20 pages in length, and an electronic file in ASCII format, or other convertible format.

The purpose of the second review is to select and recommend the best papers for the award. Recommendations for awards will be made to the panel of judges for final selection.

Publication Rights: Award winners will be invited to present their papers at the next annual APQC Benchmarking Conference. APQC retains the right to publish, in any format, any or all papers submitted for competition. Individual and team authors may also submit their papers for independent publication. All papers submitted for evaluation for the Study Prize will remain in the possession of APQC and will be available through the International Benchmarking Clearinghouse.

■ AWARD FOR EXCELLENCE IN BENCHMARKING

Purpose: The purpose of the Award for Excellence in Benchmarking is to recognize those organizations which demonstrate the consistent application of benchmarking according to the award criteria, and whose practice of benchmarking represents both leadership and innovation in their use of this process for business process improvement at both strategic and tactical levels of the organization.

Categories: A maximum of one award will be presented each year in each of the small business and large business categories.

Criteria: This award is modeled after the Award Criteria of the Malcolm Baldrige National Quality Award. This award emphasizes the approach and deployment and results of benchmarking in an organization. The full set of award criteria are contained in the following award application guidelines. Use the scoring format to complete the application, making sure to address each point and sub-point.

Achievement Categories: Applications for the Award for Excellence in Benchmarking must respond to the following five achievement categories:

    (1) Strategic Planning Integration and Information Structure (225 points)
    (2) Benchmarking Process and Support Structure (250 points)
    (3) Teamwork and Employee Involvement (125 points)
    (4) Business Alliances and Networking (100 points)
    (5) Results and Measured Improvements in Benchmarked Processes (300 points)

The purpose of the specific criteria for these categories is to evaluate benchmarking practices which may contribute to world class performance. Each year the judges will meet to review and recommend improvements to the award criteria based on the experience of the prior cycle and the developing practice of benchmarking. Specific written suggestions for improvement may be submitted to the Award Administrator by any interested party.

Evidence of Accomplishment: In responding to each of the specific achievement sections of the award guidelines, the "burden of evidence" centers on the appropriate practices which have contributed, and will contribute to world class excellence in benchmarking. Examples and objective evidence should be submitted wherever appropriate to support applicant claims. Judges will evaluate the five Achievement Categories using the scoring guidelines of the Malcolm Baldrige National Quality Award for approach and deployment in the first four categories and for results in the fifth category. Weighting of the categories and items is indicated in the criteria.

■ APPLICATION GUIDELINES

Category (1): Strategic Planning Integration and Information Structure
(225 Points)

The Strategic Planning Integration and Information Structure category examines the integration of benchmarking with the organization's planning process and how the scope, sources, and uses of benchmarking information are integrated into improvement activities. Also examined is senior management involvement and how goals, plans, and strategies are developed based on competitive information and the application of benchmarks.

A. *Strategic Planning Integration*

| 35 Points |

1. Existence of company planning documents that indicate a structured plan for benchmarking which is linked with company planning guidelines and targeted to improving performance in quality and customer satisfaction, cycle time, productivity, cost of key business processes, and support activities.

| 25 Points |

2. Activities of executives in establishing benchmarking topics and determining key benchmarking partnerships; activities of senior managers in supporting benchmarking activities, participating in benchmarking studies, and reviewing benchmarking study results.

| 20 Points |

3. How benchmarking is integrated into other improvement activities.

| 20 Points |

4. How the organization develops goals, plans, and strategies based upon projections of the competitive environment and application of benchmarks.

| 15 Points |

5. Criteria for both seeking benchmarks and identifying potential benchmarking partners.

B. *Information Structure*

| 30 Points |

1. The scope, sources, and uses of benchmark information, including, but not limited to, the following:

   a. Customer satisfaction and other customer data.
   b. Product/Service quality.
   c. Internal operations including business processes, support services, and employee satisfaction.
   d. Financial performance for overhead management, inventory management, debt management, cost of sales, etc.
   e. Environmental, safety, and health considerations of the business.
   f. Supplier performance.

| 25 Points |

2. Process for integrating benchmarking data with other competitive, market, and customer data in order to determine what to benchmark.

| 20 Points |

3. How benchmarking is used to encourage new ideas and improve the understanding of key business processes.

| 20 Points |

4. How the organization evaluates and improves the scope, sources, and uses of benchmarking data.

| 15 Points |

5. How the organization decides when to compare within and outside of its industry.

Category (2): Benchmarking Process and Support Structure (250 Points)

The Benchmarking Process and Support Structure category examines the linkage of the benchmarking process, improvement activities, resource allocation, and the deployment of training. Also examined is the adequacy of the company's support structure, including organizational structure, information repository, tracking, and review process for benchmarking studies.

A. Benchmarking Process

| 35 Points |

1. The linkage of the benchmarking process to the company's planning process and other improvement activities and how resource allocation is considered for improvements indicated as the result of benchmarking studies.

| 30 Points |

2. The benchmarking process and model used by the organization.

| 30 Points |

3. Data repository for benchmarking plans, questionnaires, studies, and reports. How this repository is developed by employees and how it is kept current.

| 20 Points |

4. The method for tracking the progress and completion of individual benchmarking projects.

| 20 Points |

5. The review process for proposed benchmarking studies (either internally or externally proposed) to assure appropriate legal and management considerations. The review process for assuring appropriate management participation.

| 15 Points |

6. The application of the Benchmarking Code of Conduct and how it is disseminated to benchmarking teams.

B. Support Structure

| 35 Points | 1. Criteria for conducting formal training in benchmarking and the extent of the deployment of benchmarking training for categories of employees (supervising or sponsoring manager, benchmarking facilitator, team leader, team member, etc.). |

| 20 Points | 2. Organization structure and job responsibilities for individuals supporting benchmarking. |

| 20 Points | 3. How benchmarking efforts are coordinated to eliminate redundancy of team efforts and to ensure that key benchmarks are refreshed periodically. |

| 25 Points | 4. Organization procedures for communicating benchmarking activities and for providing opportunities for benchmarking study teams to meet and share information about their processes. |

Category (3): Teamwork and Employee Involvement
(125 Points)

The Teamwork and Employee Involvement category examines the involvement of process owners, employees, and other stakeholders in benchmarking studies; the selection, roles, and responsibilities of team members; and how internal benchmarking expertise is deployed to support the teams. Also examined are how teams are recognized, and how benchmarking study teams communicate their benchmarking activities.

| 25 Points | 1. How cross-functional and cross-divisional needs are considered during benchmarking studies and how these concerns are institutionalized in the company's benchmarking process. |

| 15 Points | 2. How process owners and process stakeholders are involved in benchmarking study projects. |

| 20 Points | 3. The selection criteria for benchmarking teams and the roles and responsibilities of team members. |

| 15 Points | 4. How time and resources are allocated to benchmarking teams. |

| 15 Points | 5. The relationship of benchmarking team membership to the implementation team members who will pursue the recommended action plans. |

| 20 Points | 6. How the organization uses its employees with benchmarking expertise to coach, mentor, support, or lead study teams. |

| 15 Points | 7. How the organization recognizes employees for participating in benchmarking activities. |

Category (4): Business Alliances and Networking
(100 Points)

The Business Alliance and Networking category examines how an organization defines, establishes, manages, and promotes alliances and partnerships, including professional societies, trade associations, and quality-focused organizations to support benchmarking activities. Also included are how the organization uses research, competitive information, consultants, suppliers, major accounts, and common interest groups to address specific benchmarking topics.

| 25 Points |

1. How benchmarking alliances and partnerships are established and the rationale used for the selection of those organizations targeted for special relationships.

| 25 Points |

2. How the organization uses membership in quality-focused and benchmarking organizations, and professional societies and trade associations to support its benchmarking efforts.

| 25 Points |

3. How the organization uses its suppliers and major accounts to support its benchmarking efforts.

| 25 Points |

4. How the organization forms common interest groups to address specific benchmarking topics.

Category (5): Results and Improvements in Benchmarked Processes (300 Points)

The Results and Improvements in Benchmarked Processes category examines the specific benchmarks that have been identified and monitored over the past three years, and evidence of the use of benchmarking to improve these processes.

Applicants should indicate evidence of benchmarks, process goals established, and results tracked to goals to indicate trends in improvement. (The results may be normalized or indexed to protect proprietary information.) The frequency of recalibration of benchmarks should be indicated and the criteria for recycling studies should be discussed. Evidence submitted could include, but is not limited to, a discussion of the following:

| 50 Points |

1. What key measures and indicators the organization uses to evaluate and improve its benchmarking process (cycle time, access time to results, and integration of customer, market, financial, and operational benchmarking data).

| 50 Points |

2. How the organization determines objectivity and validity in the results of benchmarking studies.

| 200 Points |

3. Current levels and trends in the performance of benchmarked processes in comparison to pre-benchmarking activities. Specific benchmarks, indicators, and measures used by the organization should be appropriate to the benchmarked process. Benchmarks *could* include, but are not limited to, the following:

Customer satisfaction (segmented by customer group as appropriate)
- Customer reject rates
- Customer satisfaction levels
- On-time delivery
- Customer loss/gain
- Market share loss/gain
- Other measures of responsiveness to customers

Quality and Productivity
- Defect or error rates
- First pass yield
- Equipment downtime
- Rework costs
- Warranty costs as a percent of sales revenue

- Number of engineering change orders
- Labor productivity
- Inventory turnover
- Resource utilization

Cycle-Time
- Time-to-market for new products
- Cycle time for key business processes

Employee well-being and morale
- Employee satisfaction
- Safety
- Absenteeism
- Turnover
- Employee training and development
- Employee recognition

Environmental Impact

Scoring Guidelines

Score	Approach	Deployment	Results
0%	•anecdotal, no system evident	•anecdotal	•anecdotal
10-40%	•beginnings of approach	•some to many major areas of business	•some positive trends in areas deployed
50%	•sound, systematic approach that includes evaluation/ improvement cycles	•most major areas of business •some support areas	•positive trends in most major areas •some evidence that results are caused by approach
60-90%	•sound, systematic approach with evidence of refinement through planning, evaluation, and improvement cycles • good integration	•major areas of business •from some to many support areas	•good to excellent in major areas •positive trends-- from some to many support areas •evidence that results are caused by approach
100%	•sound, systematic prevention approach refined through planning, evaluation, improvement cycles •excellent integration	•major areas and support areas •all operations	•excellent (world-class) results in major areas •good to excellent in support areas •sustained results •results clearly caused by approach

Eligibility: Eligibility for application for the Excellence in Benchmarking Award is unrestricted in terms of location of the firm. The sole determination for which category an organization may apply is based on the following definitions of small business and large business. A prize recipient is ineligible to reapply for the award for a period of three years.

Small Business - An independent business entity with fewer than 500 full-time equivalent employees. Part-time and seasonal employees must be considered when calculating the number of employees. A small business must apply as a whole entity. A subsidiary of a small business may not apply as a separate entity.

Large Business - Business entities with more than 500 full-time equivalent employees. Organizational units of a large business may apply individually, but must apply in the large business category. Multiple entities within one organization may apply individually in the same year, unless the applying entities comprise a clear majority of the organization, in which case the application will be automatically upgraded to an organization-wide application and then only that unit may apply. A subsidiary, business unit, or division of a large business may apply for the award providing:

-    the organization has at least 500 full-time equivalent employees and 25% of all employees of the parent firm

-    the organization has been in existence for at least three years prior to the award application

-    the organization has a clear, structural definition as reflected in corporate literature (organization charts, annual reports, administrative manuals, etc.)

Fees: An application processing fee of $750 for a large business or $250 for a small business must be submitted with the *Intent To Apply Form* on or before November 16, 1992. Application fees will be refunded if the applicant is determined to be ineligible to compete. Applicants selected for a site visit are expected to pay all reasonable costs associated with the site visit.

Confidentiality: All applications, feedback reports, commentary, and evaluation information are held confidential. All individuals involved with the review, handling, and processing of application reports sign a non-disclosure agreement which is kept on file by APQC. Examiners are assigned to evaluate applications in such a way as to avoid conflicts of interest. Firms which have a representative associated with the panel of judges or board of examiners are allowed to compete, but their representative will be disqualified from participating in the examination, review, and selection processes for the category in which they are competing.

Applicants are not expected to divulge proprietary information regarding products or processes. Information regarding successful strategies of prize recipients may be released only after written approval is obtained from the applicant. A case study summarizing award-winning programs will be prepared by APQC and must be approved by award recipients prior to publication.

Examination Process: The examination process for applicants consists of a three-phase review process. Applicants are required to submit a paper copy of the application, limited to 30 pages in length, and an electronic file in ASCII format, or other convertible format. This limit includes charts, figures and other attachments.

Phase I: Each application is scored independently by examiners to evaluate the merits of the application. This first phase is intended to identify those applications which are noteworthy and pass them on to the consensus review phase.

Phase II: The second phase is consensus review. During the consensus review an agreed-upon score is determined which is used to assess those organizations that fall into the "best practice" category. All organizations which achieve a score in the "best practice" category will be recommended for site visits. The third phase is the site visit and final selection phase.

Phase III: The site visit examination teams will be led by an experienced benchmarker and will make their recommendations of the "best of the best" to the panel of judges for final selection.

Each organization participating in the evaluation will receive a written feedback report. Those organizations receiving site visits will receive more detailed reports.

Site Visit: All reasonable expenses of each site visit not covered by the examiner or organization, will be borne by the organizations visited. Businesses being considered as finalists for the APQC Award for Excellence in Benchmarking will be subject to a site visit by a team of at least two (2) examiners. The primary objective of the site visit is to verify and clarify information contained in the written application. The companies to be visited will be notified at least 10 working days prior to the proposed site visit date. All reasonable expenses of each site visit will be borne by the organizations visited. Organizations receiving site visits will receive detailed feedback reports.

■ APPLICATION PROCESS

Timetable:

Application guidelines available:	August 1, 1992
Notice of intent to apply due:	November 16, 1992
Application submission deadline:	December 18, 1992
Site visits will be conducted between:	February 1 - March 15, 1993
(only for Award for Excellence)	
Award announcement and ceremony:	May 17-21, 1993

Application Instructions: (For All Prizes)

Step 1. Submission of the Intent to Apply Form

A letter of intent and the completed Intent to Apply Form (Appendix A), need to be submitted prior to the deadline date above. The Intent to Apply Form must be accompanied by payment of the application processing fee. Applications not postmarked by the deadlines specified in the Award timetable will not be eligible during the current Award cycle.

Step 2. Preparation of the Application

The application must be typed or printed on standard 8 1/2" X 11" inch paper using a fixed pitch font of 10 characters per inch or a proportional font of point size 10 or 12. Sheets may be printed on both sides. The body of the application is limited to 20 printed pages for the Research and Study Awards, and 30 printed pages for the Excellence Award. These page limits include figures, charts, and other attachments. For the Excellence Award the application must indicate the category and item being addressed.

All applications must adhere to the highest standards of writing competency with regard to grammar, spelling, punctuation, sentence structure, and clarity. Similar standards will apply to format including: abstract, introduction, organization, technical level, integration and presentation of ideas, and conclusions.

Applicants are required to submit a paper copy of the application and an electronic file in *ASCII* format, or other convertible format.

Step 3. Submission of the Application

Ten (10) copies of the paper, meeting all the above-stated criteria and format requirements, postmarked on or before the application deadline, should be sent to:

> The American Productivity & Quality Center
> Benchmarking Award Administrator
> International Benchmarking Clearinghouse
> 123 North Post Oak Lane
> Houston, Texas 77024-7797

■ **1992 BENCHMARKING AWARD
INTENT TO APPLY FORM**

Award Application Type (Select one per application):

Benchmarking Research Prize
    Academic Research
    Applied Research   _____

Benchmarking Study Prize
    Individual   _____
    Team   _____

Award for Excellence in Benchmarking
    Large Business   _____
    Small Business   _____

> *Note:*
> Applications for the Research
> or Study Prize which are
> submitted on behalf of more
> than one individual should
> include a separate Intent to
> Apply Form for each author.

Applicant Information:

Applicant Name: _____
Company Name: _____
Company Address: _____
    _____
    _____

Official Contact for Correspondence:

Name: _____
Title: _____
Telephone: _____
Facsimile: _____

Statement:

We understand that this Intent to Apply Form and subsequent Achievement Report will be reviewed by members of the Board of Examiners, Judges Panel, and the staff of the International Benchmarking Clearinghouse. We hereby give permission for the American Productivity & Quality Center to publish, in any format, any or all papers submitted for either the Research Prize or Study Prize, and to extract case study material from Award for Excellence applications.

Signature, Authorizing Individual: **X**_____
Name: _____
Title: _____
Date: _____

Submissions for either the Research Prize or the Study Prize should submit an abstract of less than 100 words with this Intent to Apply Form.

■ AWARD FOR EXCELLENCE ADDENDUM

Highest Ranking Official of Applying Entity:

Name: _____

Title: _____

Telephone: _____

Eligibility Information:

Sales in preceding fiscal year: _____

Number of employees: _____

Number of sites or facilities: _____

Attach a brief description and history of the organization with this form. Include information specified as business factors in the Malcolm Baldrige National Quality Award application.

Statement:

We understand that this Intent to Apply Form and the subsequent achievement report will be reviewed by the members of the Board of Examiners, Judges Panel, and the staff of the International Benchmarking Clearinghouse. If selected as a candidate for the Award for Excellence in Benchmarking, our organization agrees to host a site visit to verify information provided in the achievement report. We understand that our organization must pay reasonable costs associated with site visits.

Signature, Authorizing Official: **X**_____

Name: _____

Title: _____

Date: _____

Telephone: _____

Appendix D

Sample Benchmarking Procedure

PURPOSE

This procedure describes the roles, responsibilities, and resources for process benchmarking within Anycompany USA, Inc. (AUI).

OBJECTIVE

This procedure defines the general approach to process benchmarking that is approved for use by the AUI management team. Specific procedures for benchmarking teams are described in the "Introduction to Benchmarking" course offered through the AUI Quality Department.

SCOPE

This procedure is applicable to all individuals and teams, throughout the organization, who may desire to benchmark product, service, or process performance against external organizations.

RESPONSIBILITY

Responsibility for managerial oversight of benchmarking activities is assigned to an AUI Benchmarking Champion and a Benchmarking Steering Committee. Their responsibilities are described below.

Benchmarking Champion

The Quality Officer shall serve as the AUI Benchmarking Champion and be responsible for the development and coordination of an effective and efficient companywide benchmarking process that meets the requirements of senior management for effective management-by-fact comparisons for key business process measures and supports the strategic planning process. Specifically, the Quality Officer shall:

- Promote the use of benchmarking among the operating units;
- Coordinate and facilitate the benchmarking activities of the operating units;
- Develop and maintain a companywide process for conducting benchmarking studies;
- Ensure that AUI uses leading-edge benchmarking techniques;
- Review data collection plans and provide secondary research support;
- Provide a methodology to manage the use of external consultants;
- Serve as a clearinghouse for responding to external requests for benchmarking studies;
- Develop and deliver benchmarking training to support benchmarking study efforts;
- Provide a central repository for benchmarking information and study records;
- Retain benchmarking records for five years and then effect disposition as required;
- Communicate benchmarking activities and report study findings to all relevant parties;
- Conduct strategic benchmarking studies as required to support management initiatives.

Benchmarking Steering Committee

The Benchmarking Steering Committee shall be assigned by the corporate executive committee and shall provide management oversight for all benchmarking activities. This committee shall exercise due diligence to protect AUI intellectual property while adhering to the standards of the Benchmarking Code of Conduct for its dealings with external organizations. The specific responsibilities of the committee shall include:

- Develop a three-year benchmarking strategy to support AUI strategic plans;
- Solicit admired firms to serve as strategic partners by participating in long-range studies;

- Ensure appropriate legal review of benchmarking, especially for competitive studies;
- Review and approve all requests for participation in external benchmarking studies;
- Conduct assessments to inspect for evidence of continuous improvement in benchmarking;
- Participate annually in at least one study requested by the executive management team;
- Develop, implement, and monitor a companywide policy for protection of intellectual property and proprietary information;
- Develop, implement, and manage a companywide recognition program for benchmarking;
- Ensure that adequate resources are assigned to support benchmarking within operational units.

OBJECTIVES OF BENCHMARKING

- Support the development of the annual strategic business plan by developing realistic goals for achievement of critical success factors for the business;
- Support the continuous improvement of key business processes by identifying best practices that will enable the achievement of business improvement opportunities.

REFERENCES

1. Anycompany USA, Inc., Training Manual, "Introduction to Benchmarking," May 1992.
2. Robert C. Camp, *Benchmarking: The Search for Best Practices that Lead to Superior Performance* (Milwaukee, WI: Quality Press/American Society for Quality Control, 1989).
3. International Benchmarking Clearinghouse, *Planning, Organizing, and Managing Benchmarking: A User's Guide* (Houston, TX: American Productivity & Quality Center, 1992).
4. Gregory H. Watson, *The Benchmarking Workbook: Adapting Best Practices for Performance Improvement* (Cambridge, MA: Productivity Press, 1992).

5. Gregory H. Watson, *Strategic Benchmarking: How to Rate Your Company's Performance against the World's Best* (New York: John Wiley & Sons, 1993).

DEFINITIONS

All definitions used in this procedure and AUI training materials are consistent with the glossary of benchmarking terms contained in the AUI Training Manual and in Watson, *Strategic Benchmarking* (Wiley, 1993).

PROCEDURES

The following procedures will be followed for all benchmarking studies:

- All external benchmarking projects must be approved by a member of the executive team or the senior member of a local operating unit;
- All proposed benchmarking studies must be reviewed by the intellectual property council to determine legal risks associated with the proposed effort;
- All benchmarking teams will be briefed on the Benchmarking Code of Conduct by the Benchmarking Champion after they have filed their benchmarking study plan on the computer system's benchmarking bulletin board;
- Each team conducting a benchmarking study will take either the "Introduction to Benchmarking" course or "Benchmarking Refresher Training" after their study plan has been approved by the Benchmarking Steering Committee;
- Each team will conduct its benchmarking study using the process taught in the AUI training course;
- Teams will use quality methods and management-by-fact to document their process;
- Upon completion of the data collection plan, benchmarking teams will be assigned accounts at the corporate library for secondary research expenses;
- Upon completion of the study, the benchmarking team will file the benchmarking summary report on the bulletin board and schedule a briefing of the Benchmarking Steering Committee;
- All requests for follow-up benchmarking studies must be forwarded to the Benchmarking Steering Committee for disposition.

FORMS AND RECORDS

All benchmarking projects are required to file three reports to record their activities:

- Benchmarking study plan;
- Data collection plan;
- Benchmarking summary report.

Proformas for these reports are contained in the training materials for the "Introduction to Benchmarking" course.

Appendix E

Benchmarking Bibliography

BOOKS ON BENCHMARKING AND RELATED TOPICS

Balm, Gerald J. *Benchmarking: A Practitioner's Guide for Becoming and Staying Best of the Best*. Schaumberg, IL: Quality and Productivity Management Association, 1992.

Camp, Robert C. *Benchmarking: The Search for Industry Best Practices that Lead to Superior Performance*. Milwaukee, WI: Quality Press/American Society for Quality Control, 1989.

Emory, C. William. *Business Research Methods*, 3d ed. Homewood, IL: Richard D. Irwin, 1985.

Fuld, Leonard M. *Competitor Intelligence: How to Get It—How to Use It*. New York: John Wiley & Sons, 1985.

Harrington, H. James. *Business Process Improvement*. New York: McGraw-Hill, 1991.

Jacobson, Gary, and Hillkirk, John. *Xerox: American Samurai*. New York: Macmillan Publishing Co., 1986.

Liebfried, Kathleen H. J., and McNair, C. J. *Benchmarking: A Tool for Continuous Improvement*. New York: HarperBusiness, 1992.

Porter, Michael. *Competitive Strategy: Techniques for Analyzing Industries and Competitors*. New York: Free Press, 1980.

———. *Competitive Advantage: Creating and Sustaining Superior Performance*. New York: Free Press, 1985.

Spendolini, Michael J. *The Benchmarking Book*. New York: AMACOM/The American Management Association, 1992.

Watson, Gregory H. *Benchmarking for Competitive Advantage*. Cambridge, MA: Productivity Press, 1993.

251

————. *The Benchmarking Workbook: Adapting Best Practices for Performance Improvement.* Cambridge, MA: Productivity Press, 1992.

————, ed. *The Benchmarking Management Guide.* Cambridge, MA: Productivity Press, 1993.

ARTICLES AND REPORTS ON BENCHMARKING

Albin, John T. "Competing in a Global Market," *APICS,* January 1992.

Allaire, Paul A. "Quality: Where It Has Been and Where It Is Going," *Journal for Quality and Participation,* March 1991.

Alster, Norm. "An American Original Beats Back the Copycats," *Electronic Business,* October 1, 1987.

Altany, David. "Copycats," *Industry Week,* November 5, 1990.

————. "Share and Share Alike," *Industry Week,* July 15, 1991.

————. "Willa Martin: The Image to Survive," *Industry Week,* March 2, 1992.

Auguston, Karen A. "Warehousing Distribution: Compare Yourself to the Best . . . And Worst!," *Modern Materials Handling,* May 1992.

Bailey, Jeffrey V. "Evaluating Benchmark Quality," *Financial Analysts Journal,* May–June 1992.

Balm, Gerald J. "Benchmarking—Nicety or Necessity?," *Tapping the Network Journal,* Spring, 1992.

Band, William. "Benchmark Your Performance for Continuous Improvement," *Sales & Marketing Management in Canada,* May 1990.

Barber, Norman F. "How Good Is Your EDI Program? Part 5: Peer-Based Review," *EDI World,* April 1992.

Barks, Joseph V. "Distribution Costs: A Hard Road Back," *Distribution's Logistics Annual Report,* July 1990.

Barrett, Amy. "After-Sales Service: Infiniti," *Financial World,* April 14, 1992.

Bean, Thomas J., and Gros, Jacques G. "R&D Benchmarking at AT&T," *Research-Technology Management,* July–August 1992.

Bemowski, Karen. "Carrying on the P&G Tradition," *Quality Progress,* May 1992.

————. "The Benchmarking Bandwagon," *Quality Progress,* January 1991.

Betts, Peter J., and Baum, Neil. "Borrowing the Disney Magic," *Healthcare Forum Journal,* January–February 1992.

Betzig, Robert J., and Fleming, Laura K. "Laying the Groundwork," *The TQM Magazine*, July–August, 1992.

Biesada, Alexandra. "Benchmarking," *Financial World*, September 17, 1991.

———. "Strategic Benchmarking," *Financial World*, September 29, 1992.

———. "The Second Opinion," *Financial World*, December 10, 1991.

Blackburn, Joseph D., and Zahorik, Anthony J. "A Tale of Two Industries: Machine Tools and Plastic Injection Molding," *Target*, Summer 1991.

Bonnett, Kendra R. "L. L. Bean: A Legend in Quality," *Profit*, May–June 1992.

Bracken, David W. "Benchmarking Employee Attitudes," *Training & Development Journal*, June 1992.

Bram, James M. "Researching Requirements," *The TQM Magazine*, July–August 1992.

Camp, Robert C. "Benchmarking: The Search for Industry Best Practices That Lead to Superior Performance—Part I: Benchmarking Defined," *Quality Progress*, January 1989.

———. "Benchmarking: The Search for Industry Best Practices That Lead to Superior Performance—Part II: Key Process Steps," *Quality Progress*, February 1989.

———. "Benchmarking: The Search for Industry Best Practices That Lead to Superior Performance—Part III: Why Benchmark," *Quality Progress*, March 1989.

———. "Benchmarking: The Search for Industry Best Practices That Lead to Superior Performance—Part IV: What to Benchmark," *Quality Progress*, April 1989.

———. "Benchmarking: The Search for Industry Best Practices That Lead to Superior Performance—Part V: Beyond Benchmarking," *Quality Progress*, May 1989.

Cavinato, Joseph. "How to Benchmark Logistics Operations," *Distribution*, August 1988.

Cecil, Robert, and Ferraro, Richard. "IE's Fill Facilitator Role in Benchmarking Operations to Improve Performance," *Industrial Engineering*, April 1992.

Cedrone, Lisa. "1991 ARC Conference: Knowledge by Example," *Bobbin*, January 1992.

Chapple, Alan. "Benchmarking Pits Industry Against World's Best-in-Class," *Engineering Times*, April 1992.

Chitwood, Lera. "The People Chase," *Competitive Intelligence Review,* Winter 1992.

Davies, R. J. "Mapping Out Improvement," *The TQM Magazine,* May–June 1992.

Day, Charles R., Jr. "Benchmarking's First Law: Know Thyself!," *Industry Week,* February 17, 1992.

Delsanter, Judith M. "A Win–Win Situation," *The TQM Magazine,* July–August 1992.

———. "On the Right Track," *The TQM Magazine,* March–April 1992.

Dubashi, Jagannath. "Mastering Customized Manufacturing," *Financial World,* September 29, 1992.

Dumaine, Brian. "Corporate Spies Snoop to Conquer," *Fortune,* November 1988.

Enslow, Beth. "Benchmarkers Unite: Clearinghouse Provides Needed Networking Opportunities," *Across the Board,* April 1992.

———. "The Benchmarking Bonanza," *Across the Board,* April 1992.

Ettore, Barbara. "Give Me a 'B' for Benchmarking," *Management Review,* May 1992.

Fahey, Paul P., and Ryan, Stephen. "Quality Begins and Ends With Data," *Quality Progress,* April 1992.

Fifer, Robert M. "Cost Benchmarking Functions in the Value Chain," *Planning Review,* May–June 1989.

Fleisher, Craig S., and Schoenfeld, Gerald A. "Functional-Level Competitive Intelligence: Human Resources Management," *Competitive Intelligence Review,* Winter 1992.

Foster, Thomas A. "Logistics Benchmarking: Searching for the Best," *Distribution,* March 1992.

Frasier-Sleyman, Ken. "Benchmark Your Way to Forecasting Excellence," *Journal of Business Forecasting,* Spring 1992.

Fuld, Leonard M. "Taking the First Steps on the Path to Benchmarking," *Marketing News,* September 11, 1989.

———. "Survey Findings: Computer-Based Intelligence Systems Experience Growth and Problems," *Competitive Intelligence Review,* Winter 1992.

Furey, Timothy R. "Benchmarking: The Key to Developing Competitive Advantage in Mature Markets," *Planning Review,* September–October 1987.

Geber, Beverly. "Benchmarking: Measuring Yourself Against the Best," *Training,* November 1990.

Ghoshal, Sumantra, and Westney, D. Eleanor. "Organizing Competitor Analysis Systems," *Strategic Management Journal,* December 1991.

Gillman, Douglas, J. "Results Comparison Groups Can Bolster Analysis," *National Underwriter,* August 24, 1992.

GOAL/QPC Research Committee. *Benchmarking.* Methuen, MA: GOAL/QPC, 1991.

Gold, Jacqueline S. "Return of the Native," *Financial World,* March 31, 1992.

Graham, Scott. "Futurescape: Utilities Turn to Benchmarking," *Reddy News Sourcebook,* March 1991.

Grayson, C. Jackson. "Worldwide Competition," *The TQM Magazine,* July–August 1992.

Guilmette, Harris, and Reinhart, Carlene. "Competitive Benchmarking: A New Concept for Training," *Training and Development Journal,* February 1984.

Harkleroad, David H. "Competitive Intelligence: A New Benchmarking Tool," *Management Review,* October 1992.

Harmon, Marion. "Benchmarking," *Quality Digest,* July 1992.

Hewitt, Frederick. "A Copy of Success," *The TQM Magazine,* July–August 1992.

Hillmer, Steven C., and Trabelsi, Abdelwahed. "A Benchmarking Approach to Forecast Combination," *Journal of Business and Economic Statistics,* July 1989.

Hitchner, Earle. "Xerox Is Not a Verb," *National Productivity Review,* Summer 1992.

Hubbard, Gerald M. "Keys to Creating Performance Measures," *Facilities Design & Management,* May 1992.

Jennings, Kenneth, and Westafall, Frederick. "Benchmarking for Strategic Action," *Journal of Business Strategy,* May–June 1992.

Johnson, Samuel E. "Benchmarking Facility Management Practices," *Modern Office Technology,* June 1992.

Kearns, David. "Xerox: Satisfying Customer Needs With a New Culture," *Management Review,* February 1989.

Kendrick, John J. "Benchmarking Survey Builds Case for Looking to Others for TQM Models," *Quality,* March 1992.

Kennedy, Carol. "Xerox Charts a New Strategic Direction," *Long Range Planning,* January 1989.

Kokubo, Atsuro. "Japanese Competitive Intelligence for R&D," *Research/Technology Management*, January–February 1992.

Lee, Sang M., Yoo, Sangjin, and Lee, Tosca M. "Korean Chaebols: Corporate Values and Strategies," *Organizational Dynamics*, Spring 1991.

Lehman, William M. "A Strategic Alliance in Aerospace TQM Meets the Needs of the 1990's," *APICS*, May 1992.

Lorincz, Jim. "Purchasing Research: How Do You Measure Up?," *Purchasing World*, May 1990.

Lynch, John J. "Eliminate the Auditors?," *Internal Auditor*, April 1992.

Markin, Alex. "How to Implement Competitive-Cost Benchmarking," *Journal of Business Strategy*, May–June 1992.

Maturi, Richard J. "Benchmarking: The Search for Quality," *The Financial Manager*, March–April 1990.

McComas, Maggie, Knowlton, Christopher, and Langan, Patricia A. "Cutting Costs Without Killing the Business," *Fortune*, October 13, 1986.

McMorrow, Eileen. "Proud as a Peacock: NBC's Pedalino," *Facilities Design & Management*, March 1992.

McReynolds, J. Scott, and Fern, Richard H. "Improve Operations by Benchmarking 'Best-Practice' Companies," *Corporate Controller*, May–June 1992.

Miller, John A. "Measuring Progress Through Benchmarking," *CMA Magazine*, May 1992.

Mitchell, Russell. "The Gap," *Business Week*, March 9, 1992.

Mittlestaedt, Robert E., Jr. "Benchmarking: How to Learn from Best-in-Class Practices," *National Productivity Review*, Summer 1992.

Nandi, S.N., et al. "Interfirm Comparison Revisited," *Productivity*, January–March 1992.

Owen, Jean V. "Getting Into the Benchmarking Game," *Manufacturing Engineering*, March 1992.

———. "Benchmarking World Class Manufacturing," *Manufacturing Engineering*, March 1992.

Patrick, Michael S. "Benchmarking—Targeting 'Best Practices,'" *Healthcare Forum Journal*, July–August 1992.

Pipp, Frank J. "Management Commitment to Quality: Xerox Corporation," *Quality Progress*, August 1983.

Pontillo, Salvatore M. "Banking on Quality Improvement," *Quality Update*, January–February 1992.

Pryor, Lawrence S. "Benchmarking: A Self-Improvement Strategy," *Journal of Business Strategy,* November–December 1989.

———. *Beating the Competition: A Practical Guide to Benchmarking.* Vienna, VA: Kaiser Associates, Inc., 1988.

Richardson, Helen L. "Improve Quality Through Benchmarking," *Transportation & Distribution,* October 1992.

Rivest, Gerald. "Make Your Business More Competitive," *CMA Magazine,* May 1991.

Ruch, Daniel, and Roper, Janice John. "Greening of Corporate Canada," *CMA Magazine,* December 1991–January 1992.

Saxl, David. "It's Just Business as Usual," *The TQM Magazine,* May–June 1992.

Schaffner, Karen, and Thornton, Meg. "Follow the Leader," *Apparel Industry Magazine,* January 1992.

Schmid, Robert E. "Reverse Engineering: A Service Product," *Planning Review,* September–October 1987.

Schmidt, Jeffrey A. "The Link Between Benchmarking and Shareholder Value," *Journal of Business Strategy,* May–June 1992.

———. "A Tool to Be Best-in-Class," *Directors & Boards,* Spring 1992.

Scovel, Kathryn. "Learning from the Masters," *Human Resource Executive,* May 1991.

Sharman, Paul. "Benchmarking: Opportunities for Accountants," *CMA Magazine,* July–August 1992.

Sillyman, Steve. "Guide to Benchmarking Resources," *Quality,* March 1992.

Soderberg, Leif G., and O'Halloran, J. David. "'Heroic' Engineering Takes More than Heroes," *The McKinsey Quarterly* (1), 1992.

Sossi, Paul L. "Collaboration Speeds Waste Reduction Program," *Focus,* April 1992.

Spendolini, Michael J., and Thompson, Neil H. "Perspective—Correct Etiquette," *The TQM Magazine,* July–August 1992.

Stern, Paul G. "CFC-Free Northern Telecom Shares Its Technology for a Cleaner World," *Focus,* April 1992.

Thompson, James G. "Benchmarking Rules of Thumb," *Transportation & Distribution,* July 1992.

Thor, Carl. "Conducting an Industry Level Benchmarking Study," *APQC Notebook,* June 1991.

Tonkin, Lea. "Benchmarking Bound? Don't 'Just Do It,'" *Target,* Winter 1991.

Tucker, Frances Gaither, Zivan, Seymour M., and Camp, Robert C. "How to Measure Yourself Against the Best," *Harvard Business Review*, January–February 1987.

Tyndall, Gene R. "How You Apply Benchmarking Makes All the Difference," *Marketing News*, November 12, 1990.

Vaziri, H. Kevin. "Using Competitive Benchmarking to Set Goals," *Quality Progress*, October 1992.

Walker, Rob. "Rank Xerox—Management Revolution," *Long Range Planning*, February 1992.

Watson, Gregory H. "Benchmarking: Up-Front Preparation and Strategic Perspective Lead to Benchmarking Success," *Productivity Newsletter*, September 1991.

———. "Competitive Analysis: Coordinate Competitive Analysis Tools to Get the Total Picture," *Productivity Newsletter*, October 1991.

———. "A Process for Competitive Edge," *The TQM Magazine*, July–August 1992.

Weimer, George A. "Benchmarking Maps the Route to Quality," *Industry Week*, July 20, 1992.

Whatley, Mark, and Aaron, Howard B. "Companies That Target World Class Are Destined to Be Second Rate," *Quality Engineering* (2) 1990–1991.

Whiting, Rick. "Benchmarking: Lessons from the Best-in-Class," *Electronic Business*, October 7, 1991.

Wilkerson, David, Kuh, Anne, and Wilkerson, Tracy. "A Tale of Change," *The TQM Magazine*, July–August 1992.

Young, Steve, and Greenway, Brent. "Britain's Best Factories," *Management Today*, November 1990.

Zivan, Sy. "Are You Ready for Benchmarking?," *Distribution*, March 1992.

Appendix F

Glossary of Benchmarking Terms

Activity A series of transactions that translate inputs into outputs using resources in response to a business requirement; sequences of activities in logical combinations form processes.

Benchmark A measured, "best-in-class" achievement; a reference or measurement standard for comparison; a performance level recognized as the standard of excellence for a specific business practice.

Benchmarking A systematic and continuous measurement process; a process of continuously comparing and measuring an organization's business processes against business leaders anywhere in the world, to gain information that will help the organization take action to improve its performance.

Benchmarking Code of Conduct A behavioral convention that describes the protocol of behaviors to be used in conducting benchmarking studies. (See Appendix A.)

Benchmarking gap A difference in performance, identified through a comparison, between the benchmark for a particular activity and other companies; the measured leadership advantage of the benchmark organization over other organizations.

Benchmarking partner A relationship between two parties who associate in a collegial relationship involving close cooperation to conduct benchmarking studies—the protocol of this relationship is summarized by the Benchmarking Code of Conduct.

Best-of-breed Outstanding process performance within an industry; words used as synonyms are best practice and best-in-class.

Best-in-class Outstanding process performance within an industry; words used as synonyms are best practice and best-of-breed.

Best practice Superior performance within an activity, regardless of industry, leadership, management, or operational approaches, or methods that lead to exceptional performance; a relative term that usually indicates innovative or interesting business practices that have been identified during a particular benchmarking study as contributing to improved performance at the leading organizations.

Common interest group   A network of individuals or organizations who share a mutual interest in a specific subject and have agreed to share their experiences.

Competitive analysis   The process of analyzing the magnitude and rationale for the gap between the business performance of one's own organization and that of its competitors.

Competitive benchmarking   A measure of organizational performance compared against competing organizations; studies that target specific product designs, process capabilities, or administrative methods used by a company's direct competitors.

Core competencies   Strategic business capabilities that provide an organization with a marketplace advantage; the collective learning of an organization, which is perceived by customers to be a benefit and is difficult for competitors to duplicate.

Critical success factors   Quantitative measures for effectiveness, economy, and efficiency; those few activities where satisfactory performance is essential in order for a business to succeed; characteristics, conditions, or variables that have a direct influence on a customer's satisfaction with a specific business process; the set of things that must be done right if a vision is to be achieved.

Enabler   The processes, practices, or methods that facilitate the implementation of a best practice and help to meet a critical success factor; characteristics that help to explain the reasons for the achievement of benchmark performance.

Entitlement   The best that can be achieved in process performance using current resources to eliminate waste and improve cycle time; obvious improvements that are identified during benchmarking and may be accomplished as short-term goals.

Exchange   The act of giving or taking one thing in return for another; *quid pro quo,* or this for that.

Functional benchmarking   An application of process benchmarking that compares a particular business function at two or more organizations.

Generic benchmarking   An application of functional process benchmarking that compares a particular business function at two or more organizations selected without regard to their industry.

Global benchmarking The extension of strategic benchmarking to include benchmarking partners on a global scale.

Goal The numerical target value or observed performance that indicates the strategic direction of an organization over a three- to five-year horizon.

Internal benchmarking An application of process benchmarking performed within an organization by comparing the performance of similar business units or business processes.

Key business process The critical few business processes that influence customers' perception of a business.

Networking A decentralized organization of independent participants who develop a degree of interdependence and share a coherent set of values and interests.

Operational definition A description of a process critical success factor in terms of observable characteristics or measurements.

Performance benchmarking A comparison of the performance measurement of one organization's product against another's, using a standard testing procedure to establish relative superiority in the capability of specific product features.

Process A series of interrelated activities that convert inputs into results (outputs); processes consume resources and require standards for repeatable performance; processes respond to control systems that direct the quality, rate, and cost of performance.

Process benchmarking The activity of measuring discrete performance and functionality against organizations whose performance is excellent in analogous business processes.

Process owner The individual who possesses managerial control over a particular business process.

Protocol A set of conventions governing the actions of individuals, organizations, or nations, as specified by a written agreement; a code prescribing adherence to correct etiquette.

Recalibration To adjust the measurement alignment of an instrument against a recognized standard; to standardize by determining and correcting the deviation of a measure from a standard.

Recycling To reprocess in order to gain additional information; to return to an earlier condition so that an operation can begin again.

Reengineering The radical redesign of business processes, organizational structures, management systems, and values of an organization, to achieve breakthroughs in business performance.

Reverse engineering   A comparison of product characteristics, functionality, and performance with those of similar products made by competitors; the tear-down of competitive products to their fundamental subassembly level by engineers, in order to evaluate design characteristics.

Root cause   The fundamental causal reason for a particular observation; the result of asking "why" five times to determine the basic cause in a chain of causal relationships.

Secondary research   The practice of searching for information about a particular subject from indirect sources, using information service resources.

Strategic alliance   A strategic bond or connection between organizations that have common interests; an association to further the common interests of participants.

Strategic benchmarking   The application of process benchmarking to the level of business strategy; a systematic process for evaluating alternatives, implementing strategies, and improving performance by understanding and adapting successful strategies from external partners who participate in an ongoing business alliance.

Strategic intent   A statement of the persistent ambitions of a company, used as an aid to guide its decisions for resource allocation and goal setting.

Strategic plan   A road map to gain competitive advantage by achieving goals that define business objectives for critical success factors.

Target   A mark to shoot at; a short-term goal to be achieved.

Total quality management   A customer-focused management philosophy and strategy that seeks continuous improvement in business processes by applying analytical tools and teamwork, including the participation of all employees.

Vision   The achievable dream of what an organization wants to do and where it wants to go.

World class   Leading performance in a process, independent of industry or geographic location, as recognized using process benchmarking for comparison to other worldwide contenders.

Index

About the Author

Gregory H. Watson is currently vice president of quality for the Office Document Products Division of Xerox Corporation in Rochester, New York. He served as vice president, benchmarking services at the American Productivity & Quality Center during the establishment of the International Benchmarking Clearinghouse and has previously held quality management positions at Compaq Computer Corporation and Hewlett-Packard. He has been a member of the Board of Examiners for the Malcolm Baldrige National Quality Award, a judge for the Texas State Quality Award, a senior member of the Board of Examiners for the New York State Excelsior Award, and a judge for the IBC Benchmarking Award. Watson is the author of *The Benchmarking Workbook: Adapting Best Practices for Performance Improvement* (1992), editor of *Planning, Organizing, and Managing Benchmarking: A User's Guide* (1992) and his next book, *Benchmarking for Competitive Advantage,* will be published in 1993. He is a senior member of the American Society for Quality Control and a Certified Quality Engineer. He and his family live with their two golden retrievers in Victor, New York.